To my four beautiful daughters:
Meghan, Shannon, Bridget, and Molly

PERSONAL FOUL

TIM DONAGHY

The publisher offers discounts on this book when ordered in quantity for
special sales. For more information, please contact:
(727) 531-2911
info@vti-group.com

For information on obtaining permission for use of material from this
work, please submit a written request to:
VTi Group, Inc.
13141 66th St. N.
Largo, FL 33773

ISBN-10: 0615306039
ISBN-13: 978-0-615-30603-2

First Edition

10 9 8 7 6 5 4 3 2 1

What lies behind us
And what lies before us
Are tiny matters
Compared to what lies within us.
—Ralph Waldo Emerson

Contents

Foreword

"I can get to anyone you need, John. All I do is find their weakness and hook him."
—Gambino family soldier to John Gotti, circa 1985

I worked with scores of cooperating witnesses throughout my FBI career, and their transition from subject to cooperating witness was never routine. Their motivations, expectations, and individual baggage were unique to the individual. For many, their past lifestyles and trappings of power, wealth, and influence—rooted in the superficial notion that material wealth and influence is all the power one needs in life—were major obstacles in their deciding to turn their backs on what had become false and destructive. The allure and pleasures of their past continued to test their resolve.

The FBI, on the other hand, is guided by establishing an honest relationship rooted in trust, obtaining the evidence, and corroborating the story. After vetting and reexamining the details of their recollections, one point holds true: if there is a verifiable inconsistency, all bets are off.

Every morning, those witnesses who succeed remind themselves of the eternal meaning and purpose in their lives and work at restoring honor and excellence to them. They recognize and internalize the value of virtue and integrity and feel connected to the FBI and law enforcement. In most cases, the effects of an honest transition yield peace of mind, honest relationships, and the awareness that virtue is its own reward. Those who attempt to beguile the cooperation agreement for the purpose of returning to their old patterns do not have a good track record of remaining on the straight and narrow.

Once the government offers the witness a cooperation agreement, it places an expectancy of trust on everything the witness relates concerning the case, their lives, and their criminal history. From that point forward, being completely candid and honest is the only game in town. At trial, it is not uncommon for witnesses to testify, during direct and cross-examination, to being a liar, a cheat, and a thief, because that, in many cases, is the life of a career criminal.

Tim Donaghy came from a very good family, was educated in private schools with excellent academic credentials, and started his adult life on a solid foundation. Unfortunately, he started making decisions that at first didn't appear to be all that wrong or serious, but over time, the subtle crossing of too many ethical lines led him to the point where those lines no longer existed. His fast-paced lifestyle—motivated by the desire for excitement, power, and monetary wealth—melded his character from something honorable into a personality identified by the characteristics of self-indulgence, pride, greed, deceit, and gambling, to a point where he didn't recognize himself.

When Tim came in for the first proffer, I could sense that he no longer wanted to carry the burden of deception. There appeared to be true contrition, but even with the catharsis of confession, facing and recounting all your sins takes time. After all was said and done, Tim understood that cooperating with the government meant being unconditionally truthful and that any lie would immediately breach that agreement and significantly change the circumstances considered by the prosecutors and the federal judge.

The fact that one has a cooperation agreement, however, doesn't absolve or make right the wrongdoings of the past. But it does mean that the individual has agreed to be cooperative, forthcoming, and candid for the purpose of relating the facts and circumstances of the case to a jury of his or her peers in a truthful, reliable, and credible fashion. In working with Tim and other former FBI cooperating witnesses, it was my hope and belief that as a result of confronting their past from a new perspective and a continued relationship with law enforcement they had a great start on the road to recovery and honest success. Tim—after confessing his sins, taking full responsibility for his actions, paying his debt to society, and finding the humility to completely display his past vices for the purpose of resurrecting himself without excuses and blaming others—is now able to stand tall again before his children, family, and all those who may learn something from the lessons he learned and the chilling effects of diminishing the integrity of the soul.

After almost 30 years in the Criminal Division of the FBI's New York office, it never failed to amaze me how the Bureau's highly specialized team of agents, support, and special-operation operatives revealed and solved significant and sometimes heinous crimes that perpetrators thought were foolproof and beyond scrutiny.

This case—that of former NBA referee Tim Donaghy and organized crime's involvement—was identified and solved as a result of a 30-year network of institutional knowledge, state and local law enforcement partnerships, and an intelligence framework. It was initiated by two of my predecessors—J. Bruce Mouw and George Gabriel—and the past and present Special Agents of the New York FBI's "Gambino squad" (C-16).

I became involved in this case because at the time I headed the FBI's Gambino squad. The squad normally would not investigate a gambling matter unless it had been determined that the proceeds were providing large sums of cash to organized crime families. That finding is what brought this case to light.

In telling his story, Tim Donaghy gives me much too much credit for solving this case; in truth this case was identified in part by the archival evidence gathered during 30 years of FBI organized crime investigations. Specifically, success was the result of collaboration by Paul Harris, a very focused and talented case agent; Frank Scalera, an enthusiastic and determined intelligence supervisor; and Tom Seigel, a motivated and experienced federal prosecutor.

Once identified, the case was given the full access and support of the entire FBI's investigative and intelligence resources. Those resources provided the additional intelligence and prospects necessary to build a viable case. That meant eliminating the source of illicit funding to organized crime cabals and making interested parties more aware of the importance of integrity.

Success in this case also depended on the insightful cooperation and talented and wise leadership of the FBI's New York office, namely: Mark Mershon, David Cardona, Kevin Hallinan, and David Shafer; FBI co-case agents Gerry Conrad, Beth Ambinder, Chris LaManna, and Rita Steiner; and the entire Gambino squad. Credit is also due to the United States Attorneys' Office of the Eastern District of New York and the prosecutorial wisdom, relentless work ethic, and leadership of Thomas Seigel and Mitra Hormozi. Defense attorney John Lauro was an excellent advocate and a "Class A" gentleman. Finally, crucial to success in this case were retired FBI agent Warren Flagg, the defense's ever enthusiastic P.I., and naturally, the early cooperation of Tim Donaghy.

The additional issues of employment-contract breaches by the NBA referees, alleged misconduct, manipulations, associations, and sport integrity were peripheral aspects of our investigation. We left those issues to others who wished to call attention to the culture of officiating. We concerned our investigation with aspects of illegal gambling and the directions of its revenue stream, as well as with organized crime factions targeting individuals with something to hide. Outside of the guilty pleas of Thomas Martino, James Battista, and Tim Donaghy, the professional gaming cabals and culture were put on notice of our awareness and the significant potential economic losses that had been prevented.

The far-reaching effects of the investigation and Tim Donaghy's cooperation had placed significant concerns on the radar screen. Future law enforcement scrutiny, a vigilant press, and the voice of public opinion have had a positive effect on restoring the sport's traditional American values to the game.

Phil Scala

Retired Supervisory Special Agent, FBI Squad C-16 (Gambino Family) (02/29/2008)
Founder and CEO, Pathfinder Consultants International, LLC
P.O. Box 7537, Garden City, NY 11530

Introduction

I'm guilty.

For 13 years I was a referee in the National Basketball Association, living a glamorous life on and off the court, rubbing elbows with superstar players and celebrity A-listers. I suppose many would say that I had it all—a great job, money, a wonderful family—but it was all an illusion.

You see, during my last four years in the NBA, I led a secret life that would ultimately cost me everything: my integrity, my reputation, my career, my livelihood, my marriage, my family, and my freedom. During those four years, I placed illegal bets on NBA games for four years, many of which I officiated as one of three referees on the court. My dalliance with sports betting started innocently enough, but it quickly became an obsession and addiction, one that would consume my life and destroy everything I once cherished.

For 13 years I lived the dream and experienced a thrill ride on the court alongside the best players in the world. As an NBA referee, I had a front-row seat to the greatest show on earth. I was a courtside witness to the greatness of Michael Jordan, Kobe Bryant, LeBron James, and Shaquille O'Neal. I casually mingled with Hollywood icons like Jack Nicholson and Spike Lee. I traveled around the country 26 days a month, made more than $250,000 per year, and distinguished myself on the court as a high-quality referee with a bright future in the league.

Along the way I married a great woman, had four beautiful daughters, and earned the respect of my father. For me, life was more than good; it was overwhelmingly great! But somewhere in my subconscious, there was an insatiable need for more action and more thrills, along with a dangerous impulse toward risky behavior. That unyielding need was satisfied, or so I thought, when I embarked on a dark affair with the seedy world of illegal gambling. It all started innocently enough, but my flirtation turned into an addiction, one that could never be satisfied and one I didn't want to stop. I became an out-of-control juggernaut hell-bent on self-destruction. My days and nights were consumed with thoughts of finding some action, placing a bet, and risking it all.

My road to ruin was punctuated by a shameful relationship with underworld figures who would stop at nothing to squeeze every ounce of dignity out of my soul. It didn't really matter. My soul had turned into a void as I placed my fixation on gambling above everything that was important in my life—my career, my family, and my freedom.

My involvement with illegal betting was more than a crime; it was a betrayal of the profession to which I had devoted my entire adult life. During this dark period, I associated with sleazy bookies and reputed mob figures, slowly becoming someone my family and friends no longer recognized. I passed inside information to wiseguys who were making millions of dollars on my picks and lining the pockets of Mafia heavyweights.

When the bubble finally burst, I was actually relieved to get out from under the threats and pressure brought to bear by my underworld coconspirators. And I made a choice that would both set me free and put me behind bars—I decided to confess my crimes and set the record straight.

* * *

They say a man's character is defined by the choices he makes in life. Of course, a man's character is also revealed by his willingness to accept responsibility for his actions, learn from his mistakes, and move forward in a positive, healthy, and honest way.

The mistakes I made were tremendous and life-changing, but I was determined not to let them define my character. Over the objections of my lawyer, I sat down with an assistant U.S. attorney and several FBI agents and confessed. As my addiction to gambling spun out of control, I had finally come to the painful conclusion that my life was a disaster and that it was time to salvage what remained of my soul. I told them everything: the bets, the lies, the betrayals, and things they had no idea existed. My reckless behavior set the stage for a free fall. My confession was the equivalent of the hangman pulling the lever and opening the trapdoor. It was finally over.

I resigned my position as an NBA referee and began a perilous and uncertain journey as a government witness. The FBI had a difficult time accepting the fact that I could so easily pick the winners of NBA games and probed me for more information. Along the way, FBI agents wanted to know if I, or any other referee, deliberately "fixed" games. The subsequent investigations, including one done at the NBA's request, revealed that a culture of favoritism and manipulation existed in the NBA, a culture that often affected the outcome of games. I was all too familiar with that "culture" and used my insider's knowledge to engage in illegal conduct, not for the purpose of affecting the outcome of a game, but for picking a winner and placing a bet. For me, it was as simple as knowing which referees were working a particular game; the rest was merely academic. I knew these guys. I knew who they liked, who they despised, who they would bend over backward to help, and who they would screw over at the drop of a hat. In fact, I knew them so well that they became consistently predictable, and I used their patterns to make predictions and place bets.

It wasn't just the referees who tipped their hands and made my job of picking winners easy. It was clear to me that the league was complicit in the culture of fraud and often wielded its awesome power to steer and direct the way games were played, officiated and, worst of all, decided. Protecting superstars, ensuring marquee big-market matchups, and prolonging playoff series were of primary concern to NBA big shots, and the faithful throng of referees did its part to please the bosses in the league's New York office.

I've seen all the skeletons in the NBA's closet. When I sat down with FBI investigators, they wanted to see those skeletons for themselves. In giving this account of my life in the NBA, I am making public the events that unfolded as I worked with the FBI in its effort to obtain a full picture of my involvement regarding betting on professional basketball games.

After my fall from grace, many people encouraged me to write a book and share my experiences. There were times when I winced at the notion of opening myself up to further public scrutiny. But in the end, the decision to write this book afforded me the opportunity for genuine self-examination and introspection. What personality traits do I possess that compelled me to lie and deceive? Why would I engage in risky behaviors when my life was so completely satisfying? How could all this happen to a nice kid from suburban Philadelphia who was living his boyhood dream?

The answers to those questions are painful to admit, but admit them I do. More importantly, I have embraced my faults with vigor and have developed a healthy desire to keep them in check. After writing this book, I sat back and read it beginning to end, shaking my head and wondering who in the heck this guy named Tim Donaghy was. For me, there have been times when he was incredibly difficult to recognize.

Despite much public speculation, gossip, and rumor, it is often the case that only those on the inside truly know the full story. Keeping in mind that the truth is usually stranger than fiction, this book is my inside account of the wild and often predictable world of NBA basketball. This is my story.

Ba Ba and the Black Sheep

Tommy Martino drove a Lotus. So when he pulled up to the curb behind the wheel of a four-door Honda that night, I had a bad feeling. It was December 12, 2006, and I had been patiently waiting for Tommy in front of the Philadelphia Marriott near the airport. Reaching for the front passenger door, I glanced through the window and laid eyes on the last guy in the world I wanted to see. There he was, James "Ba Ba" Battista, flashing me a crooked smile that could only mean one thing: trouble.

Like Tommy and I, Ba Ba was a student more than 20 years ago at Cardinal O'Hara High School in Springfield, Pennsylvania. Ba Ba played football with my older brother Jim and with Tommy's brother Johnny. Back in those days, Ba Ba thought he was a big tough guy, always lifting weights and wearing tight shirts that showed off his pecs; I thought he was kind of goofy, a cartoon character who was constantly flexing his muscles. Ba Ba never saw a mirror he didn't like. We were both Catholic school guys in small-town Pennsylvania and always friendly to each other, but I never considered him my friend. As a matter of fact, I thought I was better than he was. Better family, better looks, better athlete, better future. Little did I know that one day our names would be linked and that we would wear the same badge of dishonor for the rest of our lives.

By contrast, Tommy was a true friend whom I maintained contact with over the years. He was the quintessential mob-guy wannabe, always dressed to the hilt with perfectly groomed black hair, a dark Mediterranean complexion, and flashy jewelry. Only 5'4", he may have been slight of stature but he walked tall with style and confidence. Tommy had a heart of gold and a knack for being hilariously funny. And as for the women, he always wore the best-looking girls on his arm. It was hard not to like Tommy.

Although I stayed in touch with Tommy, I hadn't seen Ba Ba in years. I knew that Ba Ba was a bookie and a professional gambler; Tommy had told me that much. Apparently, Ba Ba was doing very well—a nice house, wife, and kids. Tommy, on the other hand, had a job as a computer technician at a local bank. He never went to college, but he was a smart guy and a straight shooter. At least that's what I thought.

* * *

Since graduation, I had been pursuing my passion officiating basketball, and in 1994 I made it all the way to the top: I became a referee in the National Basketball Association. That same year, Tommy called me at my home in Havertown, Pennsylvania. "Ba Ba wants to talk to you," he said. By then Ba Ba was heavily into gambling, a guy who in his own words "makes bets, places bets, and moves money." He considered himself a professional money mover, and he actually listed his occupation as "professional gambler" on his tax forms.

"Why does he want to talk to me?" I asked cautiously.

"Are you gonna be on the up and up with the NBA games?" he asked me. In other words, would I be willing to give Tommy and Ba Ba inside information on how the games were going to come out?

I was enraged and demanded that Tommy get Battista on the phone. "Don't ever call me again," I warned him. "I'll turn you in."

They backed off, and a dozen years went by before Tommy raised the subject again. By 2006, Battista had become a high-level bookmaker with connections to the Gambino crime family. Tommy served as his driver, running him from Philly to New York to pick up or drop off large sums of cash. I knew Tommy was involved with Ba Ba, but I didn't know the whole story. To be honest, I really didn't *want* to know. It turns out that Battista, who had long since quit working out and had ballooned to over 300 pounds, was not an actual member of the Gambino crime family, but Tommy did talk about how he was "connected." If Tommy and I were talking on the phone and he mentioned that Ba Ba was in the house, I'd tell him, "Okay, I'll talk to you later." To his credit, Tommy had told Ba Ba after that initial approach in 1994 that I was really pissed and that I wanted nothing to do with him. Supposedly, Ba Ba let it go…at least until that night at the Marriott.

Over the years, I had become quite the sports gambler myself. Maybe it was all that downtime on the road as an NBA referee. Maybe I just needed something to fill my days. Whatever it was, I began betting on golf, baseball, football, and eventually pro basketball.

Lots of people make bets, but for an NBA referee, gambling is seen as the kiss of death. The NBA was so concerned about the integrity of the game that it *contractually required* referees to abstain from all forms of gambling, with the sole exception of horse racing during the off-season summer months. No casinos, no cards, no office pools, not even a wager over a friendly game of golf. Nothing! For a good Catholic boy from Philly, an innocent wager might qualify as a venial sin, at worst. But in the NBA, gambling was a mortal sin punishable by eternal damnation. I knew the rules going in, but for reasons that to this day are difficult to articulate, I did it: I gambled. And worst of all, I bet on pro basketball.

For bets that required a bookie, I relied on the connections of Jack Concannon, yet another high school friend of mine. Jack and I had mixed results on most wagers, but when it came to pro basketball, our winning percentage was off the charts. The reason for our success was simple: because of my years of experience in the NBA, I was intimately familiar with the other NBA referees, their strengths and weaknesses, and their unique relationships with various players, coaches, and team owners. That's all it took. If I knew which referees were working a particular game, I could generally pick the winner or at least cover the spread.

Predicting the outcome of a game using my subjective formula proved to be unbelievably easy. Let me explain.

Allen Iverson provides a good example of a player who generated strong reaction, both positive and negative, within the corps of NBA referees. For instance, veteran referee Steve Javie hated Allen Iverson and was loathe to give him a favorable call. If Javie was on the court when Iverson was playing, I would usually bet on the other team to win or at least cover the spread. No matter how many times Iverson hit the floor, he rarely saw the foul line. By contrast, referee Joe Crawford had a grandson who idolized Iverson. I once saw Crawford bring the boy out of the stands and onto the floor during warm-ups to meet the superstar. Iverson and Crawford's grandson were standing there, shaking hands, smiling, talking about all kinds of things. If Joe Crawford was on the court, I was pretty sure Iverson's team would win or at least cover the spread.

That's how it went with referee after referee, player after player, team after team. Some referees hated Mark Cuban, the outspoken owner of the Dallas Mavericks. Others despised Robert Sarver, owner of the Phoenix Suns. Depending on which officiating crew worked their games, those teams could be in for a long night.

My system took various factors into account, including injuries to players, game venues, and specific directives from the league office, just to name a few. However, my picks were based mostly on my knowledge of which referees were working a game. Each game day, the NBA prepared a master list of referee assignments. The list was private and was not made available to anyone in advance other than the referees and a few high-ranking league officials. That list was virtually all I needed.

Of course, not everyone knew the details of the referees' relationships with players, coaches, and teams. But I did. I knew the referees who had personal vendetta against a player or a coach. I also had an inside advantage because of my access to pregame meetings. It was common for my fellow referees to voice their opinions about who they expected to win on a given night. Those opinions were often based on their knowledge of confidential inside information pertaining to players and teams, such as injury reports unknown to the general public.

I would take all the information I could find and create my own betting line for games. Initially, I did it for games I didn't referee, and then, to my greater shame, games that I did referee. I compared the line I created with the betting line in *USA Today*. If there was a disparity of more than five points, Jack and I would bet the game. It sounds astonishing to some, but we won 70 to 80 percent of our bets. Great results for sure, but astonishing? Not to me.

If Jack and I had bet exclusively on NBA games, we would have made a fortune. But we weren't satisfied with stopping there; we bet on virtually every sport we could. We would bet on 15 NFL games, a dozen college football games, or anything and everything else that had a line. On other sports, we were up some and down some—generally more down than up, like most sports bettors. But when it came to the NBA, our bets were golden. Every now and then we would come to our senses and say, "This is stupid. Let's not do this anymore. We're crossing the line here." And then we would stop betting on NBA games for a while. Eventually, one of us would go to a casino and lose $10,000 or $15,000, and all of a sudden we were back in business.

I didn't realize that Jack was telling other people about our unholy alliance, but he was. Jack placed our bets with a bookie named Pete Ruggieri, who was excited to say the least when Jack told him about me. I can just imagine the look on Ruggieri's face when Jack told him he was getting his picks from an NBA referee. Talk about winning the lottery—Ruggieri probably had a new Rolex on his wrist and a shiny Caddy in the driveway before Jack got the words out of his mouth. I can't believe how naïve I was when I occasionally reminded Jack not to tell anyone what we were doing. I never thought it would go any further than the two of us.

But as usually happens in situations like this, Ruggieri was so giddy over his newfound good fortune that he had to share it with someone else. He gave the information to—you guessed it—James "Ba Ba" Battista, and although I was not aware of it at the time, Ba Ba and his crew immediately began to secretly bet along with us, initially placing $25,000 a game on my picks. Why did Ruggieri have to tell Ba Ba, of all people? Why couldn't he tell a stripper during a lap dance or share a little pillow talk with his mistress? No, it had to be Ba Ba!

Finally, in early November of 2006, I just said, "Jack, I don't feel comfortable doing this anymore. Let's quit. We're never going to do this again." Jack understood, but then word traveled down the line that I was no longer making picks. Jack told Ruggieri, who in turn told Ba Ba.

That's when Tommy Martino started calling repeatedly to tell me that Ba Ba wanted to talk about something important. At that point, I didn't know Ba Ba was connected to the Gambinos, and I didn't know that he had been using my picks to make bets of his own. I didn't know exactly why he wanted to talk to me, but I figured he was going to get me in trouble. Later, I learned from the FBI that Ba Ba had been making millions on my picks. So that's why, on the night of December 12, 2006, Tommy and Ba Ba turned up in a four-door Honda at the Marriott Hotel in Philadelphia.

* * *

As soon as I saw Battista, I thought to myself, *Oh shit, nothing good is going to come of this.* I debated turning around and going back into the hotel, but I decided I might as well get it over with and hear what they had to say. I was shocked by how much Ba Ba had changed since high school. He was a blob of a man, nothing like his days of bulging muscles and tight-fitted shirts. Then the terrible thought ran through my mind: *I wonder if he knows what I've been doing.* That's when it hit me. He wasn't there to catch up on old times. He was there for one reason only: to put the squeeze on me, to shake me down.

Tommy started driving, telling me that he needed something at the convenience store. As he drove, Ba Ba turned to me and said quietly, "We know what's been going on."

"What do you mean?" I asked.

"We know you've been giving information to Jack," Ba Ba said. "Jack's been booking his bets with Pete, and Pete's been telling us."

Suddenly, I was sick to my stomach. I didn't know where this was going, but I knew I was in a major jam. It was a cold winter night in Philadelphia, but I felt like sweat was pouring down my forehead.

"You're better off going through me," Ba Ba said. "You don't want the NBA to find out about this."

The NBA? In my mind, Jack and I had already stopped betting on NBA games; it was over, a thing of the past. Now, suddenly, Ba Ba was trying to drag me back into it, but on a much bigger scale. *There's got to be some way out of this,* I thought, but as I sat in the back of that car, I was numb. We reached the convenience store, Tommy and I went in, and I immediately laid into him.

"What the fuck are you doing?" I asked angrily. "Bringing him down to me?"

"Tim, he's like a wart up my ass," Tommy responded. "I can't get rid of him." I just shook my head.

Tommy bought a ChapStick or something like that and we got back in the car and returned to the Marriott. We went straight to the restaurant, but I was so nauseated that I couldn't eat. Ba Ba, however, ordered 10 appetizers and the table was quickly covered with platters of food.

They told me how we were going to set the whole thing up. "For every correct pick you give me, I'll give you $2,000," Ba Ba explained. "By the way, it's going to be 2,000 'apples.' From now on, we talk about money, it's 'apples.' It'll be 2,000 'apples' for you, and 2,000 for Martino over there."

"Ba Ba," I explained desperately, "I can't do this. This is going to get me in a lot of trouble."

Ba Ba looked me right in the eye. "You don't want anyone from New York visiting your wife and kids in Florida, do you?" he asked, his threat hanging in the air.

Right then and there, I knew it was take it or leave it. He was willing to drag my wife and kids into it. I wasn't sure if the threat was real or not, but he seemed very serious that night and I wasn't going to take any chances.

After dinner, the waitress brought the bill to the table. It was like a scene straight out of *The Sopranos*: Ba Ba pulled a folded wad of greenbacks wrapped with a rubber band out of his duffel bag and peeled off enough cash to pay the $150 bill and leave a $100 tip.

"You're coming to Martino's house tomorrow," Ba Ba demanded, "and you're going to tell us how to bet the game tomorrow night, Philly against Boston."

I was scheduled to referee that game—that's why I was in town. And now this. The entire time they were eating, I was looking around the restaurant, afraid that somebody might recognize me and the two thugs at my table.

After dinner, I headed to my hotel room knowing that I had been hooked by Ba Ba. At that very moment, I understood with perfect clarity that there was no way this thing could end well.

Pathetically, I still clung to the notion that I might somehow be able to hold onto my job. I figured that since the NBA didn't know about the gambling I did with Jack, I might be in the clear on all of that. I even tried to convince myself that the whole thing with Ba Ba would only run until the NBA Finals, and then he would cut me loose. Clearly I was grasping at straws, trying to keep myself from facing the horrible reality of what was occurring. The lives of my wife and children had been threatened. Harm would come to them, to me, or to all of us if I didn't give picks—*winning* picks—to this low-rent hoodlum.

I always stayed close to my wife and daughters during the season, and when I was on the road, I would typically call them on the phone five or six times a day. That night, my wife Kim called around 10:00 PM and she could tell I was not myself. Obviously, I couldn't tell her what had just happened. She was peppering me with all kinds of questions: "Is everything okay? Did you see your mom and dad? What's going on?" I just told her I was tired and we said good night.

In bed, I tossed and turned, thinking, *There's got to be a way out of this.* I couldn't go to law enforcement. Can you imagine what that conversation would have sounded like?

Donaghy: Ba Ba threatened me and said that if I didn't give him my NBA picks, he would do something to my wife and kids.

FBI: Why did he come to you?

Donaghy: Because he knew I had been gambling on NBA games for years.

FBI: Oh really?

The next morning, I visited my parents as I always did on trips to Philadelphia. I also saw a buddy of mine who was struggling with cancer. I never said a word to anyone. Instead, I dutifully showed up at Tommy's house at 2:30 that afternoon. Tommy was divorced with no kids and lived in a middle-class neighborhood in the Philadelphia suburb of Chichester.

When I entered the house, Tommy's handgun was on the kitchen counter; he explained that the gun was for "protection." *What am I doing here?* I thought to myself, feeling trapped. *Why did I ever bet on NBA games?*

In the end, I did exactly what they wanted me to do. I told them that Allen Iverson was gone from the 76ers and that because it was still early in the season, the underachieving Celtics would be competitive. I told them that Boston would start tanking games in late January or early February, but for the time being they were still playing hard. On top of that, at the pregame meeting that morning one of my fellow referees, Derrick Stafford, told us he thought Philadelphia coach Maurice Cheeks didn't have a clue about coaching and that forward Chris Webber was washed up and couldn't jump anymore. So at least Stafford seemed convinced that Boston was going to win. When the refs make up their minds in the pregame meeting, it often becomes a self-fulfilling prophecy. That's the type of information I used in many of my picks. That was it: I told Tommy and Ba Ba to go with Boston, and then I got the hell out of there.

That night on the court, as the national anthem played and the Boston Celtics and the Philadelphia 76ers stood at attention, I just stared straight ahead, knowing I had given Ba Ba inside information. In a lame attempt to deny complicity in the dirty scheme, I made a personal promise that I would not make any calls to influence the outcome. I tried to put the whole thing out of my mind and do my job as though it was just another game. And then, just before the anthem was finished, I looked about 10 rows up in the crowd and thought I saw Ba Ba. *Oh my God,* I thought. *He's here to remind me of our deal.* It turned out to be just a guy who looked like Ba Ba, but the sight of that fat slob sent a chill through my entire body.

The game was a blowout: Boston won 101–81. Somehow, I was able to get lost in the game and concentrate on my job as a referee. I actually managed to put the business with Ba Ba out of my mind for a couple of hours, but then I truly disgusted myself by thinking, *Wow, I'm getting $2,000 tomorrow!*

I knew I was screwed and in a tight spot, but I also knew I was going to Tommy's house the following day and getting $2,000 in cash. My gambling instincts were taking over, and I was perversely excited.

My family, my career, and my personal freedom all hung in the balance, but I was actually juiced about winning the bet. On top of that, I still thought that somehow the whole thing might blow over and I would be able to keep my job as an NBA referee. Talk about delusional! I am a compulsive gambler and I actually thought that this mess could be resolved in my favor. It's like chasing one bad bet with another. It's all an illusion; it's smoke and mirrors. The only thing that's real is the incongruity of feeling total desperation while simultaneously experiencing exhilaration and euphoria. They call that feeling the "gambler's high," and for reasons that defy logic, I had it—and I loved it.

That night, I couldn't sleep. Ba Ba and I met the next day and he tossed me $2,000 rolled up in a rubber band. I wondered how I would hide the money; I couldn't put it in the bank and I certainly couldn't tell my wife. I began to convince myself that I was making the best of a bad situation.

Ba Ba immediately wanted my next pick for a game that night. I had already done my homework, studying the master list of referees and scoping out the matchups slated for that evening. I liked San Antonio against New Orleans, primarily because of the referees. In the NBA, three refs work a game, and that night Joe Forte, Sean Corbin, and Eli Roe would be on the court. Pop was tough on refs, and I knew he could control Corbin and Roe if they weren't giving him the calls he wanted. Corbin, in my opinion, was a weak referee, and Forte was young and not likely to stand up to the intimidating ways of a veteran coach like Popovich. So it was an easy call: San Antonio.

That night, San Antonio blew out New Orleans 103–77 and I earned another $2,000.

Through it all, I failed to realize that I had suddenly become the central figure in a Mafia-controlled gambling ring and that my picks would generate millions of dollars for the Gambino crime family. I never dreamed that within eight short months, I would be the focus of an NBA betting scandal, a target of the FBI and federal prosecutors, and a national disgrace. All I was thinking about was my $2,000 cut, what I would do with the money, and my naïve and misplaced notion that Ba Ba would eventually release me from his grasp and allow me to retreat into the shadows.

From respected NBA referee to mafioso. What the hell happened to me?

CHAPTER 2

The Education of an NBA Referee

I've loved basketball for as long as I can remember. When I was growing up in Havertown, Pennsylvania, I lived for the game. Morning, noon, and night I was somewhere, anywhere, shooting hoops, perfecting my dribble, working on my jump shot, and always dreaming of playing in the NBA. If there was a game on television, I was watching. I knew all the teams, each player, and every recorded statistic. Living near Philadelphia, I was a huge fan of the 76ers. In those days they had Dr. J, Moses Malone, Billy Cunningham, Mo Cheeks, and Andrew Toney. My favorite players were Doug Collins and Mike Dunleavy; they were scrappy guys who always hustled, real gamers with lots of heart and respect for the game. I played competitively through high school, but at 5'9", a college or pro career was not in the cards. Of course, no one could convince me of that back then. I had a dream to play in the NBA and I was determined to go all the way.

A true love of the game was instilled in me at an early age by my father, Gerry Donaghy. For upwards of 30 years, he officiated basketball games in high school and college. For the last 20 years of his career as a referee he worked big-time Division I college basketball. He was a regular in the NCAA Division I Men's Basketball Tournament and had the privilege of working the Final Four on four occasions. My dad was respected by everyone—the very epitome of honesty, integrity, and impartiality.

Being a referee was not my dad's primary job, however. He worked for more than 30 years for General Electric in Philadelphia, retiring in 1996. Still, from late November through early March, my dad had a second full-time job, one that kept him on the road and away from his family. He worked games primarily in the ACC, Conference USA, and the Atlantic Ten Conference, typically reffing six games a week. After finishing his day at GE, he would immediately jump in the car and travel to a game destination, often making a four-hour, one-way drive. It was not unusual for him to get home at 2:00 in the morning, get a few hours' sleep, and then start the cycle all over again. During basketball season, nothing got in the way of his commitment to the game—not the winter in the Northeast, not the long hours on the road, and not his wife and four boys back in Havertown. It seemed to me that he was gone all the time, and for those months during the season, he was.

Until I finally figured it out, his time away from home was a puzzle to me. He certainly didn't need the headaches of monotonous travel, bad weather, angry coaches, and boisterous fans. It was something deep within him that called his name and inspired him to get in his car and drive or fly to faraway places like Chapel Hill, North Carolina, or Morgantown, West Virginia, week after week.

He knew of my enthusiasm for basketball and began bringing me along with him to road games when I was seven or eight years old. Night after night, I studied him on the court very closely: how he moved, where he positioned himself, the quiet confidence he projected, the manner in which he handled the tough situations, and the commitment he made to letting the players, not the refs, determine the outcome of the game.

My father has always been larger than life to me; a serious man with a firm hand, a big heart, and an unimpeachable character. And there was something else. Watching him in action and listening to the reverence with which he spoke of the game, I discovered his true passion. I think that's when I made the transformation from mere basketball fan to something more. Basketball became a metaphor for something larger to me. It was about hard work, discipline, talent, tradition, fairness, and integrity.

By allowing me to get a glimpse of his world on the court, my dad unwittingly groomed me to follow in his footsteps. He knew I was nuts for everything basketball, and when he talked to me about the game he could plainly see that I hung on his every word. I like to believe that he thought I had what it took, that intangible instinct that is sometimes passed along from father to son. Although he never told me so, perhaps he wanted the Donaghy basketball legacy to continue—and I was his best shot.

If there was one thing my dad stressed to me more than basketball, it was the value of a college education. He was aware of my dream to play in the NBA, but he also knew it was a fantasy, not reality. On many occasions, he reminded me that precious few players, even talented ones, ever made it to the NBA. On the other hand, a college degree lasted forever and was something that could never be taken away. I recall driving through poor neighborhoods with my dad on frigid winter nights in Philadelphia. He would point to a homeless person huddled over a steam vent trying to get warm and say, "See that guy over there? He thought he was going to be a first-round draft pick in the NBA, so he didn't bother with an education. See what happens?" My dad knew just how to drive a point home and, as a young boy, it made me think. The only problem was school was never my strong suit.

I grew up with three brothers who had all the brains in the family— they breezed through school with straight As while I struggled to get Bs and Cs. Bringing home my report card was not something I looked forward to. School was tough for me, and I learned at an early age that I couldn't compete with my brothers' grades. My options were simple: I could either be the family screwup or the funny guy. I chose the latter. A sense of humor was my way of glossing over my academic shortcomings, and for the most part it worked. People saw me as the practical joker, the guy who made everyone laugh. In my senior year of high school, I was voted class clown.

From first grade through high school I attended Catholic school where everything was very black and white—and I'm not just referring to the traditional habit worn by the sisters. Things were done one way and one way only—very strict, very orderly—which was not the best environment for a funny kid who liked to shake things up. Most of the trouble that came my way was because I was always goofing off, and I usually didn't think of the consequences before I acted. Oh, there were other kids my age that pulled a prank or two, but for some reason I was usually the one who got caught. I suppose it was all self-inflicted. Besides, me being the master showman, my stunts were usually first-rate and always over the top—vintage Timmy Donaghy.

Sadly, my teachers never appreciated my sense of humor. In sixth grade, I once waited for Miss McNulty to walk out of the room before grabbing the only other kid in class who was smaller than me and shoving him in the closet. Then I opened the window of the third-floor classroom and waited. When Miss McNulty returned, I started screaming at the top of my lungs, "Oh my God, Miss McNulty! Richard just jumped out the window!" I thought Miss McNulty was going to die of a heart attack; she ran to the window with an ear-piercing scream. When Richard came out of the closet in one piece, she realized what I had done. Everyone in the class was laughing their ass off, but Miss McNulty wasn't too pleased. Neither was my father when he came to pick me up that day.

Like any kid, I wanted to make my dad proud, but I could never get my act together. Growing up with three brothers didn't make it any easier. We were very competitive, and regardless of the sport or activity, the goal was to bring home the first-place trophy. In my family, you simply didn't come home with anything other than first place. I remember once in high school winning second place in a three-on-three basketball tournament. On the way home, I rolled the car window down and chucked the trophy over the side of the Walt Whitman Bridge in Philadelphia. It was better to come home with nothing than to be second place. I hated the feeling of not winning and would do anything to avoid it.

My parents weren't openly affectionate, but my brothers and I knew they loved us. My mother Joan taught me the importance of family and friends. She put her family and friends above herself in a very selfless way. Mom was always there for me; she checked my homework, helped me through school, and came to every one of my baseball and basketball games. From my dad I learned the importance of a strong work ethic.

Both my parents had strong values and taught us by example. For whatever reason, I didn't always get the message. But when I messed up, my parents were adamant that I take responsibility for my actions. I was never allowed to cover anything up because "it would make it worse down the road." How prophetic those words would turn out to be.

After finishing high school, I went to night school at Villanova University and cleaned fish in the seafood department at Super Fresh Food Market during the day. After my first semester, I transferred to day school and stopped smelling like grouper and red snapper. My friends and I had some great times at Villanova. The campus was small enough that everybody knew each other, and it was close enough to my home that some of my friends from high school would come up to visit and party.

Tommy Martino was one of my friends who'd swing by Villanova from time to time. He was a lot of fun and really knew how to make the girls laugh. Tommy was the guy who had what every college kid wanted—the car, the money, and the cute girl. He didn't go to school and didn't work, so partying seemed like his main occupation. I didn't really know how he supported himself back then and I never asked. At the time, it didn't seem like it mattered.

I graduated from Villanova in 1989—not bad for a guy who never read a book and survived almost exclusively on CliffsNotes. During college, I did some refereeing on the weekends, mostly high school games and park ball, nothing serious. But a year or so after graduation, I was sitting at the kitchen table with my parents when my mom suggested I pursue a job in the NBA. Talk about out of the blue! But for some reason her suggestion hit me right between the eyes. I had three "real" jobs after college and I hated each one. I was a sales representative for a packaging equipment and supply company, an insurance adjuster, and a sales representative for a cellular phone company. There were many days when I feared growing old behind some office desk, wilting away right along with my dreams. One thing was for sure: I never stopped dreaming about the NBA, and my mother's suggestion was the only push I would need. So I took a shot, sent a letter to the NBA, and made a few follow-up phone calls. I never heard back.

In 1990, I decided to attend a camp in South Carolina for referees who wanted to improve their skills. Dr. Aaron Wade, who worked for the Continental Basketball Association and also helped train referees for the NBA, also attended the camp. Dr. Wade was the kind of no-nonsense guy you didn't speak to unless he started the conversation. So when I noticed him watching one of my games, I was hesitant to approach him. I was only 22 years old, and he was an intimidating figure. Little did I know that Aaron Wade would ultimately be a tremendous help to me over the years for which I would owe him a great debt of gratitude.

Two weeks after I got back from the camp, Dr. Wade called me. "Can you go to L.A. for two weeks?" he asked. "I'd like to watch you referee in the L.A. Summer Pro League."

I could hardly believe it. "Sure," I said. What I wanted to say was, "Hell yes!" A few days later I received a FedEx package with a plane ticket to Los Angeles. I was on my way to the big leagues.

When I arrived in L.A., I met Darell Garretson, the NBA's Supervisor of Officials. Darell closely watched all the games, and I knew that if I did well there was a chance I might snag a spot on the CBA's roster of referees. The CBA was the official minor league of the NBA. Minor or not, the league earned the reputation of being the toughest to referee because it wasn't, let's say, quite as civilized as the NBA. It was the Wild West of basketball: small towns, raucous fans, and coaches and players who were desperately trying to escape the CBA and make it to the Promised Land. The L.A. Summer Pro League was challenging, but Darell was there for me every step of the way. He helped all the guys and truly wanted us to succeed. For a referee, the name of the game is confidence, and Darell Garretson's unwavering support helped build my confidence, without which I never would have been hired by the NBA.

During the camp in Los Angeles, I kept my mouth shut and tried to listen and learn. Though I was the youngest referee there and by far the least experienced, someone must have seen some potential. By the end of the two weeks, Dr. Wade told me he was going to use me in the CBA's upcoming season. I was so excited I could have flown home without a plane—I was walking on air. If I did well in the CBA training program,

I knew I might eventually get a roster spot in the NBA. I wasn't going to make it as a player, but my dream of making it to the NBA was about to come true.

* * *

During my first year in the CBA, I only worked weekend games—usually Fridays and Saturdays. The travel was exhausting and the pay was low—just $125 per game—but I knew I had to pay my dues. The grind took a toll on my social life as well. I'd been dating a girl named Ann for five years when she came to me one day with an ultimatum: "Tim, this just isn't working for us. It's either me or the games." Wonder whatever became of her? Actually, it was a tough decision, as I had contemplated asking Ann to marry me. But I loved working as a referee and I wasn't prepared to give up on my boyhood dream. In an act of serendipity, two weeks after Ann and I broke up, I met the woman who would eventually be the mother of my four beautiful daughters.

Kimberly Strupp was the sole flight attendant on a 6:00 AM commuter flight from Rockford, Illinois, to Chicago. From the very moment I looked into her big blue eyes, I was a goner. During the flight, we exchanged some small talk and she gave me her phone number. She had an easy manner about her and a spirited sense of humor. I thought we made a real connection during the short flight and I couldn't wait to see her again.

Our first date was at Bookbinder's restaurant in Philadelphia. She was based out of Chicago at the time and caught a flight to Philly to meet for lunch. We talked and laughed for hours, and in the process discovered we had much in common. She was a sports fan, liked to travel, loved to laugh, and was very family-oriented. From that day forward we were a couple. Kim eventually transferred to Philadelphia so we could be closer to one another. She traveled with me to many CBA games and supported me in every way. My dream of making it to the NBA became her dream, too.

I worked a full slate of games during my second year in the CBA. The travel was rough, the schedule grueling, and the pay still lousy—but I was getting closer to my ultimate goal. I was constantly on the road, making stops at small arenas in towns like La Crosse, Wisconsin, Rochester, Minnesota, and Wichita Falls, Texas. To make ends meet, I worked a variety of odd jobs, anything to pick up a few bucks to pay the bills.

I was asked to referee the NBA preseason before my third year in the CBA and again just before my fourth year in the CBA. It was an unbelievable experience, one that gave me reassurance that I was up to the challenge. At the NBA level, the game is lightning-fast and all the players are enormously talented. It's the ultimate level of basketball competition, where only the elite survive.

I never made it to that fourth season in the CBA: the NBA finally called my name after all those years in darkly lit gymnasiums in two-dog towns, all those soggy sandwiches eaten out of a bag with one hand while driving down a lonely highway, and all that time away from home. It was a dream no more. It was real, and I was right where I always belonged— center court, ready for the tip-off. My starting salary that first year was $69,000—not bad for a guy who'd been cleaning fish in a supermarket just a few years earlier. I was floating on air and finally doing something that made my dad proud.

My relationship with Kim continued to blossom, and on Christmas night of 1994 I asked her to marry me. Of course, the proposal came in a hotel room in Detroit, where I was scheduled to work a Pistons game in a couple of days. In those days it didn't matter where we were as long as we were together. We later eloped to Barbados and became husband and wife. For the first time in my life, I had a partner who loved me, supported me, and shared my dreams.

Just minutes before my first NBA game, I remember telling myself, "I made it! I'm here! Stay calm, do the best job you can, and rely on what got you here." I was extremely nervous, but at the same time I was thrilled to be on the court with the greatest athletes on the planet, running up and down the floor beside them, watching them do amazing things with 20,000 fans cheering wildly. I was one of a select group of officials who were given the honor of wearing an NBA referee's uniform. It was a job I was born to do, and the uniform fit like a glove.

My first regular-season game as a referee was memorable, to say the very least. It was November 9, 1994, and the Houston Rockets were playing the Indiana Pacers in Indianapolis. My boss and mentor Darell Garretson was at the game, and I was working with referees Paul Mihalik and Blane Reichelt. The NBA had just established new hand-checking rules—no one could put a hand on an offensive player who had the ball beyond the foul line. The league was trying its best to clean up a game thought to be getting too physical; the idea was that the new rule would make the pace of the game faster, and both scoring and ticket sales would go up—always the NBA's main concern. Since this was one of the first games of the year, Garretson really stressed the hand-check rule during our pregame meeting.

We called so many fouls during the game that the fans went nuts. It seemed as though we were blowing the whistle on every other play, usually for fouls that wouldn't have been called the previous year. Between the three of us we called 69 fouls, an extremely high number for an NBA game. As a result, there was no flow to the game and the fans were noticeably irritated. And they were right—play stopped so often that the whole purpose of the rule was totally defeated.

Still, the only thing faster than Reggie Miller's trigger that night was the beating of my heart. Every time I blew the whistle, all 20,000 pairs of eyes were on me. I liked it, the same way I liked getting a laugh from my friends back in school. Talk about showtime!

At the tail end of the game, things got intense. Indiana was losing in the final minute and Reggie had the ball in the corner, about to attempt a three-point shot. He was defended by Houston's Hakeem Olajuwon, and after pump-faking him into the air, Reggie buried his shoulder into Olajuwon's neck, trying to draw a foul but knocking Hakeem down in the process. Instinctively, I called an offensive foul on Reggie. The place went nuts—as did Reggie and the rest of the Pacers. He thought I would call a foul on Hakeem and that he would go to the foul line for three shots. He was wrong.

Things got so chaotic that it took more than 10 minutes to finish the last minute of the game. The fans were throwing anything they could grab onto the court including water, beer, soda, and coins. Every time we got it cleaned up, they'd just throw more. I was standing in the center of the court to stay out of range of the flying debris; Mihalik and Reichelt stood on the baseline under the basket. Even the announcers at the scorer's table were covering their bodies and microphones with whatever they could find. I remember thinking to myself, *How the hell are we going to get this game over with?* Finally it ended, and we made a run for the locker room. During the exodus, somebody threw a full cup of beer on me. Tasted like Miller Lite.

In the locker room, Darell Garretson wasn't happy. He came down pretty hard on Matt Winick, who was in charge of assigning referees for the game. Garretson was furious that Winick had chosen such a weak crew for my debut. For the first few years, most young officials are paired with experienced refs, the type of guys who work the NBA Finals. That didn't happen in my first game. We watched the game tape back at the hotel and league officials ultimately defended the call I made on Reggie Miller—but I am sure they wished I had called a foul on Olajuwon. That night, I was one of the lead stories on ESPN's *SportsCenter*, featuring highlights of me standing on the court, debris flying all over the place. Not exactly how I envisioned my first game.

Later, someone on the NBA staff anonymously sent a football helmet to my house with a note that read, "You may need to wear this for the rest of your career!" Years later I watched the tape of the game with some other referees and we had a good laugh. At the time, however, it wasn't very funny.

After that fiasco, I started settling into my new routine. On a typical game day, I would have breakfast and get in a workout. The grind of an 82-game schedule is difficult, and physical fitness is an absolute necessity. The referee crew would have a meeting at 11:00 AM and cover a number of topics, including a discussion of players and any problems in the past games between the two teams. We would also watch plays that the league office would send to us electronically to watch on a computer. For example, the league office might want us to watch different plays intended to illustrate what was considered a traveling violation, or we might receive a video demonstrating the difference between a blocking foul and a charge. Sometimes the league was concerned that we weren't calling enough defensive three-second violations. If the refereeing staff was reticent about making a particular call, all the crews would get video of plays to review so that we would all know what to look for next time. We might hear from the league's supervisors or other referees that, for instance, Kevin Garnett travels a lot when he's in the post, or that Chris Webber moved his pivot foot in an obvious manner. This was done casually all year, but when the playoffs started the league office made a major issue of it and wanted us to blow the whistle and crack down on violations.

The tone in our pregame meetings was mostly professional, but that wasn't always the case. Sometimes a referee might say something like, "I had this guy two or three weeks ago, and he's a real asshole. If he starts this shit with me again tonight, I'm gonna get him." Of course, it wasn't only about which players or coaches we were going after. The flip side was talking about players or coaches we had to protect. Back when Lamar Odom was playing for the Miami Heat, longtime referee Dick Bavetta told me before a game, "The last time I had Miami, Odom had six fouls and the league emailed us and showed us that four or five of the fouls weren't good calls. We've got to take care of him. I can't have him think I'm fucking him two games in a row." So I would make a mental note of that. I remember thinking, *That's strange—are we calling a game as we see it or choosing sides?*

The pregame meeting lasted about 45 minutes, and then it was off to lunch. Afternoons were pure boredom. We did whatever we could to make the time pass quickly—go shopping, watch TV, go to the movies, or make phone calls.

As time passed, however, I began to realize that our job was more about refereeing specific players as opposed to uniformly enforcing the rules of the game. In other words, we were more concerned with who might be getting a foul and what point it was in the game, instead of just calling it like we saw it. I remember hearing comments from fans, coaches, and other referees along the lines of, "People don't come to see Shaquille O'Neal, Charles Barkley, or Michael Jordan sit on the bench." Our group supervisors would tell us the same thing, saying things like, "People paid $1,500 to sit courtside to see LeBron James or Kobe Bryant. Make sure if you blow the whistle on these guys, it's an obvious foul."

As a result, referees would huddle up during a game to make sure they were all on the same page. If Kobe Bryant had two fouls in the first or second quarter and went to the bench, one referee would tell the other two, "Kobe's got two fouls. Let's make sure that if we call a foul on him, it's an obvious foul, because otherwise he's gonna go back to the bench. If he is involved in a play where a foul is called, give the foul to another player."

Similarly, when games got physically rough, we would huddle up and agree to tighten the game up. So we started calling fouls on guys who didn't really matter—"ticky-tack" or "touch" fouls where one player just touched another but didn't really impede his progress. Under regular circumstances these wouldn't be fouls, but after a skirmish we wanted to regain control. We would never call these types of fouls on superstars, just on the average players who didn't have star status. It was important to keep the stars on the floor.

I was so young and naïve when I was coming up. When I was a ref in the CBA, Aaron Wade told us that there were no superstars in the league—there was no particular player whom people came to see. Dr. Wade simply told us, "If you see it, you call it." Darell Garretson would tell us the same thing during NBA training or rookie leagues. So that was the mind-set I had when I made it to the NBA.

It didn't take long to realize that my approach to officiating didn't match up with that of the veteran referees. Once I became part of the staff, I was slowly taught the craft of NBA officiating. The league continued to stress the new hand-checking rules and drummed it into our heads in pregame meetings: "Under no circumstances is a player allowed to put a hand on a ball handler who is beyond the free-throw line." Throughout that season, I was blowing my whistle all the time—but I started to notice other referees weren't.

"Why aren't you guys calling hand checking?" I asked. "They were adamant about it in the meeting."

"We're not calling it unless the hand check actually impedes another player's progress," the veteran would say.

"But that's not what they said in the meetings," I would respond, surprised.

"If you want to survive in this league," the veteran refs explained, "you'd better back off calling it."

With that advice, I started to back off. As a new ref, I was obviously receiving mixed signals. The officials in the NBA front office were telling us to do one thing, but the older veteran refs weren't complying. To fit in and "survive," I simply did what the older refs did, no more questions asked. I was slowly learning that NBA referees had their own way of officiating a professional basketball game.

After working with veteran referees for several years, I was able to predict how certain referees would call a game. For example, I was at my brother Jim's house for a birthday party when I was a young ref, and Dick Bavetta was officiating an NBA game on TV. "Watch," I told my brother. "Anytime Bavetta referees, you'll rarely see a blowout. When a team gets up by 20, he starts blowing the whistle like crazy." And sure enough, that's what happened—one team got way ahead before Bavetta whistled the other team back into contention.

By 1996, I had been in the league a couple of years, still trying to do things the right way. I'll never forget a pivotal moment in a game in Philadelphia I was refereeing with Ed T. Rush. The 76ers' opponent was the Chicago Bulls. That year, the league office showed us film of a particular spin move players were utilizing on the baseline. By rule, if the ball wasn't out of the player's hand before he lifted his pivot foot, he should be called for a traveling violation. The trailing ref was supposed to watch for that play because the other referee would be under the basket with an obstructed view. I was the trailing ref that night when Michael

Jordan made that exact spin move on the baseline, and I called a travel. I waved off his basket and 20,000 people—presumably Philadelphia fans—started screaming at me. I couldn't believe it.

A timeout was called and Jordan and Bulls coach Phil Jackson rushed over. Jordan was in shock. He wasn't angry—just puzzled. His attitude seemed to be, it's okay to call that violation, but don't call it on me!

By the time Phil Jackson reached me, he had his hands in the air. "What are you doing?" he asked, stunned by the call.

"Phil," I said, "that's the travel they told us to call."

"They don't want that called on *him*," Jackson said, pointing at Jordan. And Jordan added, "You're gonna call that on *me*?"

I recall thinking, *What is everyone complaining about?* The Bulls knew what was expected of them. I was just as puzzled looking back at them as they were looking at me. Nobody had any answers for me, and it was something I definitely wanted to talk about with the other referees after the game. It was strange; the whole place was booing me. Why were the Philadelphia fans upset at me for calling a travel on the Bulls? The simple answer is that everyone—even the 76ers fans—paid to see Michael Jordan work his magic with the basketball. It was basically a show, and my call was getting in the way of the star performer.

After the game, I went over to Ed T. Rush, one of the top referees on the staff, and said, "Ed, that's the spin move we saw on the tapes. Why did I catch so much heat?"

He shook his head and looked at me as if I had just fallen off the back of a cabbage truck. "You have to think about who you're calling it on," he said.

Wow, I thought. *I didn't realize I was supposed to blow the whistle based on who's playing.* However, back in those days, when a senior referee told you to do something, you didn't talk back. You listened and you kept your mouth shut.

It was a defining moment for me, because the referee's manual explicitly states, "Don't call personalities." But here was a respected referee telling me that's how the game was played. Sometime later that season, I was given a picture of Michael Jordan and me on the court, both of us standing with our hands on our hips. I brought it with me the next time I worked a game in Chicago and one of my fellow officials said, "We'll send it in and he'll sign it for you."

Sure enough, after the game the ball boy returned the signed photo along with a personal message from Michael: "Next time, do a better job and give me some calls!"

CHAPTER

Down the Rabbit Hole

"Hi, my name is Tim, and I'm a compulsive gambler. I placed my last bet on March 18, 2007."

That's how new members introduce themselves at a Gamblers Anonymous meeting. It's how I did it. Obviously, I didn't just wake up one morning and realize I was a gambling addict. No, that discovery took some time. So how does a nice Catholic boy from suburban Philadelphia end up as the poster child for illegal sports gambling in America? That's a great question.

Jack Concannon and I have known each other for a long time. During our teenage years, he was a star on the Monsignor Bonner High School basketball team in Drexel Hill, Pennsylvania. Bonner was a big rival of my school, and we got to know each other on a casual basis. We never really hung out together; Jack was a couple of years older than me. I would see him at basketball games and around town on occasion, but that's about it.

At 6'5", Jack had an impressive game and led the Bonner team to the Philadelphia Catholic League Championship in 1983 and 1984. Jack was all about defense, a rugged guy who completely dominated weaker opponents. He always struck me as the kind of guy who would sink his teeth into something, or someone, and never let go. He just didn't quit; a real determined, win-at-all-costs competitor.

Beneath the ruthless exterior, Jack was one of the nicest guys I've ever met. We reconnected in the late 1990s on a golf course, of all places.

My wife and I became members of Radley Run Country Club in West Chester, Pennsylvania, in 1998. I had been working in the NBA for four years and the pay was getting pretty good. I always loved golf and liked the idea of belonging to a private and exclusive club. Enter Jack Concannon. Jack was also a country-clubber just down the road from Radley Run. It was common for area clubs to invite each other to golf tournaments and social gatherings, and as it turned out a mutual friend and fellow member invited Jack to play with us. I hadn't seen him in several years, but he still looked the same, with one exception. Now in his midthirties, he had distinctive salt-and-pepper hair that complemented his boyish looks. We hit it off right away and reminisced about the good old days in high school. Jack had heard about my job in the NBA and said everyone back home was very proud of me. He had married his high school sweetheart, Ann, and they had two girls and a boy. By that time, Kim and I were a happily married couple with three girls of our own and a fourth on the way.

It was amazing how much we had in common. Jack owned a successful insurance agency and was doing well financially. He was a devoted family man still living near his Pennsylvania hometown. Jack was a huge sports fan and an avid golfer—a nouveau country club social climber. He was Catholic, with a middle-class upbringing and a real soft spot for the hometown team. All just like me. And I was about to find out that I would soon share one of Jack's greatest passions: gambling.

While playing golf that first day, we had a blast and became fast friends. Jack and I played every chance we could, talked on the phone regularly, and even attended parties and family functions together with our wives. Kim and Ann became friends and our kids played together—the whole thing was like Philadelphia's version of *Leave It to Beaver*.

Since Jack owned his own business, he could play golf anytime he felt the itch—and he was always itching for a game. I had summers off, so I was always ready to go. We became so close that whenever he called on the phone and my wife answered, she would sarcastically say, "Tim, your girlfriend is on the phone."

Jack drove a big black Mercedes-Benz with a trunk full of Polo, Izod, and Tommy Hilfiger golf shirts. I used to call him "Superman" because he would fly into the country club parking lot, change his clothes out of the trunk of his car, play a fast round of golf, down a few beers, play some cards, change back into his work clothes, and still be home in time for dinner with June, Wally, and the Beaver.

Naturally, the golf course was where my gambling adventure with Jack began. We started out with modest wagers of $20 per hole and gradually got carried away to the tune of $200 or $300 per hole. It was exciting and a bit nerve-racking the first few times I stood over a $2,000 putt on the 18th hole, but I quickly realized that I had a steady hand under pressure and didn't rattle easily. After all, what could be more pressure-packed than reffing an NBA playoff game with the score tied and 1.8 seconds left in regulation? No sir, I didn't rattle easily, and the action was a thrill.

After 18 holes of golf, it was off to the clubhouse for a shower, dinner, and a friendly game of blackjack. The country club set is always flush with cash—guys we used to call "heavy pockets." The stakes were high and the bourbon smooth, just the way Jack and I liked it. Talk about Butch and Sundance! We were in our element and loving every minute of it; two downtown guys rubbing elbows with the uptown crowd and draining their pockets dry, at least most of the time. Winning or losing $5,000 or $10,000 at cards was par for the course. The lawyers, bankers, and traders never batted an eye. They just casually pulled a diamond-studded money clip out of their pocket and counted off the C-notes, one at a time. They'd mutter, "One, two, three, four, five," with little or no emotion. Jack and I were a little less polished. "And a one, and a two, and a three," speaking loudly in our best approximation of Lawrence Welk.

One of the big events at Radley Run was the Member-Guest Golf Tournament. Held every summer, each participating member invited a nonmember to join him in a two-man best-ball competition. The golf was fun and the cash prizes were sizeable. But it wasn't until after dinner was served, the prizes had been awarded, and the three-piece jazz ensemble had played its last set that Jack and I got down to business. The real action was on a table in the back parlor. And yes, the room was smoke-filled and players swished their brandy in expensive snifters. For Jack and me, however, it was a couple of longnecks and a shot of Jack Daniels.

I walked up to the table that night with $10,000 in my pocket and a firm understanding that I would either double or triple my wad or lose it all. This wasn't a penny-ante card game with the in-laws around the kitchen table on Christmas Eve. No, this was all about the thrill of laying our hard-earned money on the table and rolling the dice, so to speak. We took turns dealing—a very risky venture. A player loses only once per hand, while the dealer can lose as many hands as there are players in the game. Of course, the same principle applies to winning hands. Lots of upside, lots of downside, but I guess that's why they call it gambling.

Lady Luck was fickle that evening, and I walked out of the club with two golf tees and some lint in my pocket. Sitting alone in my car, tired from the long day and emotionally drained from the nonstop action upstairs, all I could think about was finding another game the next day. Ten thousand dollars gone, just like that. The funny thing is it took me years to realize that it was never really about the money—it was about the risk, the adrenaline, the juice of standing over that four-foot putt or flipping an ace or a king over someone's two queens. That's what it was about for us, and Jack and I couldn't get enough. On to Atlantic City!

Atlantic City, New Jersey, is a quick 80-minute drive from Philadelphia on an expressway paved with hope and lined with greed. Jack and his best buddies had been making the trip for years—sometimes two or three times a week—just to try their luck at the tables. Jack eventually invited me along, and I walked into a world that blew me away.

Jack's favorite casino was the Borgata, a big, flashy monument to the excesses of the fast life. Everyone was there: the blue hairs playing bingo and nickel slots, the poor folks betting their last dime, and the high rollers indiscriminately dropping thousands in exchange for being treated like royalty by the casino. Jack's crew fell into the last category. The casino rolled out the red carpet for Jack, giving him complimentary food, drinks, show tickets, luxury suites, and limos. He knew all the names of the dealers and the pit bosses, and they knew his. He strolled in like he owned the joint, waving to employees as if they were lifelong friends. Of course, we were all just playing a big game, but it was intoxicating and I couldn't wait to breathe it in.

Jack had his favorite table, his favorite dealer, and his favorite seat—it was a ritual he followed religiously. The game was always blackjack and the stakes were usually high. The minimum bet was $100, the maximum bet was $5,000, and I never saw Jack bet the minimum. Our group was loud and we often attracted a large flock of onlookers. After winning a big hand on a big bet we would all scream and curse for joy, and the gathering crowd would multiply. Our table became the real show on the Boardwalk, not the transvestite cross-dresser singing Bee Gees songs in the lounge or the washed-up '60s folk singer asking, "How many roads must a man walk down, before he knows he's a man?" Let me tell you, the answer wasn't blowing in the wind; it was staring Jack and me directly in the face. Should he split those 8s or double-down on a 9 when the dealer was showing a 6? You bet he should! After all, we didn't come for the buffet; we came to play!

My junkets to Atlantic City with Jack weren't limited to the summer off-season months. There were occasions when I was working a game on the West Coast and was scheduled to fly home the following morning for a few days off. Instead, I would finish the game and grab a taxi to the airport to catch a red-eye flight to Philly, usually arriving around 6:00 AM. As I strolled off the plane, eyes bleary from the restless flight, my good pal Jack was there to greet me with a devilish grin on his face. "Let's go, T.D.!" he'd say. "Time's a wasting and I'm feeling lucky!" Like a shot of black coffee on a cold Philadelphia winter morning, I immediately perked up and was ready to roll. I could already hear the sounds of the casino beckoning me to the Jersey shore for another roller-coaster ride of emotions. An hour and a half later and we would be sitting at the blackjack table, waiting for that ace to fall and our luck to turn.

At the same time, Kim was anxiously expecting me to pull into the driveway at 5:00 PM. Since I was on the road most of the month, living out of a suitcase in hotels across the country, Kim treated our rare evenings together as though it was our first date. My short stops at home were like long layovers in an airport during a winter storm. She probably thought I was still on an airplane, eating a bag of stale pretzels and sipping a ginger ale. But I wasn't. I was in Atlantic City, drinking beer and playing cards for hours with our good family friend, Jack Concannon. That was where the lies began: secret trips to the casino when I should have been home with Kim and our girls. I always felt guilty, but not guilty enough and not for very long. I had an itch to scratch and no matter how hard I scratched, the itch just wouldn't go away. I didn't want it to.

Those trips all ended the same way. With our pockets full or our pockets empty, we jumped in the car late in the afternoon and arrived back in Philly just in time. As I walked into the house, Kim would give me a big hug and the girls would scream, "Daddy's home!"

"How was your trip, honey?" she'd ask sympathetically.

"It was fine," I would reply. "Just like all the others."

I was back home, insulated from the world, protected by my family, and sheltered from my demons. Yeah, right—who was I kidding?

During the NBA season, I was away from home for 26 days of the month. Including the playoffs, I was a traveling nomad for eight to nine months of the year. But whether I was home for a three- or four-day break or the entire summer, gambling had begun to consume my life. The secret trips to the casino became as regular as getting a haircut, gassing up the car, or going to church. When the weather permitted, I played golf all day and cards all night. I invited gambling into my house along with Jack and some buddies for a night of blackjack in my swank subterranean game room. My daughters would take turns sitting on my lap while I dealt cards to the guys. I should have been upstairs, reading Dr. Seuss to the girls until they drifted off to sleep. But no, I was teaching them how to signal for another card by tapping the table or how to stay by waving off the dealer. It was so wrong, but I couldn't walk away. I justified my behavior in so many ridiculous and silly ways. I actually convinced myself that we were spending quality time together, but nothing could be further from the truth. I was becoming emotionally bankrupt, willing to risk it all for one more crack at the cards. Little did I know that I was just getting started.

I suppose the highlight (or lowlight) of my casino escapades with Jack and the boys came on a beautiful summer day in—where else?—Atlantic City. I told Kim we were playing golf and would be home by 6:00 PM. She told me not to be late, as she would have dinner on the table at 6:00 sharp. But we never played golf that day. Instead, we headed straight for the Borgata, where a legend was about to be born.

Jack and I would regularly play golf with a friend of ours I'll call Fred, who, like Jack, owned a company and was master of his schedule, free to jump in the car and head for the shore anytime he liked. Fred had both of his hips replaced during the previous couple of years and walked with a noticeable limp. Walking down the fairway or strolling through the Borgata, Fred looked like a toddler in diapers taking his first few steps.

As usual, our game was blackjack, and Fred wasted no time betting big—at times he was playing three hands of $5,000 or $6,000 apiece—and he was drunk off his ass. With each winning hand, another beer went down and we all laughed like hell. A crowd began to gather and before it was over they were 10 rows deep. He was like a cartoon character, shouting, roaring, and cursing every time the dealer had to pay.

"Winner, winner, chicken dinner! Pay the boys, Mr. Banker!" he cackled. The joint was jumping and people were taking notice, and I'm not just referring to the pretty cocktail waitresses trolling for tips. The floor bosses didn't think it was so funny, especially when Fred went up $150,000 for the day. I had just finished reading *Bringing Down the House*, the story of a group of MIT students who took the casinos for millions by counting cards. When the casinos got wind of their scam, the kids were escorted to a back room and roughed up.

So there I was, watching the whole thing unfold when I noticed the pit bosses whispering to each other. But Fred kept winning.

"How do you like me now, banker boy?" Fred barked.

Okay, okay, settle down big guy, I was thinking to myself. But there was no stopping him. As Fred's stack of chips grew, he stuffed them into his pockets, giddy as a schoolboy who had just copped his first feel. He leaned back in his chair and stared up at the ceiling cameras, extending his arms and pulling back his sleeves as if to say, "Nothing up here, boys!"

He was actually *taunting* these people.

One pit boss became two, two became three...well, you get the picture. Guys with names like Vincent, Salvatore, and Dominic were staring at us, arms folded across their chests, and I was starting to sweat. I wasn't even playing, but I smelled trouble. Just then, a stout little man with a round face and a Jimmy Durante nose walked right up to me. Damn it, why me? Did I have "NBA REF IN DEEP SHIT" written on my forehead?

"You look familiar," he casually said while thoroughly looking me over. "Where are you from? Would you like to fill out an information card?" I pretended that my cell phone was ringing and promptly excused myself.

Fred's lucky streak continued and he tossed me a $1,000 chip. I played the next hand and won. By that time it might as well have been *Monopoly* money. Nothing was real anymore, except the laughs and the kick I was getting from the adrenaline rush. We were eight guys at the table—eight guys with $1,000 chips up to their chins.

"Deal the cards, mister," I cracked. "I've gotta be home by six or my wife will have my ass."

With $150,000 in his pockets, Fred's day was through. We shut it down and headed straight for the dining room, arms around each other's shoulders. Supper was a veritable orgy of food and drink. Appetizers of fried calamari, oysters, clams on the half-shell, and stuffed mushroom caps were followed by fresh Brazilian lobster tails, jumbo prawns from northern California, and 16-ounce king-cut prime ribs, medium rare. The dinner bill was over $3,000 for the eight of us—compliments of the very good luck of our good friend Fred. We were all stuffed, collectively a modern-day tribute to the gluttony and excess of Roman soldiers on holiday in some faraway conquered land.

We crawled to our cars and drove back to Philly reliving the moments of glory ad nauseam. I pulled up to my house with 10 minutes to spare and went inside.

"How was the golf?" Kim asked.

"Good, I really kicked Jack's ass, but Fred was unbelievable. He couldn't lose," I replied.

"Hope you're hungry, I made your favorite: Tuna Helper," Kim boasted.

I sat down for dinner that night with two things on my mind. First, that I couldn't swallow another bite if my life depended on it. Second, I wondered if I could get out of the house the next day and coax the boys into another road trip. Can you believe that? I hadn't even come down from that day's high and I was already looking for more action. Unbelievable!

* * *

On a warm day in October of 2002, Jack and I were sitting around the clubhouse at Radley Run Golf Course after playing a big-money match against a couple of friends. It was football season and we were talking about an acquaintance of ours named Pete Ruggieri. Ruggieri had attended high school with Jack and still lived in the Philadelphia suburbs. Back in those days, he was a big football star for Bonner, a nose guard with the tenacity of a pit bull. At 5'7" and 250 pounds with orange-red hair, he definitely stood out in any crowd. Ruggieri was married with four kids, but didn't have a job—at least not a 9-to-5 job. Pete Ruggieri was a professional gambler; that's how he supported himself and his family. It was working out quite well for him, though. He had a nice house in a nice neighborhood and a summer home at the Jersey Shore.

Like the rest of us, Ruggieri loved to play golf, and he would frequently join us for a round of 18 holes. Jack and Pete had a much closer friendship than Jack and I did. They both belonged to the same country club and had remained friends since high school.

When we played on Fridays, Pete was constantly on his cell phone, always excusing himself to take a "business call." I asked Jack about all the calls and that's when he told me that Pete was a professional gambler, a bookie—and a good one at that. I knew that Jack liked to bet on college and pro football—he was always looking at the point spreads in the newspaper. He told me he would bet 15 college games on Thursday and

Saturday and another 15 NFL games on Sunday.

"I get the picks from Pete," he told me. "What do you say we go in together as partners?"

My first thought was my contract with the NBA. I was not supposed to gamble, plain and simple. I never really looked at a friendly golf wager or a trip to the casino as a big deal, but illegal sports betting was a totally different can of worms. But then I started thinking—or should I say, rationalizing: *Shit, everyone on the staff bets.* If gambling was so wrong, why were NBA referees regularly betting on NCAA football pools and frequenting casinos around the country? The behavior of most NBA referees was the opposite of what the league expected of us, so I convinced myself there must be nothing wrong with a little betting. I thought back to our preseason meetings where some 30 NBA refs played a high-stakes game of Liar's Poker in a hotel bar. We all sat around the table, watching and laughing as hundreds of dollars passed hands.

Yes, Jack's invitation was too good to pass up. Like a pot smoker moving up to cocaine, I was making a dangerous leap to the sleazy world of sports betting. The ride would be fast and exhilarating, and ultimately it would cost me everything. But that wasn't on my mind back then. No sir, I was having the time of my life, and the odds appeared to be in my favor.

We did well that first weekend. My share of the winnings was $1,100, and I remember saying to Jack, "This is unbelievable! It's easy money!" I was hooked, and from that moment on we bet games every weekend. In addition to football, we expanded our partnership to include baseball and hockey. We didn't make money every week; our fortunes went up and down like a casino elevator shuttling its patrons back and forth from the slots to the cots.

I knew Jack was getting the picks from Pete—that was understood. But Pete was never supposed to know that I was placing bets along with Jack. I was a silent partner; I had too much at stake to go around telling anyone that I was a big sports bettor. I trusted Jack with my life and never imagined he would be flapping his jaw about me. Well, he wasn't—at least not until much later when we took another huge leap.

The gambling got so infectious that we always found a justification for continuing, even when we were getting killed. If Pete gave us bad picks on three or four consecutive games, I would tell Jack, "He's not gonna lose five in a row. Let's triple the next bet." We would bump the bet up to $5,000 on the game, watching every play on television as if our lives depended on it. And wouldn't you know it, we would win and recoup our previous losses. When Pete was hot, he was smoking! The money came pouring in so fast that I could barely keep up. We had no idea what system Pete was using, and we didn't care. Jack and I joked that it might have been, "Eeny, meeny, miny, moe."

For the next three and a half years, I was consumed with gambling. I made bets every day. Even at home, I was preoccupied with betting: blackjack games in my card room, analyzing the betting lines in various newspapers, or checking game scores on television and on my laptop. Heck, if the kids couldn't agree on whose turn it was to walk the dog, we rolled dice to pick a loser. I had a short fuse in those days, pacing around like an alley cat in heat, waiting for the games to go final, calculating wins and losses in my mind. On weekends, Jack and I would be on the phone 10 to 20 times a day, sharing updates and planning our next move. Kim would say that I seemed on edge. If she had only known the kind of money—*our* money—I was playing around with. On edge? Baby, I was *over* the edge, staring into the black abyss, clinging to the magic powers of a short fat guy with red hair and hoping, always hoping, for a big score.

When we won, Jack would deliver my share before we teed off for a round of golf or over a plate of linguini in clam sauce at some cheap diner. He would give me a wad of bills under the table or wrapped in a linen napkin—sometimes as much as $5,000 or $10,000. On one occasion I met him at Philadelphia International Airport, where I was catching a flight to the West Coast to ref a game. He handed me $6,000 in twenties and fifties and I thought, *How will I get this through security?* I started stuffing wads of cash into my socks and underwear and quietly passed by the TSA agents with a grin on my face and a sigh of relief.

There were times I was so flush with cash that I didn't know what to do with it. I would blow it as fast as I could on hotels, golf outings, blackjack at the casino, and any card game I could find. I bought luxury items for our house, diamonds for my wife, new suits for myself, and toys for the kids. I even purchased basketball shoes for everyone in our neighborhood. If they had only known where the money was coming from…

Men in Stripes

L ong before Charles Barkley was coaxed into paying off his $400,000 marker at a Las Vegas casino in 2008, gambling was a firmly entrenched form of entertainment within the NBA family. Being an NBA referee means having lots of downtime. Games typically start at 7:00 PM local time, and we were generally out of the building by around 11:00 PM. A quick trip to the airport the next morning and it's on to another city, sometimes a day or two before the next game. If the weather was good, we might play golf. If the weather was bad, we would do anything to pass the time and escape the boredom. Referee Mike "Duke" Callahan and I would occasionally sit in a hotel room and roll a golf ball toward the front door for hours at a time. The game was called "rolly bolly," and we would bet $20 a roll to see who could get it closest to the door without hitting it. Now *that's* boredom.

During training camp we played Liar's Poker. The games were competitive because we were all good liars, but Mark Wunderlich was by far the best bullshitter I've ever met. He owned me in Liar's Poker. Once on a U.S. Airways flight from Chicago to Philly, Wunderlich, Callahan, and I played Liar's Poker for the entire trip, passing cash back and forth from one seat to the next. We even asked other passengers to provide change for our larger bills. The flight attendants thought we were nuts!

When veteran referee Joe Crawford was charged and convicted for failing to report all of his NBA income on his tax return, he became very depressed. To cheer him up, the other refs in the Philadelphia area and I chipped in and bought him an expensive poker table. On many occasions we would play cards at Joe's house and have a lot of laughs.

Betting on golf was also popular with the referees. Mark Wunderlich and I would meet up with Steve Javie and his friend J.D. for a round of golf at private courses near Philadelphia. We started calling J.D. "the Fish" because he was so easy to beat. On a golfing road trip to Whitemarsh Valley Country Club in Lafayette Hill, Pennsylvania, we stopped at a Super Fresh Food Market and bought a large fish head to put in J.D.'s locker. When he opened the locker and saw those fish eyes staring right back at him, he said, "What's this?"

"Luca Brasi sleeps with the fishes," I replied, laughing so hard I almost pissed my pants.

Wunderlich and I always cleaned up on Javie and J.D., pocketing several hundred dollars each.

It wasn't just golf and cards. There was always a racetrack or a casino to visit when we were on the road. The casinos were a magnet for referees, especially in a city like New Orleans where Harrah's was only a few blocks from the hotel where we stayed. There were also casinos in the Seattle area and in Vancouver, British Columbia. On one particular trip, Steve Javie, Tommy Nunez Sr., and I drove from Portland, Oregon, to Vancouver to work a Grizzlies game. Along the way we stopped at three casinos and stretched a three-hour drive into a 15-hour odyssey. When we finally arrived at our hotel in Vancouver, we immediately went to the casino in the lower level and gambled the night away. Although I loved casinos, I was always concerned that someone might recognize me. Some guys ran into players and coaches and got scared. That's when we decided to drive down the highway to out-of-town casinos just to be on the safe side. The last thing a referee wants is for a player or coach to get some "dirt" on him.

Referees Scott Foster, Bernie Fryer, and I used to joke around about going to Vegas after we retired and playing in the World Series of Poker while wearing our NBA jackets. We played Texas hold'em all the time and had gotten pretty good. We got a kick out of imagining ourselves playing in the final round, televised by ESPN, surrounded by stacks of chips, wearing the NBA logo for the entire world to see.

Even when we hit the court, the friendly wagers didn't stop. Joe Crawford, Steve Javie, and I would place bets on all types of promotional events held during timeouts. Most arenas have some sort of animated race on the overhead scoreboard; for example, a race between three computer-generated M&M candy contestants. Sounds silly, but we weren't about to be left out of the action. Looking up at the scoreboard during a timeout, the conversation would sound something like this:

> "Who do you have, 1, 2, or 3?"
>
> "I like 3 for $20."
>
> "I'm going with 1. Have your cash ready, you rat bastard."

The crowd roared as the M&Ms raced down the homestretch. The winner was No. 1, and one of us would walk out of the arena with an extra $20 in his pocket.

We would also bet on kids pulled from the crowd who raced around the court on bikes or ran up and down the floor wearing the oversized shirts and shoes of NBA players. Since there wasn't much for us to do during timeouts, we either stood around and stared at the cheerleaders— Dallas had by far the best—or we bet on the timeout entertainment. We always had a $20 bill to put down on something.

I even made a bet once with one of the highest-ranking executives in the NBA's league office. The 2001 NBA All-Star Game was played at the MCI Center in downtown Washington, D.C. I was assigned to referee the three-point shooting contest during All-Star weekend. Just prior to the event, I was standing at the scorer's table with Stu Jackson, the NBA's Executive Vice President of Basketball Operations.

"Who do you think will win?" I asked Stu.

"Ray Allen," he replied.

"I like Peja," I countered. Peja Stojakovic was a deadly three-point shooter for the Sacramento Kings, and I thought he would win.

"No," Stu insisted. "Ray Allen."

"You wanna bet?" I boldly asked.

Keep in mind that we weren't sitting in a noisy bar a thousand miles from the scene. We were courtside, at the scorer's table, and Ed T. Rush, the Supervisor of Officials, was sitting next to Stu, listening to the entire conversation.

"Twenty bucks," Stu replied.

"You're on!" I exclaimed.

The three-point contest was an event I could actually influence, if I had chosen to do so. As a referee, I had to decide if a basket was good, if the shooter's feet were behind the line, and if the last shot left the shooter's hand before the buzzer sounded. However, once we got started, I just put the bet out of my mind and did my job. And wouldn't you know it, Ray Allen had the magic touch that night and won the event. I looked over at Stu and he was sitting there with a big smile on his face. That's when I realized, *Oh shit! I lost $20! I gotta pay the man!* I was hoping that because Stu was my boss and he was getting a kick out of all of this, that maybe I'd be in his good graces. Perhaps I would be assigned to ref an extra round of the playoffs and make an additional $15,000 or $20,000. Stu was having fun with it, I was having fun with it, and everyone around us was laughing. I figured the $20 was a small investment in my future and money well spent.

Before Stu joined the NBA's front office, he had an undistinguished career as head coach of the Wisconsin Badgers as well as the NBA's New York Knicks and Vancouver Grizzlies. He also served as Vancouver's general manager, and as I handed the money to Stu, I couldn't resist taking a shot at him.

"Stu, if you would have made draft picks as well as you called this event, you'd still be a general manager in the league!" I said.

When Ed T. Rush heard my remark, he just about fell over laughing. So there we were, a top NBA executive and a veteran referee settling a bet, courtside, at the three-point shootout of the 2001 All-Star Game. Go figure!

* * *

The big question on everyone's mind is, "Did Tim Donaghy fix games?" The answer is no. I didn't *need* to fix them. I usually knew which team was going to win based on which referees had been assigned to the game, their personalities, and the relationships they had with the players and coaches of the teams involved.

Joe Crawford and Dick Bavetta are two of the NBA's top officials, but the only thing consistent about their refereeing styles is the inconsistency. It was almost impossible for a referee to watch Joe one night and then work with Dick the next. Let's start with technical fouls. Crawford would give guys a T if they looked at him funny. Bavetta, on the other hand, acted like he didn't hear a player who called him a "no-good motherfucker" right to his face. We often joked about how Crawford would let a guy get killed driving to the basket, while Bavetta would blow the whistle if a defender breathed on someone too hard.

Their reasoning behind how they called a game was different, too. Crawford wanted the game over quickly so he could kick back, relax, and have a beer; Bavetta wanted it to keep going so he could hear his name on TV. He actually paid an American Airlines employee to watch all the games he worked and write down everything the TV commentators said about him. No matter how late the game was over, he'd wake her up for a full report. He loved the attention.

Many of my fellow referees would do anything to get "face time" on the networks, and they worked hard to cultivate novel tricks to attract the camera's eye during a game. It could be as simple as spinning the ball on one finger, calling fouls in an over-the-top and highly animated way, "checking on something" at the scorer's table to get the attention of the game announcers, being overly aggressive in calling technical fouls, hamming it up with the cheerleaders or team mascots, or even having the floor wiped with a towel so that the camera would zoom in for a close-up. The glitz and glamour of an NBA contest is addicting, and referees are certainly not immune from being caught up in the bright lights. At times, I had the impression that some referees thought the fans showed up to see them and not the game.

Veteran referee Jess Kersey was one of those guys who clearly loved the attention that went with a career as an NBA ref. Kersey managed to get knocked down by players so frequently—consequently getting himself some TV time—that it became an inside joke among the other referees. A real character on and off the court, Kersey was the kind of likeable guy who would show up on an airplane with a pizza for the flight attendants. Unfortunately, he was also known for consuming large quantities of Gatorade and vodka immediately after a game. A few years back, I worked a game with him and Dee Kantner in Milwaukee. After the game, Kersey partook of his favorite elixir and proceeded to drive us to Chicago in a rental car for a game the following evening. During the drive, he slammed the car into a toll booth, causing considerable damage. The accident landed him in rehab, where he began a long journey to recovery. To his credit, he faced his demons and conquered them.

* * *

When the NBA hired referees, talent and ability were well down on the list of job requirements. Nepotism ran rampant, and sometimes getting a job often had little to do with how good an official you were; it was all about who you knew, or better yet, who you were related to.

Darell Garretson was the first to hire his son, Ron, back in the 1980s. Ron was able to move up the ladder fast since his dad was the boss, but most of the staff thought his skills were only on par with an average referee.

People naively thought this display of nepotism wouldn't happen again, but then Joe Borgia was hired. Joe was the son of Sid Borgia, a former referee who himself became a supervisor. The NBA also hired James Capers Sr.'s son, James Capers Jr. Fortunately for James Jr., James Sr. was a group supervisor and had input on which referees advanced in the playoffs. Scott Wall's father Bill was in charge of USA Basketball and a friend of David Stern's. Matt Winick, who assigned referees to games, thought Wall never should have been hired, and he made derogatory comments to staff members about Wall's ability. I can't claim immunity from favoritism, either—when I was hired, Billy Oakes was a top official on the staff. Billy also happened to be my uncle. So I benefited from my connections, too.

Ronnie Nunn took the league's nepotism to a whole new level when he became the boss. He hired Tommy Nunez Sr.'s son, Tommy Jr., as well as old friends from years past. Robbie Robinson wasn't even refereeing basketball when Nunn called and told him to start working again. He was fired two years after he was hired. But Nunn still didn't learn his lesson. He hired David Guthrie, the son of John Guthrie (John had been Nunn's college basketball coach at George Washington University). Zach Zarba was a local guy Nunn had known for years, and Nunn tried to push him up the ladder until Stu Jackson stepped in and put a stop to it. Many officials were linked to someone, and no one cared enough to question it much less stop it.

* * *

There were certain refs I never wanted to work with, and if I got partnered with them for a crew, I knew I was in for a trip from hell. I remember one nightmarish game I worked with Joe Crawford and Phil Robinson. Minnesota and New Orleans were in a tight game going into the last minute, and Crawford told us to make sure that we were 100 percent sure of the call every time before we blew the whistle. When play resumed, Minnesota coach Flip Saunders started yelling at us to make a call. Robinson got intimidated and blew the whistle on New Orleans. The only problem was it wasn't the right call. Tim Floyd, the Hornets' coach, went nuts. He stormed the court and kicked the ball into the top row of the stadium. Robinson had to throw him out, and Minnesota won the game.

When our crew went into the locker room to review the play, Crawford let Robinson have it. He started screaming, "Didn't I tell you not to blow your whistle unless you knew what the hell you were calling? You screwed up this whole game!"

Robinson started screaming back, "I'm a grown man! Do not talk to me like that!"

They just wouldn't let up. To make matters worse, when we called the office they wanted a full breakdown of the game by the next morning. That meant we got to stay up all night and bang out stats from the tape. Lucky us.

I'm not a big drinker, but that night I thought about becoming one. Just when I thought my referee duties were done for the night, I had to go back to the hotel and referee the two guys from my crew while they got loaded and tried to break down the tape. After a bottle of Jack Daniels and two six-packs of beer, Crawford and Robinson were so hammered they were screaming and laughing the entire time we were filling out the reports. As it turned out, we had a blast.

Later that week, Ronnie Nunn told me that we could have made something up at the other end against Minnesota to even things out. He even got specific—maybe we should have considered calling a traveling violation on Kevin Garnett. Talk about the politics of the game! Of course the official statement from the league office will always read, "There is no such thing as a makeup call."

* * *

The NBA has been dominated by men for a long time. After all, the players are male, so it seems to make sense that the refs are, too. But about 12 years ago, two women were suddenly hired: Violet Palmer and Dee Kantner. How did that happen? A woman named Sandy Ortiz successfully sued the NBA on grounds of gender discrimination seeking a referee's position. The NBA had to pay her a large amount of money, and they must have wanted to forestall any other legal action by female referees. So they went into the college game and chose Kantner and Palmer, one white and one black. We all liked Palmer, who had a terrific way with people. Kantner was a little more abrasive, and her strong and cocky personality probably had something to do with the reason she was fired after five seasons. Well, that and her performance.

Quite frankly, I thought they were both terrible referees, and many others agreed. Joe Crawford used to say he wouldn't use either of them to referee a high school JV game. Because most of their experience was at the collegiate level, both Kantner and Palmer had trouble with the pace of the NBA game. But that didn't really matter—the fact that they were women was the only thing the league seemed to care about. Occasionally, the NBA would pluck a top referee from the college ranks, but those guys can make more money than a first-year NBA ref so it was hard to convince them to leave their jobs. Kantner and Palmer appeared pretty much out of nowhere. It was obvious to me they were brought in to quell an unpleasant public relations and legal situation.

I remember calling a Utah Jazz game one night with Dee Kantner. Jazz coach Jerry Sloan had one of the foulest mouths in the NBA, and he was on Kantner throughout the game like white on rice. He would be yelling things like, "What the fuck are you fucking doing out there? You don't know what the fuck you're doing! That's a fucking foul down there!"

While he was yelling at her during a free-throw attempt, I was standing all the way on the other side of the court. Again, you could hear his foul language from at least 10 rows up; everybody could hear him. As I started walking over, Jerry started going off on me. "And you!" he yelled, pointing at me, but before he could get out another word, I T'd him up.

He just laughed. He had been trying to get Kantner to give him a technical foul the whole time. He was just trying to see how far he could push her, testing her limits like a five-year-old. Either she was too scared to call a T on him, or she probably thought the technical fouls would just bring attention to her, and, therefore, she'd have to explain it to the league office.

Kantner was really hot at me as we headed to the break. During halftime, she picked up a water cooler and threw it at me.

"Who the fuck do you think you are to ride in on your white horse to save me?" she demanded.

"Obviously you didn't hear what he said to you," I responded, trying to give her the benefit of the doubt. "Because if you had heard what he said, you'd have given him a T yourself."

Instead, she was just furious at me for giving Sloan the technical that, if she had been the least bit courageous or even professional, she would have given him herself. But she's not the only one—plenty of refs would let players and coaches call them motherfuckers up and down the court and act like they had never heard a thing. The referees were just too scared of giving guys a T and getting in hot water with the league office. The postscript to Kantner's story is that after she was fired, there were rumors that she was going to sue. Suddenly, she found herself with a job working with the referees in the WNBA.

* * *

When I came into the league, Darell Garretson was the Supervisor of Officials. Garretson was a tough guy. I would sometimes be in the room with him when he got phone calls from coaches and general managers who would complain about referees. He would literally tell those guys to go fuck themselves, in that specific language. He wouldn't take shit from any of those guys, but he left his position in 1998.

At the time, there was a debate going on in the NBA as to what the "clear path" rule meant. A clear path situation was also known as a "breakaway." It's when a defender steals the ball and sprints down the court for a layup, and a player from the other team fouls him from behind. Does the offensive player have a "clear path" to the basket if there is a defender parallel to him? It sounds confusing, and it is. We were having a referees meeting prior to the 1996–97 season, and all 60 regular referees were in the room. Darell Garretson and his boss, Executive Vice President of Basketball Operations Rod Thorn, were debating the clear path rule in front of all the refs. They couldn't agree about what the rule meant and subsequently got into a shouting match.

"Don't tell me about the rule!" Thorn yelled at Garretson. "You weren't at the competition committee meeting where we talked about it. You elected not to go!"

"I'm just trying to clarify it," Darell shot back heatedly.

Thorn turned to the audience of referees. "Does anyone in the room not fucking know what I mean by a clear path rule?" he asked angrily.

We were totally silent, like kids watching a teacher and the principal getting into an argument. We had never seen anything like it. I'll tell you this—none of us dared to challenge Thorn, who was the boss of our boss. To be honest, we were confused ourselves about the clear path rule—it's a confusing rule. But by then the tension in the room was so thick we thought Garretson and Thorn might start throwing punches. Suddenly Bob Lanier, who was working in the NBA front office at the time, got up and shouted, "Whoa, whoa, whoa! Timeout! All referees out of the room! Let's talk about this without these guys in here."

So the 60 of us quickly filed out of the room, and through the closed door we could hear Thorn and Garretson screaming at each other, calling each other motherfuckers. We were actually laughing, saying things like, "Who's got money on Rod and who's got money on Darell?" as if they were going to get into a fistfight.

That was the end of the line for Darell. He "resigned" the next year and was replaced by Ed T. Rush. Rush took a very different approach with the coaches and general managers. He told them, "We want to have open communication. If there's a problem, call me." So the coaches and general managers would get on the phone with Rush whenever they had a problem. Even Dallas Mavericks owner Mark Cuban would call him to discuss things. But Rush inevitably gave the benefit of the doubt to the referee. He always had excuses like, "That was a hard game to call." Cuban finally got frustrated with what he considered Rush's line of bullshit and tried to get him fired. To his credit, Cuban wanted the game called by the book—a travel is a travel, a palm is a palm. He would say, "I want to have my team built and coached the right way. Call the game as it is in the rules." But he was a lone voice in the wilderness trying to get rid of the special treatment for certain players, coaches, and owners.

Ed T. Rush had been working as an NBA ref since 1966. Injuries forced him to retire following the 1996–97 season, and the NBA office hired him as the Director of Officiating in 1998. Since the retirement plan didn't pay nearly as much as disability did, a lot of refs approaching retirement managed to get "injured" and took the disability plan instead.

As director, he hired a large staff of assistants to help him. Too many cooks spoil the broth, and too many assistants made our life a living hell—no one did things the same way. Rush was a champion bullshitter. He was one of those guys who wanted everyone to agree with him, and as a result he was two-faced. Rush told one referee what he wanted to hear and then turned right around and told someone else the exact opposite. This put the staff in a constant state of confusion.

Rush loved to play favorites, and instead of moving the best referees up the ladder, he moved his buddies up instead. Referees are rated by five separate entities: the coaches, the general managers, the group supervisors, the Director of Officiating, and the Executive Vice President of Basketball Operations. Those last two count the most, and Rush was a master of office politics, moving refs up and down based on friendships or personal feelings instead of their talent on the floor.

As it turns out, I wasn't the only one who saw through Ed T. Rush. In a 2002 interview in the *Dallas Morning News*, Mark Cuban said, "Ed Rush might have been a great ref, but I wouldn't hire him to manage a Dairy Queen. His interest is not the integrity of the game or improving the officiating. The No. 1 priority of Ed Rush is maintaining power. There's no question in my mind that [NBA Commissioner] David Stern is not the most powerful man in the game. It's Ed Rush." As usual, the NBA office didn't respond well to that level of honesty: Cuban was later fined $500,000 by the league.

But Cuban had it right. Rush did think he was king of the NBA. He even went so far as to change the rating system that had been in place for years so that no one could question his decisions. Referees were no longer privy to their rating on the staff. It's like Rush thought he could control and convince anyone of anything. Eventually, his bullshit caught up with him and he was replaced.

For some reason, the NBA refused to hire experienced former referees like Hue Hollins and Mike Mathis as group supervisors. Both were veteran referees who had worked the NBA Finals—they were very talented and would have been tremendous supervisors. Instead, the NBA turned to average, substandard, and low-achieving former referees who had nothing to offer the referees they would be supervising. The guys they hired merely filled their positions, beholden to the NBA for giving them a job and more than willing to do the front office's bidding when a message had to be delivered to the rank-and-file referees.

By 2003, Ed T. Rush was out as Supervisor of Officials. After that, Rush's job went to Ronnie Nunn. I remember standing in line with Nunn when the NBA started the drug-testing program for referees back in the 1990s. He hadn't read the information packet the league sent out and was in a panic over the test. He told me about how he took walks in the woods with his buddies during the summer and smoked weed to help him relax. Nunn asked me, "How long does it stay in your system?"

I laughed. "Do I look like a doctor?" I said.

Mark Wunderlich, one of the other referees, used to joke that Nunn was lifelong buddies with Cheech and Chong.

The group supervisors were one step below the supervisor position. Their job was to watch the game and "observe" our performance. For the 2006–07 season, we had four group supervisors: Jim Wishmier, Mike Lauerman, Tommy Nunez Sr., and Jim Capers Sr. (Every once in a while, Joe Borgia, who was in charge of training and development, would also show up to observe a game.)

I was totally amazed that these five guys were chosen as supervisors. Wishmier and Lauerman were both fired during their referee careers. Tony Brothers, a referee who was hired around the same time I was, once told Stu Jackson, "It's no big deal getting fired from this job, because I can always come back and be a supervisor!" A truer statement has never been spoken. I can't think of any other business where you can get fired and come back as a boss.

Nunez had a 30-year career, but many of the refs knew he wasn't meant for a management position, and he sure as hell couldn't train officials. Talk about a guy who liked the action—Nunez had been going to casinos for 25 years and could barely pass a corner market without buying a lottery ticket. The people in the NBA office knew about his hobby, but as usual, they closed their eyes and kept paying lip service to the idea that there were no gamblers in the league. Nunez never stopped talking about the slots and blackjack tables. And we were supposed to take direction from him? The only thing he could give me direction on was how to play craps at the casino. He even went so far as to tell us that he had connections for free rooms in Vegas if we ever needed them.

Maybe one of the reasons Tommy got a group supervisor position was that he was a terrific guy to hang around with. He was funny as hell and always had something going on. But that didn't mean the "something" was always above board. My favorite Tommy Nunez story is from the 2007 playoffs when the San Antonio Spurs were able to get past the Phoenix Suns in the second round. Of course, what many fans didn't know was that Phoenix had someone working against them behind the scenes. Nunez was the group supervisor for that playoff series, and he definitely had a rooting interest.

Nunez loved the Hispanic community in San Antonio and had a lot of friends there. He had been a referee for 30 years and loved being on the road; in fact, he said that the whole reason he had become a group supervisor was to keep getting out of the house. So Nunez wanted to come back to San Antonio for the conference finals. Plus, he, like many other referees, disliked Suns owner Robert Sarver for the way he treated officials. Both of these things came into play when he prepared the referees for the games in the staff meetings. I remember laughing with him and saying, "You would love to keep coming back here." He was pointing out everything that Phoenix was able to get away with and never once told us to look for anything in regard to San Antonio. Nunez should have a championship ring on his finger.

I wasn't betting at the time of the 2007 playoffs, but if I had been, San Antonio was a sure pick. When you review the tape of Game 3, you will see that San Antonio was able to get the benefit of every critical call, and non-call, throughout the game. After that game, I was surprised there wasn't more of a public outcry from the press. The whole series was a disaster; it was poorly officiated from the opening tip of Game 1.

* * *

In the midst of my gambling free fall, a situation arose that placed my job in jeopardy. Pete Mansueto was a friend of mine and a fellow member at Radley Run Country Club. We had a casual relationship that was primarily confined to the golf course, but Pete did become aware of my involvement in high-stakes golf matches, freewheeling card games, and trips to the casinos in Atlantic City.

Pete and his new wife Lisa purchased the home next to ours and promptly moved in with their two children and mixed-breed pit bull. For the first few months we got along fine, but eventually we had a dispute over the removal of some trees from an adjoining lot. One thing led to another, tempers flared, the police were called, threats were made, and we were at war. I believe Pete eventually informed NBA officials that I was a heavy gambler and that I frequented casinos in Atlantic City.

I received a call from Stu Jackson who told me the NBA had received some complaints about my ongoing problems with Pete Mansueto. Stu asked me to appear in his office two days later to address the allegations and answer a few questions. I took the train from Philly to New York, completely unaware that I was about to be grilled about my gambling habits.

The meeting was held at the NBA's headquarters in Manhattan. A secretary escorted me to a conference room where I nervously waited for 15 minutes. All of a sudden, the door opened and four of the league's heavy hitters waltzed in looking very somber and serious. The inquisitors included Stu Jackson, Deputy Commissioner Russ Granik, General Counsel Rick Buchanan, and Vice President of Security Bernie Tolbert. Holy shit! All of this over a pissing match with my neighbor?

Granik, the commissioner's right-hand man, made a few opening remarks and then passed the ball to Buchanan. He opened up with a few general questions about my disagreements with my neighbor and then, out of the blue, he hit me with a quick barrage that left me reeling like Joe Frazier at the Thrilla in Manila.

"Do you bet?" asked Buchanan. All eyes were glued to me in anticipation of my reaction and answer.

"Just on golf with my buddies," I replied.

"How about football?" he continued.

"No."

"Baseball?"

"No."

"Pro basketball?"

"No!" I said with a look of disbelief on my face.

"Do you go to the casinos?"

"No."

There it was: the cat was out of the bag and I was now on the NBA's radar screen. All those years sneaking around, wearing a baseball cap pulled down over my eyes in the casinos, and avoiding NBA players and coaches by going to out-of-town joints were for naught. All those years of high times and fast living had finally caught up with me. When Buchanan asked those questions, my pucker factor went into overdrive.

After my denials and lies, Granik told me that if I liked my job in the NBA I should seriously consider moving to a new neighbor. Kim and I had already put the house up for sale and were planning our escape to Florida, so I figured I was in the clear.

A couple of weeks after the meeting in New York, I received a follow-up call from Bernie Tolbert. He flat-out asked me if I had gambled at the Borgata in Atlantic City. *How the hell did he find out about that?* I thought.

"No!" I emphatically stated.

Reflecting back on that wild day at the Borgata, I was paranoid that the league would review the casino's security tapes and see me and the guys acting like fools. I lost many a night's sleep over this and even placed an anonymous call to the Borgata and asked how long they kept their tapes. They wouldn't tell me, of course, and I was left agonizing over the seemingly real prospect of being discovered and exposed.

The NBA went so far as to hire an outside investigator to assist in its inquiry. That agency eventually prepared a written report that was submitted to the commissioner. The report was then supposed to be forwarded via email to the various officials who attended my meeting in New York City, including Bernie Tolbert. Only one problem: the report was erroneously forwarded to NBA referee Bernie *Fryer*, not Bernie *Tolbert*. Oops! Fryer promptly called to let me know that a private investigator had been hired by the NBA and had been on my tail for weeks. I was shocked and thanked him for the heads-up.

When the investigation was complete, the NBA was unable to substantiate allegations that I bet on NBA games. The league subsequently closed the investigation but did penalize me for exercising bad judgment in the way I handled the dispute with my neighbor. That year, I was not permitted to officiate as many playoff rounds as I had the prior year—which meant a loss of approximately $15,000 in wages. I could certainly live with that! I escaped detection, at least for the moment, and breathed a heavy sigh of relief. The smart play would have been to immediately stop gambling and change my errant ways. The rational person would have carefully weighed the benefits versus the risks. Any person with a brain would have been scared shitless. Not me; I was already itching to place some bets and get back in the game, and my friend Jack was ready, willing, and eager to get back to business.

At home, the mood had been tense for quite some time. The investigation certainly didn't help, but it was only a symptom of a growing cancer. My fuse was short, my attention span was limited, and my preoccupation with gambling was overwhelming. I was taking the important things in life for granted. My wife and kids were playing second fiddle to the drumbeat of cards being shuffled or of dice bouncing along a craps table. Gambling had a stranglehold on me and it wouldn't let go. I didn't want it to.

Kim was increasingly suspicious of my actions, and rightfully so. The lies were piling up and my behavior continued to be erratic. I purchased a safe and kept it in my bedroom closet. On any given day, it contained upwards of $20,000—my stash for a rainy day and my stake for the next outing. One night after dinner, Kim demanded that I open the safe. While her attention was diverted for a few minutes, I emptied the safe and stuffed the money into the pockets of my suits hanging just a few feet away. When I opened it for her, she almost looked relieved to see that it was empty. The next day, I went out and bought a couple more suits for the closet. A man never knows when he's going to hit the jackpot, after all.

As soon as the season ended, Kim and I packed up the kids and headed for the Gulf Coast of Florida and a fresh start. Unfortunately, there would be no fresh start, just a continuation of old habits and a rendezvous with disaster.

CHAPTER 5

The Players' League

Basketball is a game of personalities. Today, more than ever, the game's allure is based on the big-name, big-money superstars who dominate sports television highlight reels and single-handedly fill arenas to capacity night after night. Of equal importance, these walking conglomerates increase ratings, expand market share, guarantee exclusivity contracts, and generally fill the coffers of that seldom-scrutinized sporting entity known as the National Basketball Association.

Although the fundamentals of the game have expanded from shooting and rebounding to balance sheets and revenue projections, it all still begins with the product on the court and the talented players who perform amazing feats of athleticism in front of cheering fans across the country. Their names and faces are as well known in American homes as some of the biggest brands in the world. Nike, Rolex, and Porsche? How about Kobe, LeBron, and Shaq?

We have all witnessed the tongue-wagging acrobatics of Michael Jordan, the inspiring toughness of Allen Iverson, and the physical dominance of Shaquille O'Neal. We've also winced at the cross-dressing antics of Dennis Rodman and the brute-force tactics of Ron Artest. Television has brought all of this into our homes in living color. But there is another side to the game that few ever witness, a side that is punctuated by profanity, intimidation, manipulation, favoritism, retaliation, and humor. Only the true insider has seen this hidden face of pro basketball. Only those who run up and down the court, sweating and bleeding, know that there is something else going on in the NBA besides jump shots and rebounds. For 13 years, I was an on-the-floor witness to the reality of professional basketball. It wasn't just the long-range three-pointers or the supersized slam dunks. I'm referring to the action inside and outside the lines that could affect the outcome of a contest, and often did—what I call the game within the game.

The game within the game is played by players, coaches, owners, referees, NBA league officials, broadcasters, and even some fans. Obviously, the players and coaches are the most high-profile in this sideshow. In many respects, observing and interacting with these characters was very exciting, especially during my first few years in the league. Of course, there was always the jerk who could make any game a real headache—that's part of being a referee at any level of competition. In the NBA, game day is a wild ride filled with anticipation, exhilaration, confrontation, and exasperation. Through it all, there was this exclusive club of oversized, multitalented egomaniacs known as NBA players— and I was privileged to watch them play.

* * *

I first heard about Kobe Bryant when he was playing at Lower Merion High School in Ardmore, Pennsylvania, which is about 20 minutes from my hometown of Havertown. I had been reffing NBA games for a couple of years and there was already a buzz in the league about this phenomenal young player. I was so intrigued that I actually went to see him play in the Pennsylvania high school state championship game. The actual game could have been renamed "the Kobe Show." There weren't any set plays, no half-court game. They just gave the ball to Kobe and got out of his way. Kobe's team naturally won the game, and to no one's surprise, he was on his way to the NBA.

I first met Kobe at the Summer Pro League in L.A. I introduced myself, told him I was from Havertown, and wished him good luck on the upcoming season. We shared some small talk and he thanked me for the good wishes. He seemed like a good guy; a talented young man with a brilliant future ahead of him.

The next time I saw him was on the court in an NBA game. He was the budding superstar for the Lakers, and I was still a junior referee in the league. As his star power rose over the years, so did his obnoxious complaining and whining. Kobe wanted a foul called every time he went to the basket. He would scream on his way to the rim just to goad the referees into blowing the whistle. Sometimes this tactic actually worked, depending on who was reffing the game.

Michael Jordan had done it much the same way, but he was less verbal about it. Michael just sort of glanced at the referee as if to say, "Aren't you going to call that a foul? It's me, Michael Jordan." Kobe wasn't about to rely on subtle facial gestures. He was constantly in your face and in your ear.

Often when someone else was shooting free throws, Kobe would seek out one of the referees and start jawing: "Come on now, you owe me one. You missed that one, don't miss another one. Come on now."

On those occasions when we did actually miss a call, the best approach for a referee was to acknowledge the mistake: "You know, you're probably right. I probably missed that one." However, that line can't be used too often or the player starts asking, "When are you going to *stop* missing them?"

For the young or less-confident referee, Kobe's verbal jousting and maneuvering could be very effective. For those close to the court, it was obvious when he intimidated a ref into a call.

Let's face it, referees are big basketball fans, and we enjoy watching the big guns do their thing. I was on the floor for several of Kobe's high-scoring games and it was amazing to watch. He would throw up long-range jump shots with three defenders hanging on him and find nothing but net. During timeouts, the refereeing crew would marvel at his performance. We couldn't believe those shots kept going in. Yes, Kobe was relentless in his approach, but it never seemed personal. He was constantly fighting to gain the edge. Upbeat and friendly or down and dirty, Kobe was all business as he tried to win the game. For Kobe, that's what it's about—winning.

When he was at the height of his powers, Shaquille O'Neal was the supreme physical presence in the NBA, and the only way opposing teams could slow him down was to repeatedly foul him—the infamous "hack-a-Shaq" approach. Of course, Shaq is not exactly known for being a sharpshooter from the free-throw line—no one in the league throws up more bricks than Shaq.

Shaq never gave the referees much lip. If he didn't like a call I made on him, he would just drop the ball, give me a dirty look, and head in the other direction. He has, however, been known to remind referees that the fans didn't come to see Superman sit on the bench.

Above it all, Shaq was a funny guy, quick with a joke or a prank and never a jerk. I once worked one of his games just after I received a particularly bad haircut. As I was retrieving the ball for a free-throw attempt, I sensed the enormous center looking down at me—after all, I'm only 5'9". I looked up to make eye contact and he wryly asked, "Who the fuck cut your hair?" I just looked at him and laughed. "I got a bad chop," I sheepishly replied. Actually, it had been on my mind all day. Here we are in the second quarter of a rather intense NBA game, and I could feel my face getting flushed with embarrassment. That's Shaq.

Tim Duncan of the San Antonio Spurs never showed much of a sense of humor; he was very serious and never appeared to be having fun on the court. Dick Bavetta and I were reffing a San Antonio game one evening when Bavetta made a call that infuriated Duncan. They argued back and forth for a couple of minutes and finally bet a hamburger on who was right and who was wrong. Getting Duncan to bet a burger on the call was Bavetta's way of getting him to calm down for the rest of the game.

Later that night, Bavetta watched the game tape and realized he had indeed blown the call. So when he had a Spurs game a few weeks later, Dick stopped at McDonald's on his way to the arena and picked up a burger, fries, and a Coke. He had the meal sent to Duncan in the Spurs locker room prior to the game and everyone was happy.

At least one superstar player in the league engaged in outrageous conduct that left many referees scratching their heads. Kevin Garnett is one of the more vocal and provocative players on the court. During his years of dominance at the Target Center as a member of the Minnesota Timberwolves, Garnett was known to be particularly fond of using the n-word when addressing teammates and opposing players. It was a common occurrence, one I witnessed many times, for Garnett to shout the expletive at the top of his lungs while running up and down the court.

"Give me the fucking ball! That nigger can't fucking guard me!" he'd shout.

Throughout the game, Garnett spewed a continual barrage of the word so loudly that he could be clearly heard 20 rows up in the stands.

Now, boys will be boys, and we were all men on the court, but the NBA promotes a fan-friendly atmosphere in the arenas and a decision had to be made. One particular fall at our annual preseason referee camp, the referees in attendance raised the issue and debated whether a player's use of the n-word should generate a technical foul. After considerable and rancorous discussion, it was decided that if a player yelled "motherfucker" there would be no technical foul. However, use of the n-word during game action would result in a quick technical.

Despite the decision, many refs chose to ignore the rule, not wanting to limit Garnett's enthusiastic style of play. When it came to Kevin Garnett, referees either loved him or hated him; there was no middle ground.

Relationships between NBA players and referees were generally all over the board—love, hate, and everything in-between. Some players, even very good ones, were targeted by referees and the league because they were too talented for their own good. Raja Bell, formerly of the Phoenix Suns and now a member of the Charlotte Bobcats, was one of those players. A defensive specialist throughout his career, Bell had a reputation for being a "star stopper." His defensive skills were so razor sharp that he could shut down a superstar, or at least make him work for his points. Kobe Bryant was often frustrated by Bell's tenacity on defense. Let's face it, no one completely shuts down a player of Kobe's caliber, but Bell could frustrate Kobe, take him out of his game, and interrupt his rhythm.

You would think that the NBA would love a guy who plays such great defense. Think again! Star stoppers hurt the promotion of marquee players. Fans don't pay high prices to see players like Raja Bell—they pay to see superstars like Kobe Bryant score 40 points. Basketball purists like to see good defense, but the NBA wants the big names to score big points.

If a player of Kobe's stature collides with the likes of Raja Bell, the call will almost always go for Kobe and against Bell. As part of our ongoing training and game preparation, NBA referees regularly receive game-action video tape from the league office. Over the years, I have reviewed many recorded hours of video involving Raja Bell. The footage I analyzed usually illustrated fouls being called against Bell, rarely for him. The message was subtle but clear—call fouls against the star stopper because he's hurting the game.

As much as the league worked against players like Raja Bell, it worked in favor of the big-name players who consistently packed arenas all season long—even if the player was sometimes too outspoken for his own good. Sound like anyone you know? Yes, I'm referring to Charles Barkley of the Philadelphia 76ers, Phoenix Suns, and Houston Rockets. Barkley was an awesome talent with a big mouth and a knack for finding trouble. Still, he was quite the character and a tremendous fan favorite—at least in the city he was playing for.

I once worked a Rockets-Clippers game with my partners Duke Callahan and Bernie Fryer. Barkley was complaining about a foul I called and simply refused to let up. Up and down the court, in my ear, in my face—he was absolutely relentless. Finally, I hit him with a technical foul.

Rudy Tomjanovich, who was coach of the Rockets at the time, jumped into the fray and decided to double-team me.

"You blew that one, Tim. Charles would never act like that unless you were wrong!" Rudy jabbed.

"Really?" I snapped back. "He acts like that every night."

Tomjanovich just shook his head and said, "You're wrong, Tim. And I'll bet you dinner on it."

After the game, I marched straight to the VCR in the referees' locker room and reviewed the game tape. I watched it several times and was convinced I made the right call. I grabbed the portable VCR off the training table, took it to Rudy T, and replayed the tape two or three times.

"Shit," he said. "You're right. I owe you an apology."

I immediately barked back, "I don't want an apology, I want my dinner!"

Rudy said he would send some coupons for McDonald's over to our locker room. Then he added with a sneer, "That fucking Barkley made me look like a fool. I'm gonna bust his balls."

I went back to the locker room to catch a quick shower. Meanwhile, Rudy was apparently ripping Charles a new one—and Charles didn't like it. He grabbed a Gatorade container full of ice, walked right past security into the referees' locker room, and hunted me down in the shower stall. Within seconds I was doused with the bucket of ice and cold Gatorade. All of my extremities immediately went into shrink-shock and I lurched forward, banging my head on the shower nozzle. With shampoo running into my eyes, I heard Charles Barkley laughing his ass off like a little kid who just egged the principal's car. I turned to curse him out, but he quickly pranced out of the locker room like a ballerina in *The Nutcracker*.

Obviously, I could have made a big stink and reported Barkley to the league office. That kind of stunt is frowned upon—even for a star like him—and a large fine or suspension would have been likely. Before I did something rash, my crew chief Bernie Fryer raised a good point. "If you let it go," he cautioned me, "he'll owe you forever." So I shut my mouth and never notified the NBA. The next time I saw Barkley, he gave me a huge smile and whispered, "Thanks." From that day forward, I never had another problem with the Round Mound of Rebound.

It turns out that little encounter wasn't the only thing Charles and I had in common: we both loved to gamble. In recent years, Barkley was sued by a Las Vegas casino for several hundred thousand dollars in unpaid markers. Charles subsequently admitted to the public that he lost upwards of $10 million gambling over the years. At least he didn't bet on basketball, I guess.

One of my all-time favorites in the league was Charles Oakley, formerly of the Knicks, Bulls, and Raptors among others. On the outside, Charles could be one of the toughest, meanest-looking enforcers you would ever see in the NBA. The guy was a brick wall, an impenetrable force, and funny as hell. He could be unbelievably goofy, making weird faces and off-the-wall comments. For some referees, Oakley was trouble waiting to happen. Not for me, though; I got a kick out of his antics and we enjoyed a spirited banter on the court.

One night I was working a game in Toronto when he approached me during a timeout. He started bitching and complaining that he was getting mauled on rebounds and that I wasn't making the call. So I decided to have a little fun and bust his chops.

"You're supposed to be one of the toughest fucking guys in the league," I provokingly said, "and you're complaining to me? Don't ask me for any favors. Go handle it yourself and quit crying!"

Before I got the words out of my mouth, his muscles tightened up and his eyes bulged out of their sockets. He looked like an eager Hugh Hefner gulping down a cocktail of Viagra and ginseng surrounded by a harem of ovulating 19-year-old Playmates.

Well, the next time down the floor, a shot went up and Oakley crashed the boards. One problem—he didn't go for the basketball, but rather the groin of the opposing player. The guy went to the floor on his knees writhing in pain, groaning in gonad agony. I was in perfect position to make the call. Flagrant foul, right? Wrong. All eyes were on me, waiting for the whistle to blow, but I just looked the other way like I hadn't seen a thing. After what I said to Oakley, there's no way I was going to make that call. I certainly didn't want my comments repeated in the press the next morning or sent into the league office when Oakley was asked why he did it.

During the next timeout, Oakley slowly walked past me with his chest pushed out and said, "Yeah, I've got to take care of it myself." We both cracked up laughing.

"You do that again," I warned him, trying to be serious, "and we're going to have a major problem."

Actually, I thought I might have a problem with the league for not making the call, but nothing was ever said.

* * *

For every funny guy or likeable character in the NBA, there was a real asshole—the kind of selfish, profane, self-absorbed spoiled brat who the referees just couldn't stand. My all-time top five on this list are Gary Payton, Rasheed Wallace, Antoine Walker, Chauncey Billups, and Stephen Jackson. These guys could make your life a living hell, and they usually did.

To have a little fun at the expense of the worst troublemakers, the referees working the game would sometimes make a modest friendly wager amongst themselves: first ref to give one of the bad boys a technical foul wouldn't have to tip the ball boy that night. In the NBA, ball boys set up the referees' locker room and keep it stocked with food and beer for the postgame meal. We usually ran the kid ragged with a variety of personal requests and then slipped him a $20 bill. Technically, the winner of the bet won twice—he didn't have to pay the kid *and* he got to call a T on Mr. Foul-Mouthed Big-Shot Du Jour.

After the opening tip, it was hilarious as the three of us immediately focused our full attention on the intended victim, waiting for something, anything, to justify a technical foul. If the guy so much as looked at one of us and mumbled, we rang him up. Later in the referees' locker room, we would down a couple of brews, eat some chicken wings, and laugh like hell.

We had another variation of this gag simply referred to as the "first foul of the game" bet. While still in the locker room before tip-off, we would make a wager on which of us would call the game's first foul. That referee would either have to pay the ball boy or pick up the dinner tab for the other two referees. Sometimes, the ante would be $50 a guy.

Like the technical foul bet, it was hilarious—only this time we were testing each other's nerves to see who had the guts to hold out the longest before calling a personal foul. There were occasions when we would hold back for several minutes—an eternity in an NBA game—before blowing the whistle. It didn't matter if bodies were flying all over the place; no fouls were called because no one wanted to lose the bet.

We played this little game during the regular season and summer league. After a game, all three refs would gather around the VCR and watch a replay of the game. Early in the contest, the announcers would say, "Holy cow! They're really letting them play tonight!" If they only knew...

During one particular summer game, Duke Callahan, Mark Wunderlich, and I made it to the three-minute mark in the first quarter without calling a foul. We were running up and down the court, laughing our asses off as the players got hammered with no whistles. The players were exhausted from the nonstop running when Callahan finally called the first foul because Mikki Moore of the New Jersey Nets literally tackled an opposing player right in front of him. Too bad for Callahan—he lost the bet.

I became so good at this game that if an obvious foul was committed right in front of me, I would call a travel or a three-second violation instead. Those violations are not personal fouls, so I was still in the running to win the bet. The players would look at me with disbelief on their faces as if to say, "What the hell was that?"

Another night in Charlotte, I worked a game with Dee Kantner and Joe DeRosa. Kantner ended up calling the first foul. Lee Jones, one of our supervisors, was in attendance at the game that night. After the game, Jones made his way to our locker room and told Kantner that she missed several calls in the first few minutes of the game. To our great shock, Kantner actually told him that the reason she hadn't called the fouls was that she didn't want to lose the bet! Joe DeRosa and I almost fell off our chairs—we couldn't believe she said that to our supervisor. But as usual, nothing ever came of it, not even a verbal reprimand.

Of course, it wasn't all fun and games. Sometimes a rather insignificant event would trigger a major confrontation. It usually occurred between players, but every once in a while, it was between a player and a referee.

On the night of January 15, 2003, I was working a game in Portland between the Trail Blazers and the Memphis Grizzlies when a small on-court incident actually spilled over to the street. It started out like any other game, with both teams ready to go and the Rose Garden Arena rocking. At the 9:45 mark of the third quarter, referee Scott Wall called a personal foul on Trail Blazers forward Rasheed Wallace. Wallace responded by returning the ball to Wall when he wasn't looking, resulting in the ball striking Wall's leg and bouncing away. The ball wasn't thrown particularly hard, but it was clearly an act of disrespect toward the referee. I casually but pointedly told Wallace, "There's no need to throw the ball toward him when he's not looking."

"Fuck you!" Wallace screamed back at me.

I immediately gave Wallace a technical foul and the game continued without further incident. The Trail Blazers won the game and Wallace had a big night, scoring 38 points and shooting 16-of-20 from the field. I certainly had no problem giving Wallace the technical—his profane comments were completely unacceptable. Besides, like most referees in the league, I disliked Wallace. He was incredibly difficult to get along with and we all wanted to stick it to him every chance we got. Fortunately, he gave us many opportunities. As an added bonus, Steve Javie paid me twenty bucks for winning a bet with him.

After the game, I was walking in the arena parking lot when Wallace jumped from behind a pole and confronted me. "I'm going to get my money back for that bullshit technical foul," he said.

The league assessed a fine of $1,000 for a technical foul, and despite their multimillion-dollar contracts, players don't like giving any of it back to the NBA front office.

"It wasn't bullshit," I said. "You deserved it!" I smiled and walked away, thinking he was just kidding around.

I was wrong about that. Wallace went berserk and ran toward me with his fists clenched and raised up in the fighting position. At 6'11" and 230 pounds, Rasheed Wallace is an imposing and menacing figure.

When I realized he was completely serious, the thought crossed my mind that I was a dead man.

"You better look out you punk-ass motherfucker!" he screamed. "I'm gonna kick your fucking ass!"

After what seemed like an eternity of unbelievable screaming and tension, security personnel grabbed Wallace by the arms and restrained him. It was the longest 30 seconds of my life and I remember thinking, *Where the hell is my backup? Where's my crew? Where's security?*

Scott Wall was already in the car, and when I finally got in I barked, "Where the hell were you? I could have used a little help back there!" What a partner. I had his back on the court, and he had his ass in the car at the first sign of trouble.

Steve Javie was our crew chief that night and he walked onto the scene just as it was ending. When he got the whole story, he said, "Shit, Timmy. You should have let him hit you—you could have owned this place." I'm sure the money would have been nice, but it wouldn't have been too cool eating through a straw for the rest of my life.

We were up all night preparing a written report of the incident for the league. For his few minutes of lunacy, Wallace was suspended for seven games without pay. That's approximately $1.26 million out of his pocket. I'm sure that $1,000 fine didn't look so bad then!

After his suspension ended, I was again lucky enough to be assigned to a Trail Blazers game, this time in Philadelphia. In the first quarter, I called a personal foul on Wallace and his coach, Mo Cheeks, took him out of the game. As Wallace walked to the bench, he was cursing me out and making aggressive gestures with his hands and arms. I immediately hit him with a technical foul.

Scottie Pippen, who was playing for Portland at the time, came up to me during a timeout. "When we found out you were reffing the game," Pippen said, "we all took bets on how long it would take you to give him a technical." He thought it was hysterical. I guess he won the bet.

NBA basketball can be very physical, and there are plenty of tough guys in the league who aren't afraid to fight. I'm not just talking about players mixing it up with other players. It seems that night after night, arenas throughout the league are loaded with wisecracking, inebriated hecklers who are just itching for a fight. Players and fans jaw back and forth all the time—that's just part of the action. Some nights, it seems as though the players are fed up with all the bullshit and are more than happy to oblige an invitation to rumble. That's exactly what happened at the Palace of Auburn Hills on the evening of November 19, 2004.

It was a highly anticipated televised matchup between the Pistons and the Indiana Pacers. The Pistons had knocked the Pacers out of the playoffs the year before in a rough-and-tumble Eastern Conference Finals that left a lot of bad blood. The league office loves this kind of drama, and the game was heavily promoted on ESPN. In the referees' locker room, we were expecting a very physical game, one that would have to be controlled carefully from the opening tip-off.

Much to our surprise, the game was fairly uneventful until the very last minute. With 45.9 seconds to go and Indiana up by a comfortable margin, a fight broke out between the Pistons' Ben Wallace and the Pacers' Ron Artest. Both players were generally regarded as tough competitors who could snap if they were pushed too far. Our referee crew jumped in immediately and separated the two before any real damage was done. Artest laid down on the scorer's table while order was being restored...only to have a flying cup of soda hit him on the chest. That's when all hell broke loose. Artest zeroed in on the cup thrower who was grinning at him from the stands. As Artest turned to run into the stands, I grabbed his jersey and was literally dragged off my feet. I lost my grip and Artest pounced on the hapless fan like a tiger on a wounded animal. Fists were flying everywhere as other Indiana players joined in the melee; 7'0" center Jermaine O'Neal delivered a monstrous overhand punch right to the face of a fan who came onto the court. As the blow landed and the dude's head snapped back, I thought for sure he was dead.

About the same time, Pistons coach Larry Brown screamed at me to do something.

"Are you kidding me?" I yelled back. "You do something, you're the coach!"

Coach Brown actually got on the P.A. system and begged for calm. Police officers, security personnel, players, and coaches finally stopped the carnage, but the building was out of control and total bedlam, and we never finished the game. We made a run for the locker room with chairs and debris flying all over the place. It was absolutely amazing that no one was seriously hurt.

Running through the tunnel, it felt as though the building was shaking at its very foundation, and we were concerned that we were being chased by an ugly mob. Security was nowhere to be found and our locker room door was locked. We heard the players running through the tunnel screaming and whooping all the way—it was a madhouse.

We eventually got out of there, but the aftermath of the game was ugly for the NBA. Yearlong suspensions, criminal charges, lawsuits, and a black eye for a league that seemingly could no longer police itself. What a frightening night at the arena, and what a nightmare for NBA Commissioner David Stern.

Larry Brown's reaction that night was typical. There's no question he's had a successful career on the bench, but like so many other coaches, he simply can't keep his players under control. Too many coaches live in fear that their players will turn on them and ultimately cost them their jobs. Of course, if a coach won't reprimand his players, he's got to take it out on someone.

Brown is a classic whiner who is constantly lobbing verbal assaults at the refs. I'm talking about back-alley profanity that seemed to comfortably roll off his tongue. I suppose you can take the kid out of Brooklyn, but you can't take Brooklyn out of the kid. The only time Brown toned down his potty mouth was when his son served as the ball boy during a game. When I reffed a Larry Brown game, the first thing I did was look around to see if his son was the ball boy. If he was, I knew it would be a much easier night.

That was Larry Brown on the court, not the nice, soft-spoken Larry Brown whom fans watched during television interviews. In reality, he is a great guy, but for 48 minutes on game day, he is a master strategist, employing any and all means to accomplish his ultimate objective: to get a win. His game of intimidation through constant whining is designed to wear down the weaker referees and get the calls that can turn the tide in a close contest. It wasn't very pretty, but it was effective as hell. I saw younger and weaker referees fold under his barrage of insults night after night. His strategy worked, plain and simple, and he's got the wins to prove it.

Regardless of Brown's raunchy demeanor during a game, he has racked up impressive numbers during his coaching career. On the night of January 3, 2004, Brown's Pistons were taking on the Golden State Warriors in Auburn Hills, and the coach was going for his 900th career victory as an NBA coach. I was working the game along with Dick Bavetta and Pat Fraher, an experienced crew chosen by the league office to officiate the momentous occasion.

The Pistons were a rough team with lots of talent and a track record of being difficult to referee. That night was no different: Coach Brown and several of his big stars were mouthy as ever, challenging most calls and generally being a pain in the neck. However, on this night it wasn't the coach or the players who caused the most trouble—it was the officiating crew.

With just over four minutes left in the third quarter, I gave Pistons guard Richard Hamilton a technical foul for excessively arguing a call. As the free throw was about to be attempted, I noticed Pat Fraher standing by the Detroit bench getting an earful from Brown. Suddenly, Fraher turned around and tossed Brown out of the game. My first thought was, *Holy shit! What did Brown say to get bounced from his 900th career win on only one technical?* In the NBA, it usually takes two technicals for a coach to be sent to the showers. Whatever the reason, Brown headed for the locker room, grumbling all the way.

I walked over to Fraher and asked what Brown had done to earn an ejection after only one technical foul.

"One tech?" Fraher asked, looking at me funny. "What are you talking about? You gave him the first one, right?"

I looked Fraher straight in the eye. "The first one was on Hamilton," I said.

Obviously, we had a situation on our hands, so we told Bavetta what happened and the three of us huddled up to find a way to cover our asses. I suggested that we tell the league that Brown said something outrageous to justify his expulsion—a common tactic that was used often.

So there we were, on Larry Brown's historic night, and he's in the locker room stewing over how the referees screwed him. The right thing to do was to send someone to the locker room, admit the mistake to Brown, and tell him to rejoin his team. Bavetta finally made that decision and it was announced that Brown could return. Only one problem: Brown was so upset that he got in his car and left the arena. Because of a referee's mistake, Larry Brown wasn't even in the building to enjoy his 900th win.

We knew there would be questions to answer after the game from both the press and the league office. As reporters began filing into the locker room, Bavetta told us, "I will handle the media. Don't talk to anyone."

Bavetta had just gone into the shower when the Pistons' radio announcer, Rick Mahorn, waltzed into the locker room. Bavetta came running out of the shower, buck naked and covered in soap, to see if Fraher and I were talking with reporters.

"C'mon, Dick," Mahorn pleaded, "put a fucking towel on. That's the ugliest body I've ever seen."

Fraher and I almost fell over laughing, but the laughs didn't last long for Fraher. Bavetta basically threw him under the bus and laid the blame on his crewmate. Yes, it was Fraher's mistake, but as a crew we should have stuck together and shouldered responsibility as a team.

Bavetta took the same approach with the league office, and Fraher received a verbal reprimand. It was one of those nights where a simple mistake became a major disaster, but as usual, there were a few laughs along the way.

Pat Fraher's mistake wasn't the only time an NBA referee needed damage control after a game—far from it. On January 16, 1998, I worked a Vancouver Grizzlies–Washington Wizards game with veteran referee Joe Borgia. Late in the game, Borgia called a foul on hometown favorite

Chris Webber. Immediately after blowing the whistle, Borgia realized it was Webber's sixth foul, meaning an automatic ejection from the game. Borgia always liked Webber and decided to reverse course and issue the foul to another player, thereby keeping Webber in the game. The foul went to guard Calbert Cheaney, who was nowhere near the action when the foul was called. Predictably, Cheaney went nuts until Borgia, in an effort to calm him down, explained the situation in a very loud voice.

"I know, Calbert, but it would've been Webber's sixth foul, so I gave it to you!" he said.

Needing Webber on the floor, Cheaney immediately calmed down, but the damage was already done. Borgia spoke so loudly that announcers, reporters, and fans clearly heard his explanation.

Borgia insisted to me on the court that it was the right thing to do in order to keep Webber in the game for the fans. He was trying to teach me something he felt was important, although I had seen it done before.

Borgia was in a panic after the game as reporters swooped in to grill him about the call. We tried to concoct an explanation, but Hue Hollins, the third ref on the court that night, would have none of it. Hollins hated Borgia and he was more than delighted to watch him squirm.

The next morning, Rod Thorn called Borgia and almost fired him on the spot. Not because of what he did, but because he did it in such a vocal way. It was a rough couple of days for Borgia, but all's well that ends well. Fast forward a few years and he was—you guessed it—put in charge of referee development.

* * *

Having a run-in with a coach is a big part of the game within the game. It's all about intimidation and manipulation—the strong standing over the weak—and the desire to gain a competitive edge by any means necessary. Inexperienced referees are immediately tested by NBA coaches and ultimately, the choice is clear: either earn the coach's respect or prepare to be a punching bag every time you work his game.

Early in my career, I was officiating a game in Philadelphia between the 76ers and the Milwaukee Bucks, coached by George Karl. Karl had a reputation for being nasty to young officials; he was a virtuoso in the craft of verbal intimidation.

The game was highly competitive and eventually went into overtime. During the last few minutes of regulation play and then in overtime, Karl was riding my ass. I had every justification to give him a technical foul and toss him out of the game, but I didn't want the contest determined by a free throw. I let it go, knowing my time would come.

After the game, supervisor Wally Rooney came into the locker room and praised me for the great restraint I had shown in not giving Karl a technical foul. I told Rooney that I was looking forward to seeing Karl in Indianapolis about two weeks later. The date was circled on my calendar: January 19, 2000.

I was unusually nervous about the situation with Karl and asked my fellow refs Steve Javie and Joe Crawford for some advice. They warned me that Karl would continue to ride me until I took a stand—I had to earn his respect or he would never let up. Like any profession, politics and personalities always play a role, and NBA basketball was no exception.

We decided that the only way to end his nonsense once and for all was to toss him out of the game the first time he jumped on me. There would be no restraint this time, no patience, no deference paid to the veteran coach—it would be two quick technicals and an ejection.

My fellow referees for the Pacers-Bucks contest were Mike Mathis and Tommie Wood. I told them in our pregame meeting that I was done taking Karl's shit. They loved my plan and had a good laugh in anticipation of the unceremonious but highly scripted ejection. Actually, this type of payback and jockeying for respect was not unusual in the NBA. Coaches dumped on us, we dumped on them, but the timing was everything.

Much to the surprise of me and my partners, Karl made it all the way to the 4:54 mark of the second quarter. Mike Mathis called a foul and Karl started screaming at me. I wasn't even involved in the play, but he thought I was his whipping boy and unleashed a vicious verbal assault. He didn't mess with Mathis, who had earned his respect long ago. But I was another story, a young and weak referee who could be intimidated and manipulated…or so he thought. Not this time, and not ever again! In the blink of an eye, I hit Karl with two rapid-fire technicals and ran him off the floor. Enjoy the early beer, Coach!

The next day, Rod Thorn called me on my cell phone and demanded an explanation for the quick ejection. I told him the truth: I needed to draw a line in the sand and get Karl off my ass. Thorn wasn't pleased at all with my explanation—he loudly hung up on me.

George Karl didn't need an explanation for the quick hook. He knew exactly why it happened. After the game, he simply told reporters, "It's personal, from another game."

There was no question that I had made the right decision. The next time I worked a game involving Milwaukee and Coach Karl, it was great. He never so much as looked my way, even when I made a questionable call against his team. From that point forward we never had a problem. I had finally earned his respect.

Perhaps the best example of how a relationship between an NBA referee and a coach can create a culture of fraud involved Houston coach Jeff Van Gundy during the Rockets' 2005 playoff series against Dallas. Mavericks owner Mark Cuban, who was considered a squeaky wheel, had been complaining about Yao Ming getting away with illegal screens. Cuban had the entire referee staff scared to death—whenever we had a game in Dallas, we were all careful of what we said in the locker room because the staff thought there might be a hidden camera or microphone planted somewhere. Ronnie Nunn constantly instructed us to be careful in Dallas because he felt that Cuban would have some of us followed. Cuban ended up getting his way after some interesting revelations that resulted in a big fine for Van Gundy—$100,000, the largest amount ever levied against a coach—and a whitewash by the NBA.

Donnie Vaden was the supervisor of the referees for this series. Vaden was a former referee with several years in the league and was one of the many refs who had retired on disability. Dick Bavetta, Jim Clark, and Luis Grillo were the crew for Game 4, and I was an alternate in case one of them got injured. That night I sat with Vaden and the crew while they discussed an email that was received from the league office that day pertaining to Yao Ming. We'd also discussed Yao at the morning meeting. Since Cuban was upset about Yao's illegal screens, the office made sure that we were told to watch him closely. We were also instructed to watch his footwork and look for traveling violations. Contrary to league policy, Vaden passed this information along to Van Gundy.

As it turns out, Vaden was providing inside information about the teams, players, and whatever else Van Gundy needed to know to help him win during that playoff series. Vaden told Van Gundy to make sure Yao avoided setting illegal screens because the referees would be watching closely. But then Van Gundy made a mistake—he slipped up during a news conference on May 1 and revealed he'd received inside information from a league official. All hell broke loose, and Mark Cuban went ballistic.

Van Gundy wouldn't disclose the identity of his source, but I knew who it was, as did many other guys on the staff. Vaden had confided to me that he spoke with Van Gundy before and after each game. Their private conversations started when Vaden was out with a back injury and Van Gundy called several times to see how he was doing. Van Gundy was smart—he built a relationship with this guy and other referees and it paid off.

In order to cover its tracks, the NBA sent out a news release stating that Van Gundy apologized for his remarks about the inside information, and that there was no proof that an NBA referee had any communication with him pertaining to the game. In other words, Van Gundy had simply "misspoken."

What a smoke screen! The league would do anything to make it look like there were no referee-coach relationships. If we had checked the phone records between those two guys, I believe they would've told a very different story from the NBA's official version. (Eventually, the NBA would admit that both Stu Jackson and Vaden had spoken with Van Gundy during the series.)

If you look at how that series played out, you can see how the league can influence which team gets an advantage. Houston was up 2–0; Dallas had a powerful owner and he started to work the system. The NBA certainly didn't want Houston to win the next two games at home—the series would be a sweep. So the office contacted Vaden, who's running the meetings before the game, and tells him that the previous crews missed several illegal screens and travels by Yao Ming. Bingo! Dallas wins the next two games and the series is tied 2–2. Great for TV and even better for the NBA.

When the series became tied, Van Gundy got frustrated and couldn't hold back what he knew. He told the *New York Times* and *Houston Chronicle* that he had "inside info" and was getting screwed. You sure got that right, Jeff, but you were supposed to keep it to yourself. Dallas ended up winning the series in seven games. Picasso couldn't have painted a better picture.

* * *

Something else that fans may not be aware of is the relationship between television announcers and referees. There are times when referees miss a call or fail to handle a crucial situation the right way. Current announcers like Mike Fratello, Doug Collins, or Jeff Van Gundy might call you over during a timeout and say, "You guys really missed that." You knew that if you were in the last minute of the game and you missed a call, you'd better make a call for the other team. Many referees would look the announcers' way after a controversial call because we knew they were looking at slow-motion replays. This was something I learned from Dick Bavetta. It was a lot easier to hear from an announcer that you missed something—so that you could make a call the other way—than to get an email or a phone call from the league office saying that your blown call had cost a team a game. If you missed a call but could still make it up and you didn't cost a team a game, then everything would be okay.

The announcers knew exactly what was going on in terms of the way we called games. They knew what was happening, but for the good of the game, they would never bury us or point out our shortcomings. The NBA actually has a guy in the East Coast office listening to everything the announcers say. If he hears something that isn't good, he'll call the truck and relay the message. For example, if an announcer is discussing a rule incorrectly or saying stuff that's out of whack, the NBA will be on the phone to the production staff in the truck and the message will get to the announcer within moments. The announcers knew that every word they spoke was being monitored by the league.

Owners also played a role, especially the loudmouth variety who NBA referees loved to hate. Mickey Arison of the Miami Heat is a prime example of an owner who hurt his team on game day. He sat courtside and constantly screamed and yelled at us, seizing every opportunity to embarrass the refs in a relentless game of "gotcha." During timeouts, Arison would get our attention and say, "I've got this little TV and I'm watching the replays. You missed the call!" The more he jawed, the more we stuck it to his team. Some guys just never learn.

Robert Sarver, owner of the Phoenix Suns, was no better, constantly whining and crying about missed calls and bad fouls. He worked tirelessly to intimidate the refs, but we always got the last laugh.

Wyc Grousbeck, owner of the Boston Celtics, was much the same, always yelling, screaming, and berating. I had never met the man and didn't even know what he looked like until a game I worked in 2004. Throughout the contest, this guy sitting courtside was incessant in his ranting directed toward the referees. Finally, I went over to the scorer's table to have security escort him from the arena.

"Before you do that, did you know he's the owner of the Celtics?" said a man at the scorer's table.

"Oh, no!" I exclaimed. "He's the owner?"

That night I backed off and let him stay, but over the years Wyc Grousbeck got plenty of payback for the way he disrespected us.

On the flipside, there were owners who were very respectful of the referees, owners who never tried to embarrass us or show us up. The late Larry Miller of the Utah Jazz was a particularly nice guy, and the NBA permitted him to come on the court and shake hands with the refs, a practice that's usually frowned upon. The Maloof brothers, owners of the Sacramento Kings, are much the same as Larry Miller, fun-loving guys who love basketball and are real gentlemen.

One of my favorite front office guys was Garry St. Jean, the former general manager of the Golden State Warriors. All the refs liked Garry and treated his team fairly. Early in my career, I was working a Golden State game and the Warriors were getting thumped pretty good by their opponent. During a timeout, St. Jean casually gained my attention and made a strange request.

"The next time up the floor I want you to throw me out of the game," he said.

I looked at him, perplexed by the odd request, but when I ran by him during the next play, he started yelling at me, so I granted his wish.

"You're out of here!" I shouted.

As he strolled out of the arena, he approached me as though he was still arguing. It was all just a cover for the team and the crowd.

"Thanks, Tim. I needed to motivate these fucking clowns," he muttered in a hushed tone.

He turned around, waved me off in disgust, and stomped off the court. Funny guy.

The best-known owner in the NBA, of course, is the aforementioned Mark Cuban of the Dallas Mavericks. Always a funny guy, Cuban was actively involved in the game from the opening tip to the final buzzer. In fact, he was so animated in his cheering on of the Mavericks that he often looked exhausted at the end of a game. Anyone who follows pro basketball knows that Cuban is the consummate bleacher referee, but to his credit, he is usually right when he complains about missed calls. I was one of the few refs in the league who would watch tape of an entire game after it was completed. Sitting in my hotel room in front of a TV, I would fast-forward or rewind until I was certain that we either got a call right or that we blew the call. Nine times out of 10, Cuban was right on the money with his assessment. A very savvy basketball guy, albeit a loud and crazy one.

I always had a friendly, easy relationship with Cuban, but I was the exception to the rule when it came to NBA referees and league officials. The league office instructed us on many occasions to avoid contact with Cuban and to ignore him when he initiated contact. Still, every time I worked a Dallas game, I would say hello from a distance.

I knew from the get-go that Dallas didn't have a chance in the 2006 NBA Finals; people in the NBA front office had no love for Cuban and the majority of the referees had even less. Because of Cuban's many suggestions directed at improving the quality of officiating in the NBA, the average workload for a referee had increased greatly. Ed T. Rush, the Supervisor of Officials, constantly reminded all of us that Cuban was solely responsible for our extra job responsibilities, mostly concerning postgame reports and statistical tracking. Any way you slice it, Dallas was always facing an uphill battle against the referees.

Ronnie Nunn, who replaced Rush as our boss, once told me that the league was "relieved" when the Mavericks were knocked out of the playoffs because the front office wouldn't have to deal with Cuban's constant phone calls, emails, and complaints. In the 2006 NBA Finals, the Mavs won the first two games of the series against the Miami Heat at home. As the series shifted back to Miami, the league office began flooding the Game 3 and Game 4 referees with video of plays from Games 1 and 2 that the higher-ups felt should have been called in favor of Miami. The message was predictable and very clear: Miami was going to have an advantage in its own building, thus prolonging the series and socking it to Mark Cuban. With millions of dollars of network revenue on the line, a sweep by the Mavs was out of the question. In a strange and almost unprecedented reversal of fortune, Miami swept their three games at home and went on to win the series in six. In Game 5, the referees handed Miami a tremendous advantage by awarding the Heat 49 free throws during the contest, compared to just 25 for Dallas. In the NBA, it's tough enough for one team's five players to beat another team's five. But when it's five against eight, and three of the eight are referees, forget about it—you've got no shot!

* * *

Perhaps the most comical aspect of the game came not on the floor or in the locker room, but from the stands: breastfeeding mothers, panty-waving groupies, pot-smoking hippies, shit-faced businessmen, and, depending on the venue, celebrities, celebrities, celebrities!

The Staples Center in Los Angeles and Madison Square Garden in New York are virtual meccas for the rich and famous, the bold and beautiful, and the A-listers of stage and screen. Look around the arena and there's Tom Brady with Gisele Bundchen. A couple of rows over are Matt Damon and Ben Affleck. There's Britney Spears, Will Smith and his son, Kate Hudson, Ethan Hawke, and the list goes on and on.

Most of the celebrities pop in for a game now and then, but a few big names are serious basketball fans, and they use all their talents and skills to influence the referees and help out the home team.

In L.A., the big gun is Jack Nicholson. Whether he's on television, in a movie, or sitting courtside, he's got the same intensity and the same look. He's wearing the dark shades, leaning back in his padded chair, the picture of calm, cool, and collected. But just before tip-off, Jack started working us—and he never let up.

"Tim, how's the family?" he asked politely. "Now listen, Tim, the crowd expects a little help tonight. You've gotta be good to my team."

I just laughed and waited for the action to start. That's when Jack came alive and started his profanity-laced tirade.

"What the fuck was that? Are you fucking blind?" he screamed. "You stupid shit, blow the fucking whistle!" When Jack got into his groove, he became the grizzled Colonel Nathan Jessup we all came to fear in *A Few Good Men*. That was Jack: treating us like imbeciles, questioning our manhood, and always trying to get in our heads and force us to make the call for the Lakers. Oh, he's still looking cool as can be, sipping on something cold with a certain glow coming from his face. Whatever was in that drink, it definitely had an amorous effect on him.

When there was a break in the action, I would notice Jack looking up into the crowd, peering through his high-powered binoculars, just salivating at the sights.

"Jack, you've got front-row seats, what do you need binoculars for?" I asked him.

"Just looking at the ladies, my boy. Just looking at the ladies," he answered, while continuing to pan the crowd as though he was on a safari.

If the Lakers won, Jack would stroll by and mumble a few semi-intelligible words: "Good job, kiddo, good job." And then he was gone into the tunnel and on his way to a waiting limousine. If the Lakers lost, there were no words at all. Just a quick glance and an extended middle finger on his left hand, standing all alone, screaming the magic four-letter word. Only in Hollywood!

In New York's Madison Square Garden it was all about movie director Spike Lee. Spike was more than just a fan; he was a cheerleader, a second coach, and always a referee.

"That's a foul, you've gotta call that one!" he constantly argued.

If a call went against the Knicks, Spike was up on his feet, turning and twisting like Chubby Checker on *American Bandstand*. His facial expressions were particularly hilarious—you would think the man had just experienced a ruptured hemorrhoid.

Unlike Jack, Spike wasn't much for profanity. With him, it was more about histrionics. The thrill of victory and the agony of defeat, the arched back coaxing the ball into the net, the up-and-down, back-and-forth frantic movements of a cat looking for a litter box after drinking a bowl of warm milk—that was Spike Lee. He was always the master showman working the players, the crowd, and most definitely the referees. I couldn't wait to referee a game in New York, but not because of the lifeless Knicks. It was all about Spike.

As entertaining as Jack Nicholson and Spike Lee could be, my all-time favorite fan in the stands was not a celebrity at all, but rather the mother of one of the game's biggest superstars.

Cleveland's Quicken Loans Arena is home to the Cavaliers. It's also universally regarded as the palace for native son and franchise savior LeBron James. King James rules his kingdom with acts of grace and daring on the court. I've seen a lot of talented players in my day, but this guy is beyond spectacular. Still in his early twenties, LeBron is basketball's pop icon, watched and adored by fans all over the world. Still, his biggest fan and cheerleader is the petite, attractive woman with a big voice sitting in the first row directly behind the basket—his mother Gloria.

Gloria made her presence in the league known to all the very first time her son stepped on the court. Always cheering, always shouting, she was a virtual nonstop electric turbine in a nuclear power plant; she caught my eye, and my attention, right away. She knows everyone on the court by their first name and loves to turn on the charm at the first opportunity.

"Hi, Timmy, how's my boy tonight?" she chirped. "Gimme some love tonight, Timmy. We gotta get some love."

Of course, she was referring to the Cavaliers getting some love from the referees, but it sure sounded good coming out of her mouth.

"Okay, baby. I'll see what I can do," I'd respond playfully.

Whether I was directly under the basket just a couple of feet from her or on the other end of the court, I could always hear her clearly. She made her presence known and demanded attention.

When I was watching the action under the basket on her side of the court, she would attempt to quietly distract me with playful words of flirtation.

"What room are you in at the Marriott, Timmy?" she'd giggle.

There I was, closely watching the pushing and shoving under the hoop, and I was fighting back a smile. She was so close to me that it felt as though she was standing directly behind me, whispering and blowing in my ear. Although I can't offer any specifics, I'm positive she caused me to miss a few calls; when the siren sang her bewitching sweetness, I got a lump in my throat and couldn't blow the darn whistle. What a character, and what a great lady!

CHAPTER 6

How the Game
Is Really Played

For all intents and purposes, it was just another ordinary day in early November of 2003. Thanksgiving was fast approaching with Christmas right around the corner. The weather in the Northeast was turning chilly and area golf courses were getting ready to close for the season. Oh, and NBA basketball had just tipped off for another season of exciting action—on and off the court.

Jack Concannon and I had just finished one of our last rounds of golf for the season and were relaxing in the clubhouse at Radley Run. He was studiously reading the sports section of the *Philadelphia Daily News* and I was on the phone with Kim explaining that I would be late for dinner that night. Cards, of course.

As I turned off my cell phone, Jack asked me the $64,000 question that would ultimately change my life forever.

"You know who's going to win these games?" he asked, pointing to the newspaper's betting line for the NBA games to be played later that night.

It was the first time the subject of picking NBA games had come up. Ever since we started betting on major sporting events, we were focused on everything except pro basketball. In some respects, I suppose the possibility of betting on NBA games was always the elephant in the room, but it was a silent taboo, an untouchable, a place I didn't want to go. Still, my response to Jack's question that day rolled off my tongue rather easily. I took a quick look at the betting lines and zoomed in on the matchups.

"If I was betting, I'd bet this team, that team, and this team," I said, pointing to my pick for each of the three games listed.

We checked the final scores later that night and learned that two of my three picks were winners. How about that?

There were many times during my career as an NBA referee that someone would approach me at a dinner party and ask who I thought would win a particular game or a playoff series. I always politely sidestepped the inquiry and changed the subject. At that time, I was serious about my contractual agreement to avoid even the appearance of impropriety in my duties as a referee. More importantly, I was always mindful of the standard of integrity set by my father and the absolute obligation I felt to preserve the game's reputation, not to mention my own.

But it was all different now. I was a runaway train with no sense of direction. My moral compass was spinning out of control, and I was about to betray the game I loved and myself right along with it. This was the moment, like a fumble on the goal line as your team is about to go in for the winning score, or the missed three-pointer to win the game as time expires. If you don't like sports clichés, try this on for size: it was the moment when a person arrives at the proverbial fork in the road and a split-second choice can be the difference between happiness and despair, marriage or divorce, freedom or imprisonment. This was the moment that sealed the deal, and made the outcome a fait accompli.

Jack and I didn't actually bet that day; it was sort of a trial run that somehow made the inevitable a little easier to swallow. I suppose it could be equated to not sleeping with a woman on the first date, even though a strong mutual attraction is obvious and both parties are more than willing. In the ensuing days, we discussed it plenty, and Jack was eager beyond description. After all, betting on pro basketball did not require the services of Pete Ruggieri. Pete may have been the guy that made our picks for all the other bets we placed, but I was now stepping up to the plate and making the picks on NBA games. Suddenly, I was the go-to guy, the featured back, the cleanup hitter, the center of attention—and I liked it! No more middle man; just me and Jack, a tight little circle filled with friendship, loyalty, and tons of trust—blind trust. I never thought twice about Jack's dependability; he was a solid friend who always had my back. Besides, he wasn't some strung-out street criminal looking for his next fix. He was a respected businessman, a loving husband and devoted family man, a pillar of the community. Hell, he even went to church most Sundays! No, Jack was the least of my worries. In fact, I didn't really have any worries. I was certainly aware of the gravity of my involvement in betting on basketball and of the ramifications if I was to get caught. But getting caught didn't seem plausible. Jack and I were too smart for that—we were smarter than everyone else, and as long as we were careful, we couldn't lose. That was my warped mind-set at the time, the place where reality morphs into fantasy and a man's core values are overshadowed by his risky dalliances with vice and immorality. That was a man who was no longer recognizable to the people who knew him best and loved him most. That was me.

A couple of weeks later, Jack and I took the plunge. I was working on the road for most of the month, but my separation from Jack never slowed us down. We were on the phone constantly, five times per day, discussing that week's games, cross-checking the betting lines, and making our pro basketball picks. Pete Ruggieri was still giving Jack the picks for college and pro football, but the NBA picks were mine alone. Jack took care of the rest. He contacted a bookie, placed the wager, settled up with the bookie, and personally delivered my cut. I reminded Jack many times not to place the NBA bets with Pete. Because we all knew each other, I feared that Pete might eventually put two and two together and realize I was the source of the picks. Jack assured me that Pete would never piece it together and that he would never know—it was our little secret. That was good enough for me.

Our bets on NBA games were extremely selective; I only picked contests where I felt very confident about the outcome. I would typically pick one or two games out of a full slate of 10 matchups on any given night. I didn't bet the full schedule and often skipped a night or two. I never pretended to be omniscient with my predictions. Many times, I just didn't have enough information to sufficiently increase our odds of success. On other occasions, all the stars lined up and the pick was a no-brainer.

Jack and the bookie worked on a credit arrangement. Jack called in our picks and, win or lose, we racked up a tally until Jack settled at a later date. The NBA bets were wildly successful, but our continuing foray into college and pro football wagering was mixed, at best. Some weekends netted a windfall, while others were a shameless slaughter. No matter; we rarely counted the winnings and never batted an eye at the losses. The exhilaration of being a player, of risking everything, was the fuel that drove the engine.

Jack and I split the profits or paid the piper when we reached the $5,000 plateau. In those days, I always had a wad of cash, a personal stash that fluctuated like the tide in Chesapeake Bay during a full moon.

Money went in and out of my pockets like a handful of sand slips through your fingers. When it rolled in, the pockets of the suits hanging in my closet were stuffed with cash. Although I worked diligently to conceal the loot from my wife, my biggest fear was not detection but that it would all come to an end, and that I would return to a life without risk and excitement. Here I was, a veteran NBA official, traveling the country, rubbing elbows with basketball superstars and Tinseltown celebrities, earning more than $250,000 a year, and the only thing that turned me on was picking a long-shot horse to win the third race at Santa Anita Park on a Tuesday afternoon.

There was always a certain unspoken disconnect between Kim and me. As my career took off, her career ended. With four babies in six years, Kim had her hands full, especially with a husband gone 26 days of the month. Whether at home or on the road, I was usually the center of attention and Kim often faded into the background. I suppose I didn't realize it at the time, but she was living my life, not her own. Still, as selfish as I was back then, I desperately wanted to have her respect and approval and couldn't stomach the thought of being diminished in her eyes. For that reason alone, to remain a larger-than-life figure in my house, I hid my addiction from Kim and lived a total lie with the one for whom I'd promised to be ever faithful. Shit, I couldn't even be faithful to myself; how could I be faithful to her?

My real relationship was with Jack. Phone calls, golf outings, card games, trips to the casino, and money exchanging hands under the table were the basis of our friendship. Along the way, in acts of self-preservation, we evolved into pathetic souls playing a cloak-and-dagger game. We developed a paranoia complex commonplace among serial gamblers. When I checked into hotels, I would often change rooms, sometimes two or three times in one night. I began to think that NBA security or the FBI was bugging my room and silently eavesdropping on my conversations with Jack. I rarely used the phone in my hotel room and often retreated to a pay phone in the lobby or down the street. Jack and I devised a code to confuse and throw off any would-be listeners. I would talk about a particular city, tipping Jack to the game I had picked. If I followed up with a conversation about Kim, he was to bet the home team. If I mentioned his wife Ann, the visiting team was my pick. This was the excitement that I craved: living a secret life, flirting with disaster, and wanting more, more, more! There were weeks when Jack and I placed upwards of 50 bets on football and basketball, and each one was the bastard child of two misguided gamblers who risked it all on the mere chance that Lady Luck would smile favorably upon them.

Actually, when it came to pro basketball, Lady Luck didn't play much of a role. I didn't need the old girl, thank you very much. No sir, when it came to pro basketball, I didn't need a roll of the dice, a flip of the coin, a spin of the wheel, a turn of the cards, or a Ouija board. All I needed was the NBA's daily Master List of Referees.

The first time Jack and I placed a wager on an NBA game, I couldn't believe what I was doing. I knew it was wrong and that I had sunk to a new low, but the rush was overwhelming. I don't even remember which two teams played or what the final score was. But I have a crystal-clear recollection of who the officiating crew chief was for the game. You see, I checked the Master List of Referees that day and scanned the game assignments. The moment I came to one particular name, I went no further and promptly called in my pick to an anxiously waiting Jack Concannon.

* * *

NBA referee Dick Bavetta has been officiating pro basketball for more than 30 years. When it comes to blowing the whistle, Bavetta is the face of the NBA—a true legend and a certain lock for election to the Basketball Hall of Fame. Not since the legendary Earl Strom has a referee been more recognizable to the public, more accessible to the media, or more embraced by the National Basketball Association. Bavetta holds many officiating records including most consecutive games refereed. He is universally known throughout the basketball world and regarded by most as a great official and a terrific guy.

I knew of Dick Bavetta's reputation well before joining the NBA. It seemed as though every time a big game was played, Bavetta was on the court, front and center. Always the master showman, he has an uncanny way of diffusing the most volatile situations, calming nerves and restoring order to a sometimes very physical and chaotic game. In another life, he would have made a great diplomat, working through problems and finding solutions acceptable to all parties. That's Dick Bavetta, the NBA's No. 1 ambassador for everything good the game stands for—honesty, integrity, and fairness.

During my early years in the league, I relished the opportunity to work a game with Dick. To be under his tutelage was a tremendous experience for a young referee breaking into the pro game. In the NBA, the total referee pool is broken down into groups of 15. From those 15, the league office assigns three referees to officiate a particular game. I was one of the lucky ones to be in Dick Bavetta's group, and during my 13 years in the league, we worked countless games together. It got to the point where he knew me and I knew him, and that's precisely why I felt extremely confident in betting on any NBA game officiated by Dick Bavetta. Again, to me, our colleagues, players, and coaches, he was friendly, personable, level-headed, and always approachable. But when it came to picking which games to bet on, I focused on one of his other personality characteristics. At the end of the day, Dick Bavetta was consistently one thing above all others—predictable!

That very first time Jack and I bet on an NBA game, Dick was on the court. The team we picked lost the game, but it covered the large point spread and that's how we won the money. Because of the matchup that night, I had some notion of who might win the game, but that's not why I was confident enough to pull the trigger and pick the other team. The real reason I picked the losing team was that I was just about certain they would cover the spread, no matter how badly they played. That is where Dick Bavetta comes into the picture.

From my earliest involvement with Bavetta, I learned that he likes to keep games close, and that when a team gets down by double-digit points, he helps the players save face. He accomplishes this act of mercy by quietly, and frequently, blowing the whistle on the team that's having the better night. Team fouls suddenly become one-sided between the contestants, and the score begins to tighten up. That's the way Dick Bavetta referees a game—and everyone in the league knew it.

Fellow referee Danny Crawford attended Michael Jordan's Flight School Camp years ago and later told me that he had long conversations with other referees and NBA players about how Bavetta propped up weak teams. Danny told me that Jordan himself said that everyone in the league knew that Bavetta cheated in games and that the players and coaches just hoped he would be cheating for them on game night. *Cheating?* That's a very strong word to use in any sentence that includes the name Dick Bavetta. Is the conscious act of helping a team crawl back into a contest "cheating"? The credo of referees from high school to the NBA is "call them like you see them." Of course, that's a lot different than purposely calling more fouls against one team as opposed to another. Did Bavetta have a hidden agenda? Or was he the ultimate company man, making sure the NBA and its fans got a competitive game most times he was on the court?

When that first game went final, Jack and I were on the phone, naturally.

"I can't believe it was that easy!" Jack said in disbelief.

Well, it's not that easy for just anyone, I was thinking. Just anyone didn't have the same knowledge I had. Just anyone hadn't officiated hundreds of NBA games or understood the tendencies, quirks, patterns, and prejudices of the referees who called the games. Just anyone didn't know Dick Bavetta like I did!

It was strange watching an NBA game that I had placed a bet on. Typically when I watched a game I was analyzing the referees, a sort of silent critique of how they handled the game. But not this game. Instead, I was rooting for a team, living and dying with every three-pointer thrown up and every free throw bouncing off the rim. I hadn't been that involved in a game as a fan since I was a kid watching my beloved 76ers play at the Philadelphia Spectrum. Perhaps my excitement came from something more than just the fact that I had placed a very dangerous wager. Perhaps it emanated from the knowledge that I had an edge, that I knew something very few others knew, and that of those very few, I was undoubtedly the only one breaking the law. Bottom line, I knew Dick Bavetta—but I wasn't alone.

Terry Durham and Mike Mathis are retired NBA referees, each having officiated at the pro level for more than 20 years. Mathis was quite the character during his time in the league. He was known to walk right into an NBA locker room with a bag of jerseys and hustle autographs from the players for his charity events. A few years back, after their retirement from the league, Durham and Mathis were in Las Vegas having some fun at one of the casinos. They bounced into the sports book area and bet a "teaser," where the bettor is required to pick the winner of three NBA games in order to cash in. Their first two picks were winners and they needed only one more to get a payday. They watched the third game on television and saw that Dick Bavetta was the head referee working the game. The team Durham and Mathis had picked was winning by 15 points, but the spread was eight and there were still two minutes left in the game. Their bet looked pretty good, right? Not with

Dick Bavetta on the floor. Durham and Mathis just laughed because they knew Bavetta was about to do his thing. Sure enough, the whistle started to blow and the losing team cut the margin of defeat to a respectable six points, thereby covering the spread and denying Durham and Mathis the trifecta. Terry Durham later told Steve Javie and me that as soon as he saw Bavetta, all chances of winning went right out the window. The two longtime referees knew that Bavetta would make the game close, and he did.

Veteran players also knew of Bavetta's tendencies. In 2006, the Dallas Mavericks and the San Antonio Spurs were fighting it out for the best record in the Western Conference. Dallas was 45–11 and San Antonio was 44–12 going into a head-to-head matchup, and Bavetta was the crew chief on the court. The Spurs won the game on their home court 98–89, inspiring some heated postgame comments from Mavericks guard Jerry Stackhouse.

"Somebody saw Bavetta get off the bus Wednesday night and I thought, *Oh, shit!*" said Stackhouse. "I knew what was coming. It's tough to come on the road in this environment and have to play against the refs, too. Fuck Dick Bavetta. I'm tired of his shit. It's like the game is about him. He just needs to call the game and call the fouls. This game was about Dick Bavetta."

Bavetta declined to comment.

Veteran sports columnist Garth Woolsey of the *Toronto Star* got it right when he said, "Basketball, of all the sports, is the easiest to manipulate."

Of course, basketball fans across the country have always known the truth in Woolsey's statement. When opining on the far-reaching effects of my transgressions, well-known sportswriter Mike Wise of the *Washington Post* said it best:

> It will not matter one bit to the NBA consumer if [Donaghy] acted
> alone. Most fans have had their hunches about certain referees for some
> time, and one possible crooked cop among them opens up a Pandora's
> box to question an entire league's credibility.

Studying under Dick Bavetta for 13 years was like pursuing a graduate degree in advanced game manipulation. He knew how to marshal the tempo and tone of a game better than any referee in the league, by far. He also knew how to take subtle—and not so subtle—cues from the NBA front office and extend a playoff series or, worse yet, change the complexion of that series.

The 2002 Western Conference Finals between the Los Angeles Lakers and the Sacramento Kings presents a stunning example of game and series manipulation at its ugliest. As the teams prepared for Game 6 at the Staples Center, Sacramento had a 3–2 lead in the series. The referees assigned to work Game 6 were Dick Bavetta, Bob Delaney, and Ted Bernhardt. As soon as the referees for the game were chosen, the rest of us knew immediately that there would be a Game 7. A prolonged series was good for the league, good for the networks, and good for the game. Oh, and one more thing: it was great for the big-market, star-studded Los Angeles Lakers.

In the pregame meeting prior to Game 6, the league office sent down word that certain calls—calls that would have benefitted the Lakers—were being missed by the referees. This was the type of not-so-subtle information that I and other referees were left to interpret. After receiving the dispatch, Bavetta openly talked about the fact that the league wanted a Game 7.

"If we give the benefit of the calls to the team that's down in the series, nobody's going to complain. The series will be even at three apiece, and then the better team can win Game 7," Bavetta stated.

As history shows, Sacramento lost Game 6 in a wild come-from-behind thriller that saw the Lakers repeatedly sent to the foul line by the referees. For other NBA referees watching the game on television, it was a shameful performance by Bavetta's crew, one of the most poorly officiated games of all time. NBA star Grant Hill later stated on national television that Dick Bavetta was known for extending playoff series. Consumer advocate and former presidential candidate Ralph Nader went much further in his condemnation of the events. In a letter to

NBA Commissioner David Stern, Nader wrote of the erosion of public confidence in the integrity of professional sports:

Dear Mr. Stern:

At a time when the public's confidence is shaken by headlines reporting the breach of trust by corporate executives, it is important, during the public's relaxation time, for there to be maintained a sense of impartiality and professionalism in commercial sports performances. That sense was severely shaken in the now notorious officiating during Game 6 of the Western Conference Finals between the Los Angeles Lakers and the Sacramento Kings.

Calls by referees in the NBA are likely to be more subjective then in professional baseball or football. But as the judicious and balanced *Washington Post* sports columnist Michael Wilbon wrote this Sunday, "too many of the calls in the fourth quarter (when the Lakers received 27 foul shots) were stunningly incorrect," all against Sacramento.

After noting that the three referees in Game 6 "are three of the best in the game," he wrote: "I have never seen officiating in a game of consequence as bad as that in Game 6... When Pollard, on his sixth and final foul, didn't as much as touch Shaq. Didn't touch any part of him. You could see it on TV, see it at courtside. It wasn't a foul in any league in the world. And Divac, on his fifth foul, didn't foul Shaq. They weren't subjective or borderline or debatable. And these fouls not only resulted in free throws, they helped disqualify Sacramento's two low-post defenders." And one might add, in a 106–102 Lakers' victory, this officiating took away what would have been a Sacramento series victory in 6 games.

This was not all. The Kobe Bryant elbow in the nose of Mike Bibby, who after lying on the floor groggy, went to the sideline bleeding, was in full view of the referee, who did nothing, prompted many fans to start wondering about what was motivating these officials.

Wilbon discounted any conspiracy theories about the NBA-NBC desire for Game 7 etc., but unless the NBA orders a review of this game's officiating, perceptions and suspicions, however presently absent any evidence, will abound and lead to more distrust and distaste for the games in general. When the distinguished basketball writer for the *USA Today*, David DuPree, can say: "I've been covering the NBA for 30 years, and it's the poorest officiating in an important game I've ever seen," when Wilbon writes that "The Kings and Lakers didn't decide this series would be extended until Sunday: three referees did..." when many thousands of fans, not just those in Sacramento, felt that merit lost to bad refereeing, you need to take notice beyond the usual and widespread grumbling by fans and columnists about referees ignoring the rule book and giving advantages to home teams and superstars.

Your problem in addressing the pivotal Game 6 situation is that you have too much power. Where else can decision-makers (the referees) escape all responsibility to admit serious and egregious error and have their bosses (you) fine those wronged (the players and coaches) who dare to speak out critically?

In a February interview with David DuPree of *USA Today*, he asked you "Why aren't coaches and players allowed to criticize the referees?" You said, "...we don't want people questioning the integrity of officials... It just doesn't pay for us to do anything other than focus people on the game itself rather than the officiating." "Integrity" which we take you to mean "professionalism" of the referees has to be earned and when it is not, it has to be questioned. You and your league have a large and growing credibility problem. Referees are human and make mistakes, but there comes a point that goes beyond any random display of poor performance. That point was reached in Game 6 which took away the Sacramento Kings Western Conference victory.

It seems that you have a choice. You can continue to exercise your absolute power to do nothing. Or you can initiate a review and if all these observers and fans turn out to be right, issue, together with the referees, an apology to the Sacramento Kings and forthrightly admit decisive incompetence during Game 6, especially in the crucial fourth quarter.

You should know, however, that absolute power, if you choose the former course of inaction, invites the time when it is challenged and changed whether by more withdrawal of fans or by more formal legal or legislative action. No government in our country can lawfully stifle free speech and fine those who exercise it; the NBA under present circumstances can both stifle and fine players and coaches who speak up. There is no guarantee that this tyrannical status quo will remain stable over time, should you refuse to bend to reason and the reality of what occurred. A review that satisfies the fan's sense of fairness and deters future recurrences would be a salutary contribution to the public trust that the NBA badly needs.

We look forward to your considered response.

Sincerely,

Ralph Nader

Kings coach Rick Adelman looked absolutely ill after Game 6, and Lakers coach Phil Jackson strained to hold back a playful smirk when asked about the officiating. I wasn't even a member of the crew working the game, but I couldn't sleep that night. I knew that the referees, not the players, decided the outcome of the game. I don't know why it affected me that night; this was something I had witnessed many times before. Perhaps it was the magnitude of the game or the blatant and shameless manipulation of a game that was viewed by millions of fans around the world. This game wasn't stolen by a quiet thief in the night. It was no less than an armed robbery in broad daylight.

The 2002 Lakers-Kings series preceded my involvement in betting on pro basketball, and the hypocrisy of my indignation was a bit premature. But in the course of a few months, my hypocrisy would take off like an F-18 catapulting from the deck of an aircraft carrier in the Persian Gulf heading for Baghdad. It would have no limits.

With Game 6 in the Lakers' column, it was on to Game 7 in Sacramento. The Lakers won that game and went on to win the NBA championship. Most of my colleagues and I were convinced Sacramento was robbed of the Western Conference title and an opportunity to compete in the Finals.

As much as any other game or series, the 2002 Lakers-Kings matchup illustrated to me the relative ease with which I could predict the outcome of a contest simply by knowing which crew was assigned to work a game. There was another person who clearly understood Dick Bavetta's role in the Game 6 debacle. A Sacramento fan had a Lakers jersey with the name "Bavetta" printed boldly on the back. The fan angrily held the jersey up every time Bavetta reffed a game in Sacramento, and it pissed him off to no end. We wouldn't dare look at the fan or the jersey while in Bavetta's presence, and we never mentioned a word about it, not even as a joke. But it wasn't a joke—it was a statement of disgust. Actually, the fan struck a chord with Bavetta, who subsequently went out of his way to help Sacramento every chance he could after the dreaded Game 6.

The 2002 series certainly wasn't the first or last time Bavetta weighed in on an important game. He also worked Game 7 of the 2000 Western Conference Finals between the Lakers and the Trail Blazers. The Lakers were down by 13 at the start of the fourth quarter when Bavetta went to work. The Lakers outscored Portland 31–13 in the fourth quarter and went on to win the game and the series. It certainly didn't hurt the Lakers that they got to shoot 37 free throws compared to a paltry 16 for the Trail Blazers.

Two weeks before the 2003–04 season ended, Bavetta and I were assigned to officiate a game in Oakland. That afternoon before the tip-off, we were discussing an upcoming game on our schedule. It was the last regular-season game we were scheduled to work, pitting Denver against San Antonio. Denver had lost a game a few weeks prior because of a mistake made by the referees, a loss that could be the difference between them making or missing the playoffs. Bavetta told me Denver needed the win and that it would look bad for the staff and the league if the Nuggets missed the playoffs by one game. There were still a few games left on the schedule before the end of the season, and the standings could potentially change. But on that day in Oakland, Bavetta looked at me and casually stated, "Denver will win if they need the game. That's why I'm on it."

I was thinking, *How is Denver going to win on the road in San Antonio?* At the time, the Spurs were arguably the best team in the league. Bavetta answered my question before it was asked.

"Duncan will be on the bench with three fouls within the first five minutes of the game," he calmly stated.

Bavetta went on to inform me that it wasn't the first time the NBA assigned him to a game for a specific purpose. He cited examples, including the 1993 playoff series when he put New Jersey guard Drazen Petrovic on the bench with quick fouls to help Cleveland beat the Nets. He also spoke openly about the 2002 Los Angeles–Sacramento series and called himself the NBA's "go-to guy."

As it turned out, Denver didn't need the win after all; they locked up a spot in the playoffs before they got to San Antonio. In a twist of fate, it was the Spurs that ended up needing the win to have a shot at the division title, and Bavetta generously accommodated. In our pregame meeting, he talked about how important the game was to San Antonio and how meaningless it was to Denver, and that San Antonio was going to get the benefit of the calls that night. Armed with this inside information, I called Jack Concannon before the game and told him to bet the Spurs. To no surprise, we won big. San Antonio blew Denver out of the building that evening, winning by 26 points. When Jack called me the following morning, he expressed amazement at the way an NBA game could be predicted. Sobering, yes; amazing, no. That's how the game is played in the National Basketball Association.

Virtually no one outside of professional basketball has any idea how the NBA assigns referees for playoff games. Oh sure, there is a standard formula that incorporates factors such as years of service, the referee rating system, and prior playoff experience. But in my experience, final decisions were often much more subjective, made for the purpose of generating fan excitement, ensuring marquee matchups, prolonging a series, and milking television revenues for every last dollar.

Consider the 2009 NBA Finals. A matchup between small-market teams from Denver and Orlando would have been a ratings and revenue disaster.

The dream matchup in 2009 was the L.A. Lakers versus the Cleveland Cavaliers—Kobe vs. LeBron. After LeBron James' buzzer-beater winning shot in Game 2 of the Eastern Conference Finals, the NBA's marketing partners on Madison Avenue were salivating over the prospect of a thrilling Finals between the NBA's biggest superstars. Of course, Cleveland got knocked off by Orlando and the stage was set for a Finals showdown between the Lakers and Magic. From the NBA's perspective, it wasn't the dream matchup, but it was still a pretty good one—Kobe vs. Dwight Howard. In years past, the NBA has utilized the referee-assignment process to get the right result in the playoffs—that is, the right result for the league.

Game 4 of the 2008 Western Conference Finals provides a good example of how easily the direction of a series can be influenced. The game was played in San Antonio with the Spurs trailing the Lakers 2–1. A Spurs loss would result in a 3–1 deficit, a Game 5 back in Los Angeles, and almost definitely the end of San Antonio's season. Improbably, the NBA proceeded to assign referee Joe Crawford as crew chief for this pivotal contest. Yes, the same Joe Crawford who threw Tim Duncan out of a game a year earlier, subsequently challenging Duncan to a fistfight. The bizarre incident was so serious at the time that the NBA suspended Crawford from participating in the playoffs that year, costing him thousands of dollars in earnings.

In a contest of such consequence, why, of all people, would *Joe Crawford* be assigned to the game by the NBA? It was no secret that the league office wanted a Lakers-Celtics Finals that year—and only the San Antonio Spurs and their low ratings in the previous year's NBA Finals stood in the way. Enter Joe Crawford. As a strong and forceful referee, Crawford had the backbone to make calls against the home team, calls that would favor the visiting Lakers. And, of course, Crawford had no love for Tim Duncan, coach Gregg Popovich, or the Spurs.

Sure enough, the game ended on a controversial non-call right in front of Crawford that favored the Lakers. The next day the NBA had no choice but to issue a press release stating the call was "missed." The Lakers finished off the Spurs in Game 5 back in Los Angeles, and the NBA's dream matchup was a reality.

In the playoffs, the NBA initially only made referee assignments for the first four games of a series. If a series extended beyond four games, the league assigned referees one game at a time, 24 to 48 hours before tip-off. To me, the only reason to assign refs in that fashion was in the interest of prolonging a series, ending a series, or guaranteeing the desired marquee matchups. And everyone knows there are certain referees who can deliver.

In the NBA, the standards used to determine the best referees are vague and subjective—often, the results more closely mirror those of a popularity contest. The referees who "play ball" with the front office get the best game assignments and the most rounds of playoff basketball. The inequity of the NBA's system was so egregious that the referees union, the National Basketball Referees Association (NBRA), finally voted to give every referee a $20,000 playoff bonus whether they worked a playoff game or not. Still, $20,000 is a drop in the bucket compared to the kind of money a referee can earn working the playoffs. For those subjectively chosen few who work into the Finals, bonus pay can exceed $100,000.

* * *

To my knowledge, I was the only active referee to place bets on NBA games and I have no evidence to suggest otherwise. But I wasn't the only person who knew in advance how a game would be decided; most of us had a pretty good idea. And make no mistake, Dick Bavetta wasn't the only referee who influenced games. Almost every referee on the staff had an occasional agenda that could affect the outcome of a particular game. If a referee had 10 or more years in the league, there was undoubtedly some bad blood between that ref and certain players, coaches, or owners. Likewise, referees had favorite players and coaches, special relationships that generated special treatment. After all my years in the league, I knew about most of those relationships, and I used that knowledge to my advantage when making picks.

Some picks could be made with very little homework. All I had to do was keep up-to-date with current information generally available to the public. Things like slumps, injuries, and player-coach relationships were considered. Of course, my information was usually more detailed and precise than what was available to the public, but my real advantage came from knowing the other referees in the league. That's how I was able to pick the winners over 70 percent of the time. It was all about the referees, and it was all about relationships.

NBA referee Joe Crawford has long been considered one of the premier officials in the league. Like Dick Bavetta, Crawford is a master of controlling a professional basketball game, but that's where the similarities end. As much as Bavetta is the quintessential diplomat and peacemaker, Joe Crawford is the overbearing tyrant who rules the court by fear.

A former mailman from Philadelphia, Crawford was a mentor to me and one of my first friends in the NBA. I suppose it was only natural that we would become friends. After all, we attended the same high school and were Irish Catholic Philly natives following in the footsteps of our fathers—Joe's dad was legendary Major League Baseball umpire Shag Crawford.

Joe Crawford is the kind of guy who would give a friend the shirt off his back, but with a very rough temper, his demeanor could turn on a dime. On the court, he officiated with an iron fist. If a player so much as looked at him funny, he would hit him with a technical foul. This approach made for a rocky relationship between him and some players in the league. So when Crawford and those particular guys were on the court together, I was confident that I could predict the outcome of the game, and I often did.

In an April 2007 game involving Tim Duncan and the San Antonio Spurs, Crawford gave the usually mild-mannered Duncan a technical foul for no readily apparent reason while Duncan was sitting on the bench. Duncan sat there shaking his head and laughing to himself in disbelief. About a minute later Crawford then yelled, "You want to fight?" and promptly threw Duncan out of the game with his second technical from the bench. The Spurs bench went wild. Stu Jackson later called Crawford and told him he was done for the year. The early end of Joe's season, including the playoffs, cost him about $85,000 in lost wages.

In a follow-up email to the referee staff and the league office, Crawford railed about the lack of respect players had for referees and the NBA's failure to back him up. Then, in a direct shot at the league's embracing of referees like Dick Bavetta, he fired a sharp rebuke:

> I also told [Stu Jackson] that the staff is an officiating staff of Dick Bavetta's—schmoozing and sucking people's asses to get ahead. Awful, but it is reality.

Crawford also touched on the fact that he was being excluded from working the playoffs that year:

> Look on the bright side everybody, MORE playoff games for you guys and Dick, maybe you will get to be crew chief in the 7th game of the Finals, which is a travesty in itself you even being in the Finals.

Crawford is clearly no shrinking violet and is not afraid to mix it up with anyone, including coaches and owners. He really had a problem with Golden State coach Don Nelson and once threw him out of a playoff game in 2003 for staring at him.

"I'd like to stab Don Nelson in the eye with a fork," Crawford often said. He even joked about bringing a fork out on the court when he had Nelson in a game.

Mickey Arison, owner of the Miami Heat, was also on Crawford's shit list. Crawford was working a 2006 playoff game in Miami when Heat forward Udonis Haslem drove to the basket and thought he got fouled. Joe disagreed and made no call. That infuriated Haslem, who subsequently threw his mouth guard at Crawford. Haslem received a quick technical followed by an ejection, which drew a comment from the radio announcer sitting at the scorer's table.

"Fuck you, go fuck yourself!" Crawford screamed at the announcer. Everyone in the vicinity heard the remark, and Mickey Arison was so upset he tried to get Crawford fired. Nothing happened to Crawford, but his memory bank of future paybacks was increased by one that night.

Crawford also wasn't timid about screwing Dallas Mavericks owner

Mark Cuban every chance he could. Crawford was not much of a relationship-builder; to the contrary, he built walls and blew up bridges to the extent that I felt very confident in making a pick when Crawford was on the court with one of his enemies.

In one particular game against the Chicago Bulls, the Mavericks were comfortably ahead by 24 points at halftime. With a little help from Crawford, the Bulls pulled within four points late in the game—much to the consternation of Mark Cuban, who fired off a nasty email to the league office and referees union:

> In the past I have told you guys that if Joey Crawford is being challenged in the least bit, he will "show" his displeasure by sticking his hand way down his pants. It's a very obvious gesture that he makes sure is in full view of the person he has intended it for.
>
> However, when our entire bench sees it. The 2 little kids sitting next to me giggle and comment to me about it. That's disrespecting the game where the officials don't have any personal feelings toward or about any given individual. Where the officials recognize that they are highly visible representatives of the NBA.
>
> This has nothing to do with me. If he has a problem with me and my questioning some of his questionable calls, he can tell me or ignore me. It doesn't really matter.
>
> But for him to make what is the equivalent of a very inappropriate gesture well that's not good for the NBA and I find it hard to believe that any person cannot have their judgment influenced when they have reached a point that they are so upset they find the need to make such a gesture.
>
> When I brought this up in the past, Stu has denied it happens. Well, we have a bench full of players and staff who saw it. Many of whom commented that it's not the first time they have seen it.
>
> I have, the guests of a season ticketholder, who spends tens of thousands of dollars per seat, who saw it and I'm sure will mention it to them and they to me.
>
> I don't want him suspended, I don't want him fined. I don't want

anything but him to realize that if he can't respect the game by calling it as it happens and without sticking his hands down his pants to show how he feels, well maybe he hasn't learned much in his many years of officiating.

Or maybe he thinks he is above the game. Which is exactly what I think he thinks.

Joey does it his way. Which is exactly what others have told me. Which is exactly why there is little continuity in how the game is officiated from game to game.

I made it very clear to him after the game that I would be sending this email.

I await your response.

m

Cuban's criticism of Crawford drew a sharp and telling response from Lamell McMorris, spokesman and lead negotiator for the NBRA:

Mr. Cuban,

A wise person once told me that "it's hard to lead from behind." You immediately come to mind when I recall this saying. The only embarrassment to the NBA is you. As a leader (owner) in the NBA, the behavior that you consistently demonstrate is deplorable. Executives at the league office and your fellow owners may have to "tolerate" you and watch what they say but I don't.

You've created an "image" that you obviously feel must be maintained and attacking the officials is integral to your strategy. You are fostering an environment of hostility and abuse of the officials that is detrimental to the sport. What's next in your arsenal of abuse? Are owners, coaches, and players going to physically assault an official next?

Perhaps your energy will be put to better use by building a better team and being a real motivator where it's needed—within the Dallas Mavericks organization.

You, the players, and coaches will be treated with respect when you give it and especially in your case when you demonstrate that you deserve it.

Leave the refs alone. Build a strong team, and perhaps rather than going down in history as the biggest whiner in basketball, you'll be remembered as a winner.

Lamell McMorris
Principal, Founder & CEO
Perennial Strategy Group

Keep in mind this attitude toward one particular owner was being held and expressed by a *spokesman for the referees' union*. Still think personal relationships don't affect how refs call games?

Referee Danny Crawford (no relation to Joe) also had little affection for Mark Cuban and bragged that since 2001, the Mavericks were 1–15 when he worked their playoff games. One more tidbit of information for my mental rolodex of referees to watch when making my picks.

I worked many games with Danny Crawford over the years, including a contest between Orlando and Utah on March 6, 2006. The game was close throughout the evening and looked to be decided in the last seconds. On a pivotal possession late in the game, Crawford missed a foul on a Magic player, generating outrage from Orlando coach Brian Hill and the entire Magic bench. Crawford got the call wrong and he knew it, but the damage was done as several technical fouls were assessed to restore order. All of a sudden, a tight contest became a comfortable lead for Utah with just seconds remaining. Orlando lost that night, and our crew felt responsible for the poor job of officiating.

Afterward in the locker room, Crawford mentioned that he had another Orlando game in Chicago a few weeks later on March 28. That's all I had to hear.

"Jack, I've got a winner coming up on March 28. Bet Orlando over Chicago. Can't miss!" I said with confidence.

Sure enough, Orlando won that game outright, and Jack and I cashed in one more time.

Twenty-eight-year veteran referee Jake O'Donnell was another tough cookie who made enemies on the court. O'Donnell's career abruptly ended after an incident with Houston forward Clyde Drexler in a playoff game between the Rockets and Suns on May 9, 1995. O'Donnell hated Drexler and refused to shake hands with him in the pregame captain's meeting. Then, O'Donnell put Drexler on the bench after calling a cheap touch foul. When Drexler argued the call, O'Donnell hit him with back-to-back technicals and tossed him from the game.

O'Donnell flat-out admitted he was biased against Drexler on ESPN a year later, saying, "I wouldn't give Clyde Drexler much leeway because of the way he reacted with me all the time." In response, Drexler said, "It kind of tells everybody what he's about. All along I've felt that was true. You expect unbiased professionalism from a referee. It was obvious he couldn't provide that." And this was a guy who worked as an NBA referee *for 28 years.*

O'Donnell once said to me, "If players or coaches give you shit, stick it up their ass. It may take time, but they'll eventually leave you alone." Relationships, baby, relationships!

Derrick Stafford also burned a few bridges during his career. After an on-the-court clash with Sacramento center Vlade Divac in 2003, Stafford was reported to have told Kings guard Doug Christie, "Tell Vlade this is not the last game of yours I'll be working this season." And just before the 2002 All-Star Game, Stafford ran afoul of Heat coach Pat Riley, earning himself a two-game suspension for telling Riley during a game, "It's not about you. Go on TV crying."

Of course, Stafford had some friends in the league, too. I worked a Knicks game in Madison Square Garden with him on February 26, 2007. New York shot an astounding 39 free throws that night to Miami's paltry eight. It seemed like Stafford was working for the Knicks, calling fouls on Miami like crazy. Isiah Thomas was coaching the Knicks, and after New York's four-point victory, a guy from the Knicks came to our locker room looking for Stafford, who was in the shower. He told us that Thomas sent him to retrieve Stafford's home address; apparently, Stafford had asked the coach before the game for some autographed sneakers and jerseys for his kids. Suddenly, it all made sense.

Referee Jess Kersey was another one of Isiah Thomas' guys. They'd talk openly on the phone as if they had known each other since childhood. Thomas even told Kersey that he was pushing to get Ronnie Nunn removed from the supervisor's job so that Kersey and Dick Bavetta could take over. This sort of thing happened all the time, and I kept waiting for a Knicks game when Stafford, Bavetta, and Kersey were working together. It was like knowing the winning lottery numbers before the drawing!

Like Derrick Stafford, referee Steve Javie was no fan of Pat Riley and had no problem letting Riley know exactly how he felt. In a 2001–02 regular-season matchup between Miami and Cleveland, Javie approached Riley on the sideline while the Heat were losing and said, "It's giving us absolute delight to watch you and your team die!"

How's that for impartiality? Javie was fined $1,000 by the league. Do you think he forgot about that one the next time he worked a Heat game?

And then there was the ongoing feud between Javie and 76ers superstar Allen Iverson. The rift was so bad that Philadelphia general manager Billy King often called the league office to complain about Javie's treatment of Iverson during a game.

Iverson was eventually traded to Denver, and in his first game against his former team, he was tossed after two technicals. Afterward, Iverson implied Javie had a grudge against him, saying, "I thought I got fouled on that play, and I said I thought that he was calling the game personal, and he threw me out. His fuse is real short anyway, and I should have known that I couldn't say anything anyway. It's been something personal with me and him since I got in the league. This was just the perfect game for him to try and make me look bad." The league fined Iverson $25,000 for his comments, but most of the league referees thought the punishment was too lenient and were upset he wasn't suspended. As a result, we collectively decided to dispense a little justice of our own, sticking it to Iverson whenever we could.

Shortly after the Javie-Iverson incident, I worked a Jazz-Nuggets contest in Denver on January 6, 2007. During the pregame meeting, my fellow referees Bernie Fryer and Gary Zielinski agreed that we were going to strictly enforce the palming rule against Iverson. Palming the ball was something Iverson loved to do, but if he so much as came close to a palm, we were going to blow the whistle. Obviously, our actions were in direct retaliation for Iverson's rant against Javie. True to form, I immediately excused myself and made an important phone call.

Sticking to our pregame pledge, each of us whistled Iverson for palming in the first quarter—we all wanted in on the fun. The violations seemed to affect Iverson's rhythm and he played terribly that night, shooting 5-for-19 with five turnovers. After getting repeatedly whistled all night long, Iverson approached me in an act of submission.

"How long am I going to be punished for Javie?" he quietly inquired.

"Don't know what you're talking about, Allen," I responded.

In actuality, I knew he would continue to pay for his indiscretion for at least another couple of weeks. For the next several games, I picked against Denver, knowing that Iverson was growing increasingly frustrated by the payback he was receiving. I scored on two of the next three games.

I spoke to Javie after my game with Iverson and we had a good laugh. He expressed a hope that everyone on the staff would follow suit and stick it to A.I. the way we had. Soon afterward, referee Scott Foster had a Denver game and went easy on Iverson, generating a strong response from referee Bernie Fryer, who sent an email to Foster accusing him of not being a team player.

The entire Iverson saga was one brief episode out of the many that occurred in NBA arenas across the country every single night. You just had to know what you were looking for and where to look. It was all about relationships.

At times, relationships between referees and players went beyond the action on the court and spilled over to the personal lives of those involved. Referee Eddie F. Rush was known by the entire staff to be particularly close to Chicago Bulls superstar Michael Jordan. If Rush was working a Bulls game, Jordan was untouchable, but the relationship affected much more than just Jordan's on-court scoring average. In 1989, Rush met an attractive young singer named Karla Knafel at an Indianapolis nightclub. They struck up a conversation and Rush explained he was an NBA referee in town to officiate a Bulls-Pacers game. Knafel excitedly told him that she had always wanted to meet Michael Jordan. Rush casually pulled out his cell phone and called Jordan in his hotel room. Rush made the introduction and Jordan and Knafel began a 10-year affair that later made headlines. Jordan scored and NBA referee Eddie F. Rush was credited with the assist! How about a high five?

Rush had other favorites too, including legendary center Shaquille O'Neal. In a 2004 playoff game between the Lakers and Timberwolves, Rush was overheard at the scorer's table asking how many fouls Shaq had with 8:59 left in the fourth quarter. It was clear to me that he made the unusual inquiry to warn the other referees that Shaq was getting close to the limit, and that they shouldn't call a foul that would send him to the bench for the night.

Stars like Shaquille O'Neal were generally liked by referees and could expect favorable treatment. Shaq was known to occasionally get in the ear of his favorite referees and convince them to let a little air out of the basketball. The league has definite rules concerning each ball's air pressure, but Shaq liked to get that soft extra bounce on his free throws and short shots around the hoop. Of course, the big guy might have scored a few more points if he actually practiced free throws during warm-ups instead of trying to collect phone numbers from pretty girls. Before one particular Lakers game in the Staples Center back in 2003, Shaq sent a ball boy into the stands to tell a woman he wanted her phone number. Only one problem—the woman was the wife of one of the referees who was working the game that night. Oops, looks like Shaq might be in for a long night. Can someone please get me a phone?

Referees and fans alike know that marquee players are treated more favorably than lesser players, and the bigger the star, the more favorable the treatment. The league wants the superstars on the court and in the game and fully expects its referees to make sure that's where they are. Veteran referees call it "managing" the game; others call it "manipulating" the game. No matter what you call it, the practice is ripe for exploitation by an insider, and to my profound regret, that is exactly what I engaged in.

Although I relied heavily on the tendencies and practices of my fellow referees when making picks, a golden nugget of invaluable information would occasionally sneak up on me, or better yet, walk right through the door. The referees' locker room was closed to everyone except the staff, supervisors, and ball boys. Every arena in the league posts a notice on the door of the locker room prohibiting unauthorized admission. Still, on any given night the locker room can resemble New York's Grand Central Station at rush hour on a Friday night. Vendors, technicians, security personnel, celebrities, game announcers, reporters, team personnel, trainers, and even mascots popped in and out as we prepared for tip-off. We discussed players, coaches, injuries, illnesses, in-house turmoil, slumps, feuds, contract disputes, and much more—nothing was off limits.

I worked a game in Washington, D.C., on December 26, 2006, and was warming up in the locker room when I unexpectedly received a tip that I couldn't resist. The Wizards employee who was responsible for game operations checked in with us before game time. The guy was a local attorney who worked for the team as a hobby, and with more than 20 years on the job, he knew more basketball gossip than just about anyone in the league. That night, he told us that he had just spoken to Memphis coach Mike Fratello, who advised him that his players were really banged up with injuries. Fratello was just hoping he would have five guys on the floor to finish the game.

"Excuse me," I said, as I headed out the door. "I need to make a phone call."

Information like that was surprisingly available on a regular basis— all you had to do was sit tight and listen.

There were also times when the best inside information came directly from the league office or my immediate supervisors. The NBA family is comprised of a relatively small group of very rich men who pay hundreds of millions of dollars to buy a franchise and join one of the nation's most exclusive sports clubs—the National Basketball Association. Collectively, the owners are the financial engine that drives the league, without which there would be no league. The commissioner has regular, personal contact with team owners and feels a strong obligation to keep each one in the loop on matters of league-wide concern and to ensure that each team is treated fairly by league officials at every level. If a team owner or general manager thinks his team is being treated unfairly, if he thinks that referees are unevenly enforcing the rules to the detriment of his team, a simple phone call, text message, or email to the league office usually results in quick action to remedy the concerns. For the NBA, the goal is peace, order, and the avoidance of public criticism. For the referee on the court, the message is clear—even things up and give the squeaky wheel some grease. The message is either delivered directly from the front office or routed through the league's referee supervisors. The method of delivery is the "directive."

Referee supervisors would usually meet with us every two weeks, but they sent directives on a weekly basis. When they actually attended a game, the supervisors and the assigned referees would meet during the day to discuss the evening's matchup and any special concerns. This is where the directive comes into play. Typically, the supervisors would tell the game referees about problems or mistakes in previous games that put a particular team at a disadvantage, and that those matters had to be immediately remedied—as in, that night! They would tell us that a previous crew had missed calls on a certain player or team and that they shouldn't be missed again. We were given game video illustrating the missed call or the rule violation and told to get it right the next time out.

Given that "guidance," the referees were left to interpret its meaning. If a team got away with a couple of traveling violations in one game, the referee crew would double the travels called on the team in its next game. If we were informed that we missed too many three-second violations or illegal screens against a team, we gave it to them good the next time they hit the floor. If the referees had a bad game that significantly contributed to a team's loss, we went out of our way to fix the situation and make it up to that team. Directives came from the league via top brass or immediate supervisors, and the referees set a course of action to essentially manage or manipulate the action on the court. This was particularly true during the playoffs where every call, every mistake, was magnified tenfold. It got so bad that we were overwhelmed by all the armchair refereeing by our superiors. Game instruction was the focus of our pregame meetings and it was revisited at halftime. Owners and general managers would call the commissioner or other high-ranking official during the game to lodge complaints, and new directives to address the complaints would be delivered to us in the locker room at halftime. It was an ongoing process that didn't end until the final buzzer sounded—and we dutifully played along. Survival and advancement for an NBA referee requires strict adherence to the front office's directives. If they wanted us to call more moving screens on Yao Ming, we called them. If Raja Bell needed to be slowed down, we slowed him down. In so many respects, we became puppets of the league, trying to keep everyone happy while simultaneously advancing the agenda of the NBA.

For me, the league's intrusion into officiating was yet another opportunity to make a good pick. If I knew a team was going to get most of the calls, it was like taking candy from a baby. And to think—the outcome of the game, my winning pick, was often made possible by the league itself. Unwittingly, of course, but made possible nevertheless.

* * *

In professional sports, the ultimate goal is to make the playoffs and win a championship. Teams in the NBA compete all season long to reach the postseason, and if possible, to secure home-court advantage, thereby gaining a statistical edge in their quest to advance toward the Finals.

In the playoffs, players and coaches earn sizeable bonuses and owners share in the windfall profits generated by television coverage and sold-out arenas. With home-court advantage wrapped up, players spend more nights sleeping in their own beds, owners earn extra revenue from more home games, and the fans go wild as they cheer on their team in the friendly confines of places like the Staples Center, Madison Square Garden, and the United Center. And, if an NBA referee lives in the same city as your favorite team, you may not be the only one pulling for the home team and a trip to the playoffs.

Referees selected to work in the playoffs receive significant bonuses, as well as generous travel allowances and per diems for food and lodging. With four rounds of playoff games, assigned referees can make serious money above and beyond their regular-season pay. A referee working only the first round would earn more than $30,000, while a more experienced referee working the NBA Finals would earn more than $100,000. As you might imagine, playoff assignments are coveted and the battle to secure them is highly competitive. It typically takes six or seven years for referees to make the first-round playoff roster and 12 or 13 to work the NBA Finals. The selection process is based in part on a rating system developed to grade and compare referees. Throughout the regular season, referees were scrutinized and ranked by coaches, general managers, group supervisors, the Director of Officiating, and the Executive Vice President of Basketball Operations. The top 36 refs typically get to work the playoffs. I made it after seven years in the league and stayed there for the rest of my career, so I was assured of some very good bonus money every May.

For each playoff game officiated, we received an additional travel allowance of $2,000. The full allowance is paid regardless of the actual cost of travel; if a referee resides near a city where he is assigned to work a game, he pays a few bucks to gas up his car and then pockets $2,000 from the league. For a referee making it all the way to the Finals, the travel allowance could total an additional $26,000, above and beyond the $85,000 bonus pay.

Needless to say, playoff referees want to minimize their travel expenses and pocket as much of the $2,000 allowance as possible. Frequent-flier miles provide some assistance, but nothing does the trick like working a game close to home. Fire up the BMW, put on a Billy Joel CD, and drive across town for the amazing low cost of $11.36 in gasoline. Throw in a can of Red Bull and a pack of gum and we're talking $15.62. Net profit: $1,984.38.

It was commonplace to listen to referees openly talk about how they would root for teams that played close to their hometown so the team would make the playoffs and get home-court advantage. The stage would then be set to work the series and maximize the net profit on the $2,000 travel allowance.

This little piece of information was yet another factor I considered when making my picks. It certainly wasn't the most important clue I needed to make the right choice, but it was one more clue among many, and I considered them all.

* * *

So that's how I did it. I listened to the directives from the NBA office, I considered the vendettas and grudges referees had against certain players or coaches, and I focused in on the special relationships that routinely influenced the action on the court. Throw in some quirks and predictable tendencies of veteran referees and the recipe was complete. All I had to do was call it in and let the law of averages take over. During the regular season, I was right on the money seven out of 10 times. There was even a streak when I simply couldn't miss, picking 15 winners out of 16 games. No one on the planet could be that lucky. Of course, luck had little to do with it.

Jack and I were delirious with our success, but we were never satisfied. I sometimes think that the ease of picking NBA games made it somewhat boring; the risk of losing just wasn't there. Perhaps that's why we kept betting on college and pro football with reckless abandon. Perhaps that's why we played blackjack and kept traveling to Atlantic City for one more roll of the dice, one more spin of the wheel. To me, gambling was not just a flirtation with risky behavior; it was my lifeblood, a sustenance that kept me fully alive 24 hours a day. But it changed me, and there were days when even I could see the madness of it all. I was selfish, arrogant, insensitive, and constantly on edge. I placed myself above all others and lost sight of the most important people in my life—my wife and daughters. I jeopardized my career, gambled with my freedom, and toyed with total ruin. Still, these fleeting glimpses into my decaying soul never caused me to wake up from my stupor—not voluntarily anyway. It was going to take much more than introspection and personal reflection to snap me out of the fog of my gambling-induced psychosis. A Dr. Phil moment was not going to get it done.

As I rolled along betraying everything I believed in, I could never have known that hope was on the way. It wasn't going to come easy and it wouldn't arrive overnight; to the contrary, the darkest days were yet to come, and I would hit rock bottom before the candle of normalcy would reignite and the flame of life in a decent man would start to flicker. Even then, a gentle breeze could blow it away in the blink of an eye and I would be lost once again. But it was hope, and even for an emotionally bankrupt fool like me, I would eventually recognize it when I saw it. It was coming, but first came the bottom. Lord, have mercy.

CHAPTER 7

On the Take

The great showman Harry Houdini was known throughout the world for his death-defying feats of magic. Of course, magic had nothing to do with his famous brushes with mortality. No, the great master engaged in nothing more than clever tricks of illusion and sleight of hand, albeit with flair. For a three-and-a-half-year period from late 2003 to spring of 2007, I too was a master illusionist, living a lie, deceiving my audience, and risking it all. In many ways, I was having the time of my life, or so I thought. You see, for me, the illusion had become much more than just a game—it actually became my reality.

Jack and I were sprinting on a treadmill fueled by excitement and thrills, and someone kept increasing the speed. Making 35 to 40 bets per week on football, baseball, basketball, and hockey, we continued to gamble on golf at the country club, cards in the back parlor, and blackjack in the casinos. I was constantly checking the television, my laptop, and my cell phone for updates on games in progress. Jack and I spoke on the phone five, 10, sometimes even 20 times per day. We were like 13-year-old girls talking about the cute boy who just moved into the neighborhood. It was a frenzy of self-indulgence coupled with a complete absence of self-control. There were times when I had to chuckle at the sheer craziness, but the chuckle always faded as I refocused on the task at hand—make the picks, place the bet!

A year or so into this chasm of time that I now refer to as "the dark period," Kim and I packed up the kids and moved to Bradenton, Florida.

Kim's parents had a winter home down there and we were looking for a fresh start after our run-in with the neighbors in Pennsylvania. I called fellow referee Bob Delaney, who had been living in Bradenton for years, and he gave me a glowing report. There were the usual questions about schools, property taxes, and the crime rate. Yeah, whatever! The only question I wanted answered concerned the country clubs in the area and whether or not the members liked to gamble. Can you imagine it? A cocky beer-drinking kid from a working-class neighborhood in Philadelphia tossing cards to the suntanned, slick-haired, Gucci-wearing Sarasota crowd. When I got the salivating report from Delaney, it was music to my ears. In the blink of an eye, I went from being a fan of Bruce Springsteen to a devotee of K.C. and the Sunshine Band. "That's the way, uh huh, uh huh, I like it, uh huh, uh huh!"

It's hard to believe now that my biggest fear about moving was the possibility I wouldn't be able to find a card game. Oh, I would surely miss Jack and the boys back at Radley Run, but Jack loved to travel and it was just a quick flight down the eastern seaboard to the Sunshine State. I wouldn't see him nearly as much, but we still had our cell phones and the odds still appeared to be in our favor.

I was earning upwards of $275,000 a year in the NBA, and life was good. Kim and I bought a 4,200-square-foot home in a gated community with six bedrooms, four baths, a pool, a hot tub, and an outdoor kitchen with a bar. Kim shuttled the kids around town in a brand-new Chevy Yukon SUV and I eased in and out of the country club's parking lot in a shiny black BMW. While my four daughters were attending an expensive private school, Kim was receiving private lessons at the club from the hunky tennis pro who made all the ladies swoon. In between sets, Kim and her new friends dined on Waldorf salads and fresh papaya. At the same time, I was working out in a private health club, playing golf with my new crew, or dealing cards at all hours of the night. I felt like Ray Liotta's character in *Goodfellas*. The only difference was he got addicted to cocaine and I was hooked on gambling. Otherwise, we were the same—life was sweet and the ride was a thrill.

In my spare time, I was also dabbling in the stock market with reckless abandon, purchasing stock options and investing tens of thousands of dollars in companies I knew nothing about. I watched the market on my computer daily, especially when I had downtime between games. There I was, in a hotel room with the drapes pulled shut on a beautiful sunny day, glued to the screen, watching the ticker roll on CNBC as my account moved up or down by as much as $10,000 in a single morning. My trades became so frenetic that my stockbroker actually sent me a letter calling attention to the depreciation in my account and warning me about my trading habits. I lost more than $30,000 in ridiculous stock trades in just over a week, but I didn't care about a warning from some stiff in a $200 suit from the Men's Wearhouse. I knew what I was doing; I thought I had it all under control.

After the move to Florida, I continued to stay in contact with Jack. He had a winter home in Fort Myers and flew down from Philly several times a year. We kept betting at the usual clip and got together every chance we could. Between 2004 and 2006, we actually stopped betting on NBA games on a couple of occasions for one or two months at a time. Call it fear of getting caught, call it a guilty conscience, call it whatever you like. We backed off for a short time and then drifted right back into the mix—the pickings were too easy. The NBA was our ace in the hole for covering losing bets on other sports. Jack delivered my cut when I was in Philly or he was in Florida. We'd meet for lunch, I'd order pastrami on pumpernickel smothered in Grey Poupon with a crisp pickle wedge on the side, and then Jack would pull out an envelope stuffed with $20 bills totaling $5,000 and slowly slide it across the table. I would ask about his wife and kids as I reached for the envelope without looking at it, and then quietly placed it in my coat pocket. I'd arrange for a couple of tickets to the game that night to be left at the will-call window and we'd flip a coin for the bill and go our separate ways. It was almost as simple as picking up a carton of milk on the way home from a day at the office.

Jack and I placed our last bet on an NBA game in November of 2006, and that was what eventually prompted Tommy Martino and James "Ba Ba" Battista to come calling. Jack and I continued to bet on everything else, including the Super Bowl in February of 2007. We won that bet as the Colts beat the Bears. My cut was $2,000, but I never saw the money. As it turned out, it was the last bet Jack and I ever placed together.

* * *

After my unexpected contact with Ba Ba in December of 2006, I rarely spoke with him—it was all Tommy, and it was all the time. Tommy and I were on the phone as much as I had been with Jack. Daily for sure, always talking about the same thing.

"Who do you like tonight, Tim?" Tommy asked. "Got any winners for us?"

Even though Tommy and I had been friends since the ninth grade, our contact during those months in 2006 and 2007 was stressful. Ba Ba's involvement was a festering sore that wouldn't go away. Still, every time I picked a winner, the cash register in my brain would ring up another $2,000 sale. *Cha-ching!* To make those winning picks, I had to constantly work the phones, looking for a tip, an inadvertent slip, or anything else to gain an edge and beat the house. I certainly wasn't calling a psychic hotline or some betting expert's 900 number. No, I was plugged-in and stealing inside information like a pickpocket lifts a wallet from a mark on a crowded commuter train headed for the suburbs. You see, I was talking to people who knew the inside stuff, the kind of scoop that is very reliable and usually paid dividends. I was talking to my very own colleagues—NBA referees—and they had no clue what I was doing.

Although I chatted with all the referees at one time or another, I spoke with three of them on a regular basis. You could say that they were my go-to guys, but that would be unfair. The information they unwittingly passed along was just one part of the overall equation, but sometimes it was a very big part, and I never passed on any opportunity to land the big fish.

Mark Wunderlich was a Philadelphia guy, and our friendship came easy. We played golf and cards at the country club and our families socialized together frequently. Mark was a member at Concord Country Club in Concordville, Pennsylvania. Coincidentally, Jack Concannon and Pete Ruggieri were also members and knew Mark well. I played golf with Mark and Jack on several occasions and we had a ball. Mark was a real jokester and the three of us would laugh our way through the entire round. Mark also played golf with Jack and Pete on Thursdays in the summer. Mark and I spoke on the phone regularly, gossiping about other referees and the big shots in the front office. Mostly, I was looking for information relevant to games played later that night or a day or two later. I was trolling for a fresh tip, and there were moments when I felt like a streetwalker cruising for tricks on Sunset Boulevard. It was common for Mark to call and leave a teasing message on my cell phone.

"Tim, you gotta call me ASAP. I've got a big scoop!" he'd yell excitedly.

I would immediately call him back to hear the big news of the day.

"Bavetta has the game tonight and Vegas took it off the board because too much money was bet one way!" he'd report giddily.

Of course, he was only joking, but it underscored two things about Mark Wunderlich. First, he was a real prankster. Second, he knew Dick Bavetta as well as I did.

I learned early in my career that Dick was a good guy to have on your side. The front office loved him. Dick was the kind of guy who could help me advance and move up the ladder, so I stayed close to him, always mindful of his clout with the brass. Besides, he was funny as hell and had a million great stories to tell. He knew everyone and everything; he was the Dear Abby of NBA gossip and I loved to listen to his tales. Ten years into my career, when I started betting on NBA games, I spoke to Dick regularly, trying to get some good inside information that would make my pick a sure thing. If I wasn't working a game with Dick, I was working him on the phone, shooting the shit, comparing notes, and generally dissecting upcoming games. Dick and the others thought they were simply engaging in some friendly gossip and banter with another member of the family. They had no idea that I was intentionally seeking information and using it to line my pockets. It was a betrayal, plain and simple, and my trail of lies and deceit grew longer with every phone call, email, and text message.

And then there was Scott Foster, not just another patsy in my game of illusion, but a real victim of my selfish and thoughtless misdeeds. You see, Scott wasn't merely a source to exploit or a brain to pick. No, for the better part of 15 years, he was like a brother, loyal to the core, supportive, and always there for me—he was my best friend.

We met in 1990 at the referee training camp held in South Carolina. I wasn't the only attendee dreaming of the NBA, and it was clear to me that Scott was talented. He was from Baltimore, not far from my home in Pennsylvania, and we were both setting out on a journey that would ultimately lead to the NBA. We paid our dues in the CBA, occasionally working a game together, and always had a lot of fun. In 1993, we worked a game in La Crosse, Wisconsin, before a packed house of 5,000. Flip Saunders had not yet broken into the NBA and was coaching the Catbirds on their home court. Saunders loved to get on the referees and crawled all over me when I called a foul on one of his players. He wouldn't let up, so I gave him an early ticket to the showers. The fans in the small arena went crazy as Saunders stomped off the court. Scott and I were laughing like two little kids at his dramatic exit. After the game, Scott and I were cornered by Saunders in the hallway near our locker room. I tried feverishly to open the door as he ranted about our lack of officiating skills, but it just wouldn't open. Scott took over and had the same bad luck. It looked like the coach's eyes were going to pop out of their sockets when we suddenly realized he had greased the doorknob with Vaseline. Cracking up with laughter, we finally got inside the locker room and headed for the showers. Bad move! Flip had the maintenance staff shut off the water to the locker room, leaving us naked, sweaty, and fumbling with the shower handles. We quickly dressed and walked back to the hotel with the full appreciation that Flip Saunders got the last laugh that night. See you in the NBA, Flip.

Scott and I broke into the NBA in 1994. Like Kim and I, Scott and his wife Paula were busy raising a family with two boys and a girl. Scott and I became such close friends that he asked me to be godfather to his son Kyle, and I asked him to be godfather to my daughter Molly.

We understood each other—the time away from home, the grueling road trips, and the responsibility of officiating a big game under enormous pressure. Before moving to Florida, I played golf with Scott at Radley Run in Pennsylvania, and at his club, Cattail Creek, in Glenwood, Maryland. We were both very competitive and loved to wager on golf, Texas hold'em, and pro football whenever the Eagles and Ravens squared off. We spoke on the phone almost every day for 15 years, right until the end of the 2007 NBA playoffs. Phone records would later reveal that I placed 134 calls to Scott between October of 2006 and April of 2007. Many of those calls lasted no longer than two minutes, and most were placed in the hours immediately before or after NBA games. When this information broke in the media, many people rushed to the conclusion that Scott and I were involved in illegal betting together, and that we were comparing notes and making our picks just before tip-offs.

To be clear, Scott had *nothing* to do with my illegal gambling activities. Speaking with Scott on the phone was a regular and natural part of my day. We talked about our families, investments, mutual friends, and, of course, our jobs. We called each other when something crazy happened in a game and generally critiqued our fellow refs and gossiped about anything and everything going on in the NBA.

Eventually, I started to solicit more and more information from Scott, not for the purpose of having a good chat, but to get something I could use in making a good pick. At first, I didn't realize what I was doing. After all, whether I gambled or not, we would be having the same conversation. Eventually, I would come to appreciate the depth and breadth of my betrayal. Like the husband who cheats on his wife, deceiving a true friend cuts to the bone and changes a relationship forever. To say that we would have had the same conversation even if I wasn't using him is a rationalization. I abused the trust he placed in me and blindsided him by permitting my misdeeds to cast a shadow over his reputation. He deserved better from his best friend, and I will always feel deep shame and remorse for my conduct.

* * *

Armed with the toxic information I siphoned from my friends and colleagues, I was making winning picks with regularity. I was Ba Ba's boy, his man on the inside, and we just couldn't lose.

Even though Tommy didn't bring Ba Ba to me until December of 2006, Tommy and I had stayed in contact over the years, socializing with each other's families and frequently talking on the phone. Tommy was always a player, his pockets filled with cash and a nice car in the driveway. His source of income was a mystery to me until the day he told me he was selling pot. Apparently, he started out on a small scale, growing it in his basement and selling it to his friends. Eventually he expanded and established a large-scale operation with sophisticated equipment and a healthy clientele. I suppose I wasn't shocked by Tommy's admission. He liked to live fast and on the edge, and selling weed seemed right up his alley. Besides, it was none of my business, as long as he didn't try to get me involved. He never did.

While we were still living in Pennsylvania, Kim and I threw a dinner party at our home that Tommy attended. We ran out of ice, so I grabbed my keys and started toward the driveway when I saw Tommy's Lotus blocking my exit. He tossed me his keys and I took off down the street, spinning the wheels and flooring it all the way. I hadn't driven a fast car in a long time and it felt pretty good. When I sped back onto my street, ice in hand, Tommy was waiting at the curb.

"Man, Tommy, that was fun. I had it up to 70 in three or four seconds. I'm talking warp speed!" I said with a rush of excitement.

"Hey pal," Tommy responded, "you're lucky you didn't get pulled over. I've got 20 pounds of weed in the trunk. Shipment came in today."

"Holy shit! Why didn't you tell me?" I snapped.

"Christ, you were only going for ice down the street," Tommy laughed. "I didn't want you to sweat the details."

Talk about luck! Maybe I was untouchable. Maybe nothing could stop me. Maybe I could go on leading a double life. Maybe...

I didn't know it at the time, but Ba Ba wasn't messing around when he placed bets on my picks. He started out at $10,000 per game, but quickly upped it to $50,000 when he realized that I was the king of basketball prognosticators. He was laying off action with bookies all over the country and with off-shore gambling sites. Nobody in Philly was big enough to handle the amount of his bets, and word on the street quickly spread that Ba Ba had something going on. It was a recipe for disaster, but guys like Ba Ba never look at the big picture. They live for today; driving the fancy cars, wearing the imported Italian silk suits, flashing wads of cash—that's how guys like Ba Ba lived their lives. This was his world, the underbelly of society, where the rules are made to order, if there are rules at all. For Ba Ba, it was all about "business." He couldn't care less about the rush of excitement or the thrill of the win. He had obligations, the serious kind that required constant attention and a firm hand. If I was the golden goose for Ba Ba, he was the rainmaker for his bosses, and rainmakers always have a certain sway in the organization— not to mention some leeway in finding ways to drain the well dry. His connection to me was always Tommy, and Ba Ba used both of us to keep the pipeline flowing. Tommy was really nothing more than a mid- to low-level goombah, working his hustle to stay relevant on the street. In his world, hanging with guys like Ba Ba gave him status. He liked that, or at least the illusion it cast. In reality, Tommy was a doormat, a gopher, an errand boy, a bagman. Hell, I wouldn't be surprised if he picked up Ba Ba's dry cleaning for him.

It was too bad, because Tommy had the ability and the charm to make something of himself. Tommy was no gambler; he wasn't caught up in the throes of addiction. He just wanted to be somebody, to get noticed, and perhaps to earn a pat on the back. Like a monkey on a chain performing tricks at the command of an organ grinder, Tommy became the opposite of what he wanted to be. Man, Tommy, what the hell happened to you—what the hell happened to *us*?

Any way you slice it, the three of us were on the same path to ruin, but that came much later. At the time, we were living it up and the money kept pouring in. My $2,000 share of each win started to accumulate, and Ba Ba sent Tommy to meet me in cities around the country to settle up. Ba Ba stayed back in the shadows, trying to avoid any association with me that might draw unwanted attention. Too bad he wasn't more careful with his wagering practices. He was sloppy, plain and simple. There was too much action and it came too fast. Maybe he was getting pressure from his bosses to milk the cow with both hands and two feet. Let's face it; they used Ba Ba like Ba Ba used me and Tommy. The big guys were smart enough to know that nothing this good lasts forever, so it might as well be exploited to the fullest and with all due haste. That's how it went, and from December of 2006 to March of 2007, it was pedal to the metal, a rocket ride to the finish line where there are no winners, only losers.

Every time Tommy met me to deliver my share, he brought the same message from Ba Ba—bigger paydays were coming. Don't get me wrong, the money was great, but it was the rush of adrenaline that really got me off. Unlike Ba Ba and Tommy, I was hooked, a veritable gambling junkie, looking for another shot in the arm, another needle in the vein. I was no different than a drug mule strung out on crack, tweaking and geeking at all hours of the day and then looking for my next fix. I couldn't stand Ba Ba for what he made me do, but I was already doing it with Jack anyway. The only difference was some warped notion that Ba Ba was forcing me to do it against my will. Shit, I don't think I had any will left. Gambling owned my sorry ass and it wouldn't let go, at least not until I looked in the mirror and said, "Enough!" That day was nowhere in sight, so I picked a comfortable horse and jumped on the merry-go-round.

Our system wasn't without flaw. Sometimes Tommy was so stoned when I phoned in my picks that he passed along the wrong information to Ba Ba. At times, I thought Tommy might be pulling a double cross and filling his own wallet. But no, that wasn't his style; he was a loyal dog willing to take whatever scraps Ba Ba threw his way. Other times, Tommy would call me for a pick when I had no idea which team to choose. On a few occasions, when he really busted my balls to get an answer, I simply flipped a coin to get him off my ass. It made no difference to me—a win paid $2,000 and a loss was a loss. If I had been smart, I would have consistently picked losers for Ba Ba, eventually forcing him to drop me from his stable of stoolies and cheats. Of course, he was well aware of my previous success with Jack and may have smelled a rat, but it might have been worth a try. Even the best card players catch a cold streak now and then, so why couldn't I? But I didn't do it. Subconsciously, I was digging the action and riding the wave.

I did get a taste of Ba Ba's intolerance for losing when I once made two losing picks in a row. After the second loss, Tommy called for an explanation and reassurance that it wouldn't happen again.

"Tim, what the hell is going on?" Tommy asked. "Ba Ba's getting restless and he's talking stupid."

"What are you talking about? What's he saying?" I replied.

"You know, two losses in a row. He's not buying it," Tommy warned.

"Fuck Ba Ba!" I shouted. "This isn't science, it's gambling! You don't win every time! I don't need his shit!"

"Take it easy, don't talk like that. You know Ba Ba," Tommy stated with an air of caution in his voice.

"I'm doing the best I can. I'm sure it will turn around," I responded half-heartedly.

"Okay, Tim, that's what I want to hear," Tommy said, trying to sound reassuring. "Who do you like tonight?"

"San Antonio. I gotta go," I said, hanging up the phone.

I was pissed! Ba Ba was milking the cow and getting rich and he had the nerve to second-guess me? I had enough pressure in my life without his shit.

Wouldn't you know it, that night San Antonio coach Gregg Popovich gave me a rash of shit in the second quarter and I tossed him out. It started with him whining about a call against his star player, Tim Duncan.

"This is fucking bullshit, that's fucked up. Fuck you guys!" Popovich ranted.

So I gave him a quick T, his second of the night, and punched his ticket for an early trip to the showers.

"Don't you fucking tell me to get out!" Popovich screamed.

I just turned my back and walked away—early night for the coach. The Spurs won the game, but didn't cover the spread. Oops, that was three losers in a row for me.

Later that night, I received a call from Tommy back at the hotel.

"Jesus, Tim, what the fuck was that? Are you crazy? Ba Ba's pissed as hell! He thinks you're doing this on purpose," Tommy moaned.

"Don't you morons understand?" I snapped back. "I'm not throwing these games. I'm just giving you my opinion on who I think will win. Now get off my back!"

I slammed down the phone and that was the last I heard of it. Lucky for me, my next pick was a winner.

I decided to focus on the influx of cash and all that it entailed. Big house, fancy electronics, extravagant parties, you name it. For Kim's 40th birthday, I threw a big bash complete with a live band, gourmet food, top-shelf liquor, and all the trimmings. Best of all, I paid for everything with cash. I just dug into my pocket and peeled off the C-notes.

"Nice job tonight," I said to the bartender as I eased $500 into his breast pocket. "Here's a little something extra for you."

For some reason, Tommy wasn't doing as well. It seemed like his 2,000 apples were never delivered on time; his share was always coming "next week." When next week came and went, Tommy came whining to me.

Ba Ba didn't like Tommy traveling through airports with more than $10,000 in cash, so he sent him on delivery trips with exactly $10,000 and not a penny more. On January 4, 2007, Tommy flew to Phoenix with my money secretly hidden in his carry-on bag. I was in town working a Suns game, but managed to sneak away for a few hours and picked him up at the airport. We stopped at the Marriott, had a few drinks, and made plans to grab a good meal and hit the town. Before leaving the hotel room, Tommy gave me the loot, neatly wrapped in a narrow brown paper band. I took my thumb and fanned the wad across my face. It was a hot day in Phoenix, but those bills cooled my brow and soothed my tormented soul. I casually flipped the pack of cash onto the bed and strolled out the door as if I didn't have a care in the world. Ten thousand big ones laying on the bed, there for the taking, a housekeeper's winning lottery ticket right next to a room service menu and two white dinner mints. Champagne anyone?

All through dinner, Tommy kept bitching about not getting his cut. Tommy hated "slow pay." He regarded it as a slap in the face, a sign of disrespect. He was right, of course. Ba Ba was toying with him and there was nothing Tommy could do about it—except complain to me. He was relentless, like a drunk slobbering over his whiskey and repeating the same sad story over and over again. I finally had enough and offered him half of my share just to shut him up. I also wanted to keep Tommy happy. The last thing I needed was Tommy running his mouth and bringing down our house of cards. By messing with Tommy, Ba Ba was playing with fire, and I had to constantly put out the flames. You can only push a guy like Tommy so far before he kicks back. Oh, he won't do it to your face; he's not man enough for that. But he'd find a way to make you pay.

The following month, Tommy drove from Philly to Newark to meet me for lunch. It was February 26, 2007, and I was in town to work a Knicks game. My fellow referee, Gary Zielinski, joined me and Tommy for the meal and we all had a few laughs. After lunch, Tommy and I slipped away to my room in the Marriott and he made the drop. Another $10,000 and another earful of Tommy's crap. Once again, I split the proceeds and fronted him $5,000 out of my own cut.

The wins were piling up and everyone was happy, except Tommy. I found out that Ba Ba didn't pay for anything—not the drugs Tommy sold him, not Tommy's 2,000 apples, not even the lunch bill at Geno's Steaks in South Philly. Tommy was getting more aggravated as the weeks went by, and I was his sounding board, always patiently listening to his venom directed at Ba Ba. It was becoming a big problem and I felt increasingly uneasy. To make matters worse, Tommy found out that Ba Ba was betting considerably more on the games than he previously told us. He was also piling up losses in Atlantic City and had outstanding markers totaling more than $400,000.

During the entire three-month period I was making picks for Ba Ba, I earned $42,000. I gave $15,000 to Tommy with the agreement that I would get it back when Ba Ba finally paid him. That never happened.

The last game I picked for Ba Ba was on March 18, 2007, a matchup between the Orlando Magic and the Miami Heat. Joe Crawford was assigned to referee the game, and I knew he was still smarting over Heat owner Mickey Arison's attempt to get him fired as a result of a previous run-in. I also knew that Miami's young superstar, Dwyane Wade, was playing injured, and that Orlando was getting some points from the oddsmakers. I called it in to Tommy a few hours before tip-off. Tommy and I used a prearranged code the same way Jack and I had. If I was picking the home team, I would mention his brother Chuck. If it was the visitor, I would mention his other brother Johnny. That night, it was Orlando all the way.

"How's Johnny doing?" I asked Tommy.

Orlando won big that night and I scored another $2,000 for the home team—Team Donaghy, that is.

I was always aware that I was doing something wrong. Still, I found ways to justify my conduct, compartmentalize my actions, or just not think about it. As much as I had jumped onto the bandwagon, I remained hopeful that Ba Ba would cut me loose after the NBA Finals that year. I suppose at another level, I knew full well that Ba Ba would never let me go. People were making a ton of money off my picks and there was no reason in the world for them to hit the brakes on the gravy train while it was still steaming down the tracks. No, I was probably stuck for a long time unless the unthinkable occurred. The prospect of getting caught never took root with me. I've always been good at extricating myself from bad situations and I figured this would be no different. Who in their right mind would believe two petty thugs over me? I was a respected, up-and-coming force in my profession, right? *Let's not even go there,* I thought to myself. *Take getting caught out of the equation and focus on the Ba Ba problem.* Like the ostrich with its head in the sand, I was setting myself up for a real shocker.

Before that would come to pass, however, something happened that made me think the light at the end of the tunnel was growing near. Would fate whisper my name and give me one last opportunity to straighten up and fly right? Could I actually get out from under Ba Ba's thumb and breathe the fresh air of freedom? Perhaps the better question is, did I want to? Regardless of the answer, I would get my chance.

Two or three days after the Orlando-Miami game, I got a call from Tommy.

Ba Ba was in rehab.

Rehab? You've got to be kidding me! I couldn't believe it at first. Could this be my get-out-of-jail-free card? There had to be more to the story, I figured. Maybe something happened to him. Maybe he was wearing cement galoshes at the bottom of the Delaware River, or he was ground up at a rendering plant and processed into dog food. After all, he was running with some tough guys who may have caught him skimming from the take. And what about those markers he had at the casinos? A moment later, a terrifying thought occurred to me: *What if the FBI had grabbed him and he was singing like a bird?* But Tommy sounded legit when he dropped the bombshell, and I knew that Ba Ba was using cocaine and painkillers. Hell, Tommy was Ba Ba's drug supplier. I also knew that Ba Ba had trouble at home and that his wife kicked him out of the house because of his drug habit—at least that's what Tommy told me weeks before. If the story was true, it was possible I was home free.

Tommy told me to sit tight for a month or so to see how it played out. Tommy wasn't excited the way I was. He needed the money, whether he got it from Ba Ba or by mooching half of my share.

"It's all good," Tommy said. "Maybe we'll pick it up again later."

I thought, *Yeah, and maybe we won't!* This was my big chance to break free from Ba Ba—at least that's what I kept telling myself. Would I miss the action? Well, there was always Jack to fall back on. Better yet, I could completely forget about betting on pro basketball; there were plenty of other sports to bet on. Maybe this was it, a real chance for the fresh start Kim and I were looking for when we moved to Florida three years earlier. Better late than never!

Over the next few weeks I spoke with Tommy a few times, but it was just chitchat. The NBA regular season was winding down and the playoffs were right around the corner. After a few days of subconsciously thinking about my next pick, I started the process of weaning off my usual routine. No more scanning the Master List of Referees and no more targeted phone calls to my colleagues. The radar antenna slowly came down and I was feeling relieved, even more than I expected.

I saw Tommy again on April 10, 2007, in Washington, D.C. I was working a Wizards game and he was delivering another payment. He drove down from Philly and we met up and had some drinks. We talked about Ba Ba and our families, but not a word was said about making picks or placing bets. It was strange, this abrupt departure from the usual routine. Tommy wasn't pressing me for information and he wasn't whining about Ba Ba. He was eerily calm.

A week or so later Tommy called to say that Ba Ba was out of rehab and back home with his wife. Still, nothing was said about picking up where we left off. It was somewhat puzzling. Why in the world would these guys just cut off their money supply? The playoffs were coming and basketball would soon be gone until October. What happened to making hay while the sun shines? Was it possible that Ba Ba was a new man, rededicated to his wife and kids? Maybe the rehab took. Was he walking away from a life of crime and joining mainstream America? It didn't add up, and my euphoria was tempered by nagging doubts. What were these guys up to?

After the regular season ended, I worked the first two rounds of the playoffs, including a wild series between Phoenix and San Antonio. The Spurs prevailed and eventually won the championship against Cleveland. I packed my bags and made one last flight for the season—the trip home. It was a relief to pull into the driveway and know that I could relax, see my wife and kids, and play lots of golf over the next few months. I was still a year or two away from earning the opportunity to officiate in the third round of the playoffs, so I just kicked back and started to decompress.

It was the first of June and I hadn't made a bet on any sporting event since March 18. I was still betting on golf and cards and fooling around with the stock market, but nothing with Ba Ba, Tommy, or Jack. It felt good, and I pushed many of my paranoid fears out of my mind. I was back home in Bradenton and I was almost home free. That's when it all came crashing down.

CHAPTER 8

The Beginning
of the End

I was at the Lakewood Ranch Golf and Country Club near my home in Bradenton, getting ready to tee it up, when my cell phone rang. It was Tommy. He sounded so nervous that he was practically stuttering. My stomach immediately tightened and my throat went dry. I knew instinctively that something was seriously wrong. Before he said more than a few words, my paranoia kicked in and I told him to use a different phone and call me back on a different number. I quickly asked one of my golfing buddies for his cell phone and gave the number to Tommy. I didn't want anyone listening to what he was about to tell me.

Standing on the first tee, waiting for Tommy to call back, I was numb to everything and everyone around me. It was one of those slow-motion moments where you can see people talking and gesturing, but all is silent. I was in my own little world, oblivious to anything other than my feelings of desperation and quiet, internal panic. I looked down and noticed my hand trembling ever so slightly, and the thought crossed my mind that I was having a heart attack. It seemed as though time was standing still and that nothing could stir me from my semi-comatose funk. Then the phone rang, and I snapped back to life.

"It's the FBI," Tommy said, barely able to choke out the words. "They knocked on my door three or four times. We talked. They asked about all the referees in Philly. They had phone records, Tim. Lots of calls between you and me."

"Oh shit," I muttered to myself as my stomach turned upside down. I wanted to puke and I actually felt a gag reflex set in, forcing my diaphragm to twist and wrench.

I had rejected the notion this moment would arrive, but in reality it was only a matter of time. My arrogance came crashing down and I felt like a little boy getting an earful from the school principal.

Come on, Tim, pull yourself together, I thought. *Where are those nerves of steel now? It's time to circle the wagons and fight for your life.*

"What did you tell them?" I asked, still stunned by hearing those three dreaded letters. "Did they ask any questions about me?"

It was no time to be a team player. The only concern I had was saving my own selfish sorry ass. Fuck Tommy and Ba Ba and Jack; it was all about self-preservation, and the juices of instinctual survival were finally starting to flow.

"Yeah," Tommy admitted. "They asked about you the second time they came to see me."

I couldn't believe what I'd just heard: did he say the *second* time they came to see him? What the hell was going on? That dirty piece of shit! He's working with those pricks—he's actually trying to set me up. I figured the phone was bugged and that I was being recorded. *Play it cool,* I thought to myself. *Don't show your hand.*

"What did you tell them?" I calmly asked.

"I told them Tim doesn't bet!" Tommy exclaimed. "He's not allowed to. He's an NBA referee, for God's sake!"

Tommy's words, and the conviction with which he spoke, gave me some temporary reassurance that the call wasn't being recorded. The FBI wouldn't want a denial of wrongdoing by their star witness memorialized for posterity. I felt safer and decided to probe a little further.

"What else happened?" I continued. "What about Ba Ba?"

"I didn't tell them a fucking thing!" Tommy insisted. "I took the Fifth."

"What do you mean, you took the Fifth?" I shot back.

"At the grand jury, I took the Fifth," Tommy responded.

Houston, we have a problem.

"You testified before a grand jury?" I asked, dumbfounded by Tommy's statement. "They've got a grand jury going?"

I immediately formed a mental image of Tommy on the witness stand and cringed. My old friend Tommy Martino, the 5'4", jive-talking street hustler draped in Italian silk and adorned with gaudy gold jewelry, would be no match for the slick-tongued Ivy League sharks cutting their teeth in the U.S. Attorneys' Office. There would be no battle of wits, no sharp exchanges back and forth between intellectual equals. An examination of Tommy would be the equivalent of leading lambs to slaughter—shear away the outer layer of bullshit and then cut his throat and watch him bleed. My entire future rested in the hands of Tommy Martino, and all I could do was sit back and watch it disappear.

I thought about Greg Anderson, the personal trainer of slugger Barry Bonds and a key figure in the BALCO steroid scandal. Anderson was found in contempt of court after refusing to testify before a grand jury. I knew that Tommy would never spend a single night in jail to protect me. The FBI didn't want a pissant like Tommy Martino. Tommy was no more than a means to an end, a conduit to the real prize: an NBA referee betting on pro basketball. Tommy's whole life was played out somewhere in the middle. He was the buffer between me and Ba Ba, the bagman who played a well-defined role but never called the shots. I could only imagine the tactics employed by the agents working the case. All they had to do was stroke Tommy's fragile ego and make him feel important. It would be Tommy's big day in the sun, an opportunity to be someone important, his time to shine.

I knew full well who the target was, and I knew I would soon be on my own. It turned out that even Ba Ba got a heads-up from Tommy. I suppose Tommy recognized the need to keep his boss in the loop. After all, Ba Ba's friends don't look kindly upon rats. If Tommy pissed off the wrong people, he could find himself hanging on a meat hook in a refrigerated freight truck headed for Tijuana, Mexico. Tommy told me that Ba Ba even hired a lawyer to represent him. They call it "protecting your interests," and Ba Ba—always the shrewd businessman—wasn't taking any chances with his.

Over the next two or three weeks, I was a mess. I couldn't sleep, I couldn't eat, and I was shedding pounds from sheer worry and stress. My wife thought I was sick and urged me to see our family doctor. I was sick all right—sick from a binge of reckless and destructive behavior that was coming home to roost. I feared that I would eventually get the telephone call, or worse yet, an unannounced knock on the door from gun-wielding FBI agents coming to make the arrest and lock me up. My thoughts were all over the board. Gone were the days of calm and coolheaded steadiness. I spent most of my time trying to get myself together and think rationally. The rest was devoted to rehearsing answers to questions I presumed would eventually be asked by my pursuers. It would be a big-game hunt for the mother of all trophies, and my head would surely be mounted high above the mantle on the wall of a skilled marksman.

I was talking with Tommy on the phone almost every day, having thrown caution—and my better judgment—to the wind.

"What's going on?" I'd ask pathetically. "Have you heard anything?"

Although Jack and I hadn't placed a bet since the Super Bowl, we still talked regularly. Jack told me he heard from Pete Ruggieri that the cops were sniffing around Ba Ba and Tommy, but not around me. Obviously he hadn't spoken with Tommy, or at least he wasn't letting on. I started to have my doubts about Jack, and we engaged in a cat-and-mouse game to determine each other's motives. I had a difficult time wrapping my mind around the prospect that Jack was working for the authorities. We had been friends for so long, and I still naively believed in the loyalty that usually comes with a true friendship, even though I had broken that trust myself in the past. Besides, we both had so much to lose, right? Wrong—they didn't want Jack any more than they wanted Tommy. I was the prey in the crosshairs. In fact, if necessity forced the FBI to get in bed with a two-bit punk like Tommy, a working relationship with someone like Jack would be regarded as a gift from heaven. Simply put, Jack was credible, a real citizen who paid his taxes, lived in the suburbs, and looked like most of the faces in a prospective jury pool. Jack was the dream witness who could sit on the witness stand and clearly articulate our misdeeds of the past several years. The only question in my mind was whether or not the authorities were aware of Jack. Even if they weren't, it would only be a matter of time.

Pressure was building like the grinding of tectonic plates along the San Andreas Fault, and I was at my wit's end. I was talking with Tommy and Jack, but that was no more than an effort to stay close to those who could hurt me the most. It was the same thing day after day, the same questions, the same answers, the same paranoia. Finally, I decided to turn to someone outside of my secret world: my wife Kim. It was sad that it had taken this kind of trouble to force me to open up to my own wife. I had been deceiving her for years, living a separate life as a junkie, desperately addicted to gambling. She knew I liked to play cards and bet on golf, but she had no idea about the casinos and the sports betting. I think she always surmised that I was up to something, but nothing like this. It's funny how we often turn to those we hurt the most and expect comfort and a sympathetic ear. I'm not sure what I expected, but I couldn't keep it to myself for one more day—and I didn't want Kim and the girls to get blindsided.

It was a Friday night in June of 2007. Kim and I dutifully attended a dinner party at a friend's house while I struggled to find a way to drop the bombshell. I watched her throughout the evening, smiling at friends and neighbors, politely laughing at funny jokes, swaying to jazz music piped into the room, and generally having a very pleasant evening. I was like a fly on the wall, watching her, tracing her steps, knowing full well that she had no idea what was about to unfold. I hadn't looked at her like that in years, and she looked particularly pretty in the evening light. I loved the way her soft hair hung down and tickled her shoulders. I noticed little mannerisms that had held my attention for hours when we first met. Still, I found myself feeling sorry for her. In a few short weeks, her life would be thrown into chaos and she would be humiliated by my actions. Fate would force her to wear a face of strength, but it would be a façade, masking the excruciating pain of betrayal. For those fleeting moments, I was no longer focused on my problems. Kim was the focus of my concern, and I prayed to God that he would spare her from the misery that was certain to arrive, the misery that I alone had brought into our lives.

I watched the clock all evening long, waiting for the party to mercifully come to an end, waiting for the moment when the lies would stop and the truth would finally come out. We arrived home just after midnight. I was uncharacteristically aware of the symbolism of the new day just beginning. How the day might progress was anyone's guess, but a new day it was, and I was committed to making it the first day of a new life.

Kim asked for a little help with her dress, and as I eased the zipper down to the small of her back, I stopped.

"I have something to tell you," I said quietly.

As she turned to face me and our eyes met, a certain uneasy trepidation filled the room. She could clearly see in my demeanor that something was seriously wrong. She carefully stepped back and slowly sat on the side of our bed, hands neatly folded across her lap. I told her everything. The golf, the cards, the casinos, Jack, Ba Ba, Tommy, and the gambling on pro basketball. The more I talked, the more I opened up the way a husband should. It was cathartic and I just kept talking. Kim listened for the longest time, seemingly savoring every word of the first meaningful conversation we'd had in a very long time. Such a shame that it would take a family disaster, one generated by my actions, to bring this long overdue moment to fruition.

When I finally finished my confession, Kim seemed more puzzled than informed.

"I don't understand what you did wrong," she said. "All you guys bet. What are you so concerned about?"

I explained again that I actually bet on NBA games and that I used inside information to make my picks. I told her that I was working with bookies to place illegal bets and that I was getting paid for my services. She just shook her head in disbelief.

"All the stuff Bavetta does?" she said. "And the stuff the other guys do? Are you telling me you could lose your job over this? What about them?"

"That's different," I responded. "Those guys weren't telling other people how to bet on NBA games."

"I don't get it," she repeated. "It's just the boys being the boys. I think you're overreacting. I think you should just keep your mouth shut."

"I don't think you understand," I persisted. "I'm in major, major, major trouble!"

"Everybody makes mistakes," she continued. "We'll get through it together."

Maybe she didn't fully understand the gravity of the situation, or maybe she didn't want to. Whatever the case, when we went to sleep that night, I was stunned by her failure to grasp the seriousness of the matter and the predicament we were facing. As I lay there staring at the ceiling, I kept replaying her last words:

"Okay, you did something wrong, but I think you should keep your mouth shut. The worst that will happen is the NBA will give you a job doing something else."

Another job in the NBA? Was she kidding? I was a dead duck, and the life we had grown accustomed to was about to be flushed down the toilet. Kim was obviously fooling herself. Perhaps she was thinking about all of the referees charged with felonies 10 years earlier who had retained their jobs with the league. But those charges were for tax evasion stemming from an illegal airline ticket scam, not illegal gambling. Perhaps she wasn't yet prepared to deal with the enormity of the situation, the utter ruin and financial collapse that would befall our family. Perhaps she couldn't face the prospect of a total fall from grace, the end of our days brushing elbows with superstars and celebrities, and the end of private schools for the kids and tennis lessons at the country club. Perhaps it was all just too much to digest at 2:00 on a Saturday morning after years of living in the dark. Whatever it was, it all rested on my shoulders. I knew exactly the type of storm that was coming. But for the first time in a very long time, I felt the peace and calm that comes with being honest. I had told the truth to my wife and immediately felt a burden lifted from my shoulders. It was the first step on a long road back. As I drifted off to sleep that night, I felt good, almost hopeful, and I knew precisely what I had to do next. Two days later, I met with a lawyer.

* * *

Greg Hagopian had a reputation as a badass criminal defense attorney in the Bradenton-Sarasota area. That's what I was looking for. At 43 years old, the stocky former state prosecutor had more than mere courtroom savvy—he had street smarts. After years of prosecuting pimps, drug dealers, and carjackers, he made the switch and started cashing in on a judicial system that rewards lawyers who know the ropes and their way around the courthouse. I originally met him through a fellow member at Lakewood Ranch Country Club, and we played golf together on several occasions. A rabid sports enthusiast, he seemed fascinated by my position with the NBA, frequently probing me for behind-the-scenes gossip. I liked him; he was a professional guy with an edge and very down-to-earth. He also happened to live one street over from my house, and when I called two days after making the big revelation to Kim, he said he'd be right over.

Greg strolled up my front walk wearing dark-blue pleated Dockers, a pink cotton short-sleeve golf shirt, and brown deck shoes, no belt. He carried a black monogrammed briefcase with a gold lock and combination plate. He looked like a businessman taking care of some last-minute affairs before heading for the brunch buffet at the country club.

Buckle up, big guy, I thought to myself. *You're going to love this!*

We exchanged a few pleasantries and quickly retreated to my private office just off the main sitting room.

"What's going on, Tim?" he asked. "You sounded very concerned on the phone."

Concerned? What an understatement! My entire life was on the verge of collapse. I was trapped, boxed into a corner, desperately looking to navigate my way out. But first I needed a skilled lawyer to hold my hand and reassure me that everything would be all right.

I was on a roll, opening up and letting it all out, first to my wife and then to my new lawyer. I was telling the story like a lifelong sinner hitting the confessional after decades away from the church: a little timid at first, but eventually eager beyond control.

I laid it on the table, closely watching Greg's face for any reaction. At the same time, he stared at me, closely watching my face for the same. When I finally took a breath, he instructed me not to tell another soul what I had just told him. He was taking charge, and I liked it. I repeatedly pressed the point that my days of lying and deceit were over. I wanted to come clean.

"I hear you, but let's not be stupid," he said. "We've got to handle this thing on our terms, and that means you've got to keep your mouth shut. Understand?"

During the conversation, Greg admitted making an occasional bet on a game or two. He knew how it worked, and I found myself trusting him. Greg Hagopian was going to be my starting point guard against a team of special agents and federal prosecutors. I realized that I would ultimately lose the game, but I wanted to keep the score close. Too bad I couldn't hire Dick Bavetta!

When I mentioned Tommy's testimony at the grand jury, Greg's demeanor changed and he became very serious. He knew from experience that the vast majority of grand jury proceedings result in a criminal indictment in federal court. If Tommy was being straight about his denials of my involvement in betting on pro basketball, he had already committed perjury under oath and was facing a sobering five years in prison. Why would he put himself in that position? Did he think the feds were just fishing around, following up on some anonymous tip? Did he actually think he could play a game of chicken with the Department of Justice and make it blink? No, guys like Tommy understand that prosecutors don't convene grand juries unless they're on to something. But if the FBI had Tommy wired, they certainly wouldn't want him denying my complicity. They would want him to lure me into a conversation about betting on games, maybe even asking me for a few picks in the Finals. I just didn't get it. What the hell was going on?

At the time, I had no way of knowing whether the authorities were aware of Ba Ba and Jack. If they had Ba Ba, Jack, *and* Tommy, I was finished. If they didn't have Ba Ba and Jack, what led them to Tommy Martino? Was he running his mouth to stoned friends at the corner bar or did he get caught selling dope and decide to save himself? I could see Tommy getting pulled over in his Lotus with a trunk full of weed. I imagined him sitting across the interrogation table from some low-level narcotics task-force agent who just threatened him with 10 years in prison if he didn't give up his supplier. Tommy would be pissing down his stumpy little legs, groveling for mercy, when suddenly the light would go on and he would offer up a much juicier prize: me.

Could it possibly have happened that way? Regardless of how it got started, Tommy waited to call me until after meeting with the FBI three or four times and after testifying before a federal grand jury. If he was lying to me about his testimony denying my involvement, the cat was already out of the bag and it would only be a matter of time until the feds came knocking on my door.

Greg Hagopian didn't know Tommy the way I did, and he wasn't interested in an introductory course in Tommy 101. He wanted to cut to the chase and talk to someone who would have the answers.

"Call Martino and get his lawyer's name and phone number, right now," Greg said. "Just get the name and tell him you've got to go, nothing else."

I quickly called Tommy on his cell phone and told him my lawyer wanted to speak with his lawyer. He gave me the information and I told him we would talk later. We never did. Greg said he would make the call first thing the next morning and we parted company for the day. He reminded me one last time to keep my mouth shut and say nothing, and that was it. He was gone in a flash with a new client and my personal check for $20,000 in his pocket.

After a sleepless night of anticipation, I waited for Greg's call on Monday morning, hoping that the news would be good. The phone rang just before noon and Greg confirmed that Tommy had testified before a grand jury in New York—but there was more. After Tommy testified, his lawyer spoke with Tom Seigel, the Assistant United States Attorney handling the case. The prosecutor was livid, accusing Tommy of lying and threatening to bury him if he didn't come clean. Worst of all, the prosecutor specifically mentioned me by name.

"You can tell your friend Tim that he's reffed his last NBA game!" he shouted.

Hearing those words, albeit secondhand, rocked me, and I felt as though my knees were going to buckle. Since receiving Tommy's frantic phone call on the golf course, I knew my days were numbered. Still, I hadn't specifically heard the words confirming my worst fears until that moment. Greg reminded me to keep my mouth shut, but I would have none of it. Something deep within my soul told me that I had to go to New York and confess my sins. I was still unsure about Tommy, but it no longer mattered. They knew about me! Where or how they got the information that linked me to betting on pro basketball remained a mystery, but one thing was perfectly clear: the levee of deceit that had surrounded my life for the previous three and a half years was about to break. A virtual torrent of devastating consequences would soon be coming my way at breakneck speed. It was an unnatural disaster, the kind created by selfish and greedy men who feel unconstrained by the rules of the game. My entire professional career was based on enforcing rules and promoting fairness. Now the tables were turned, and I was the one hoping for a fair shake and a level playing field. Regrettably, I forfeited my right to those things the very moment I first bet on an NBA game. Bad guys don't get the breaks; they just get what's coming to them. In my case, the bad news would come in waves and I would nearly drown. I took a firm stand with my lawyer that morning and instructed him to set up an appointment with the investigating agents and the prosecutor. We were going to New York.

For some reason, my thoughts shifted to my old pal, Jack Concannon. We were still talking on the phone now and then, but nothing like the glory days of our wild binge of gambling and living in the fast lane. I wanted to let him know what had happened. I assumed Jack would eventually get caught up in the prosecutor's web of intrigue and I thought he deserved a heads-up. After finishing with Greg, I called Jack on his cell phone. There would be no picks, no wagers, no secret code language, and no plans for a junket to the Borgata.

"Jack, big trouble. I've got to see you right now," I said.

"What's up, T.D.? I'm down in Fort Myers for a few days," he replied.

"Can you drive up here today?" I pressed. "It's very important."

"You want me to leave now?" Jack questioned. "I'm sort of in the middle of something."

"Jack, it can't wait. There's a Waffle House restaurant next to a truck stop on Interstate 75, about halfway between Fort Myers and Sarasota. I'll meet you there in an hour," I said.

"I know the place," Jack replied. "What's this all about?"

"Can't talk on the phone. I'll fill you in when I see you," I responded.

"Okay, this better be good," Jack said apprehensively.

Driving down I-75, I worried that the FBI was following me. I put the car on cruise control to make sure I didn't give anyone a reason to pull me over. Was my phone bugged? Were they monitoring my calls? Just how far along had the investigation progressed? As I pulled into the restaurant parking lot, I saw Jack's car. That's when the thought occurred to me: *What if Jack already knows what I'm about to tell him? What if he has spoken with the FBI, too?*

Jack was sitting in a corner booth near the back of the restaurant, sipping on an iced tea. We shook hands and I placed my hand on his shoulder and then gently dragged it down his back and side, my fingertips subtly searching for signs of a wire. As we sat down, Jack was bursting with curiosity.

"Nice to see you, T.D. What the hell is going on?" he said.

I told him everything—the call from Tommy, the grand jury, the threats from Ba Ba, my attorney's conversation with Tommy's lawyer—everything. Jack's jaw dropped and he rocked back in his seat, seemingly stunned by the news. Mr. Cool actually looked rattled, a little green around the gills. I knew Jack could act; he was an insurance salesman, after all. Yeah, he could act, but not like this. He really didn't know. If I was 99 percent sure he was totally caught by surprise, his next question quickly inched me up to an undeniable 100 percent.

"You're not going to tell them about me, are you?" Jack asked in a tone unbefitting a man of his stature. Over the next 20 minutes or so,

Jack sought constant reassurance that I wouldn't identify him to the feds. "Tim, this will devastate my wife. I've got kids, Tim. Do you know what this will do to my business? I can't go to jail, Tim, I wouldn't make it," he pleaded.

Jack wouldn't let up and he trembled openly as we talked further, stuttering his pleas to keep his involvement a secret. His requests dissolved into begging and the scene left me feeling extremely uncomfortable.

"Jack, I have no clue what they already know, but I'm gonna be honest with them. There's no other option," I said candidly.

We talked for a while and then parted company. It was the last time I ever saw Jack or spoke with him. As he walked to his car, he looked drained with exhaustion, and I felt sorry for him. It had been a long time since our days in high school, and everything was different now. I had great times with Jack, but those days were gone; it was the end of a friendship that, ultimately, was yet one more illusion in my life. Our involvement with gambling was destructive in many ways. Too much time away from our wives and children, too much time chasing phantoms in card parlors and casinos, too much time consumed by immorality and vice. For me, there would be a heavy price to pay for my moral free fall and a very public accounting of my actions. Jack's reckoning would be different, at least on the surface. Beyond that, only he could say.

On the drive home, I called Greg and was informed that a meeting had been scheduled with federal authorities in New York for June 15. Greg spoke personally with Assistant U.S. Attorney Tom Seigel, who was overseeing all aspects of the case. Seigel was running the show and firmly delivered a stern message and warning to Greg that further confirmed all my suspicions: "You tell Tim Donaghy I know the whole story and it'll be a lot better for him if he comes up here and tells us everything. He's going to lose his job, but if we have to come to him, he's going to jail for a long time."

Hearing it from Tommy's attorney was bad enough, but getting an ultimatum from a federal prosecutor was sharply unnerving. Holy shit, this guy meant business! But there was no need for tough talk and threats; I wasn't a street thug who needed a rough kick in the ass. Hell, I wanted to tell them everything, because the pressure of living a lie was killing me. Tom Seigel didn't know with any certainty what I was thinking, but he probably believed I was some wiseass know-it-all who thought he was above the law. Seigel would learn shortly, however, that I was running scared, and more important for him, I was about to serve up a ready-made, once-in-a-lifetime case on a silver platter.

After delivering Seigel's sobering message, Greg said there was one more thing he wanted to discuss. He reminded me that he was a former state prosecutor with little experience in the federal system and that his conversation with Seigel convinced him of the need for a real heavy-hitting defense lawyer, one who knew his way around a federal courthouse. He recommended Tampa attorney John Lauro and said he had already taken the liberty of setting up a meeting for the three of us the following day. Greg was sending me a message that the stakes were getting very high and the prosecutor was clearly not to be taken lightly.

On the drive home that day, I knew my career as an NBA referee was over. There would be more time for personal reflection later, but during that moment, alone, I felt terribly sad, and my eyes welled up with tears. I thought about the long road I had traveled to the NBA. The clinics, the summer leagues, the CBA, the long hours on the road to run-down gymnasiums, the crazy fans, and the cheap hotels were all on my mind. I pictured myself standing on the court in Indiana for my first NBA game, listening to the national anthem with pride, awestruck by the realization that I was living my dream. I was fighting back tears, reminding myself that I was Gerry and Joan Donaghy's boy, and that Donaghys don't cry in the face of adversity. I remembered throwing that second-place trophy over the side of the Walt Whitman Bridge, and I wondered why the hell anyone would do something like that. And then, like an apparition to a spiritually starved wanderer, I felt my father's presence. It was warm and loving and fatherly. I was drawn to memories of watching him on the court, learning from him, discovering who he was, and always trusting him. I could hear his voice as he gently lectured me about the value of a college education. Suddenly I was 10 years old again, and through the window of my mind I could see my dad backing out of the driveway, alone, heading off to another game on a snowy night in February. I never really understood it until that very moment, but I had always wanted to be like my dad: highly regarded by friends and colleagues and thought of as a man of great integrity, a man to be respected. Of course, I couldn't cut it and I failed miserably. I am his son, but not half the man.

Overcome with emotion and sobbing uncontrollably, I suddenly realized that I was sitting in my car, parked in the driveway of my home. I had no recollection of the drive to my house; it was like waking from a dream and wondering where you are. I looked around and the yard was quiet with no one in sight. I slowly raised my head and gazed into the rearview mirror, staring into the bloodshot eyes of a man I no longer recognized. After a long pause that seemed to last forever, I noticed an orange glow surrounding my face. Turning around, I witnessed the late evening sky at dusk, ablaze with color, the sun softly slipping below the horizon while basking in a final farewell to the world. I caught my breath, wiped my eyes, and walked into the house. Trouble was no longer looming on the horizon; it had come to my doorstep. I decided to take it like a man, to be strong like my father, and to ride out the storm until a new dawn broke. What else could I do?

CHAPTER 9

Welcome to the FBI

Before heading north to New York for a rendezvous with destiny, Greg Hagopian and I drove to Tampa to see John Lauro. We met for dinner at an elegant restaurant and got to know one another over appetizers. Lauro, 50 years old but looking 35, had a tan complexion and jet-black hair, and he made a great first impression. The guy was a physical specimen, wearing a dark, athletic-cut, tailored Armani suit and a light-blue open-collared shirt. His handshake was firm and his demeanor confident and unflappable. Like Greg, John Lauro was a former prosecutor who had switched sides and now capitalized on his skills for serious profit, along the way developing a reputation as the man to see when the feds were breathing down your neck.

I gave Lauro a quick tour of my life story and Greg chimed in by relaying Tom Seigel's verbal threat from the day before. Lauro sat back and listened, occasionally turning a forkful of moo shu pork. He'd heard it all before, but even he knew this case was different. The sparkle in his eye betrayed an affection for the high-profile, publicity-generating criminal caper. And why not? The man had years of experience and tons of talent, and besides, a little recognition is always good for business, not to mention a healthy ego.

John Lauro also understood the value of a high-profile defendant to a veteran federal prosecutor hungry for a career-making case. He had been there himself, 20 years earlier. Prosecuting drug runners and bank robbers was heady stuff in the early days, but after a few years on the job, it turned bland, even stale. A case like mine was not just an attention grabber; it was a stepping-stone to a flashy high-rise Wall Street suite and a lucrative private practice where doctors, bankers, day traders, and Colombian cartel kingpins paid boatloads of money to make problems disappear. Lauro knew that my problems would never be resolved under the radar of public scrutiny. No, public scrutiny would be pursued, even chased by those holding the cards. I once again pushed my plan to make a full confession on day one, but like Greg, Lauro was against it. He wanted to feel the prosecutors out, find out what they knew, and devise a strategy. For me, it was too late for that; the game was over, and I just couldn't stomach living a lie for one more day.

We made plans to travel together to New York the following day, and Lauro told me in a matter-of-fact tone that he needed a $50,000 retainer. I cut the check and drove home to Bradenton for a restless night's sleep.

The Delta Airlines flight from Tampa to New York's La Guardia Airport was uneventful, except for my feelings of terror and panic. It wasn't the flight; I'd been on thousands of airplanes over the years. It was the uncertainty of what I was about to face. Lauro again advised me to keep my mouth shut and see how the meeting played out. Again, I insisted on telling my story and facing the music. Recognizing my resolve, he offered one last piece of advice.

"If you insist on talking, you better be honest and tell them everything you know," he said. "But keep in mind, once you take that step, there's no turning back."

No turning back? Brother, I didn't ever want to turn back. It was time to turn the page and move forward. I was ready to march right into the U.S. Attorneys' Office and give it up without a fight. My only remaining hope was that my honesty would be rewarded.

We arrived in New York at roughly 9:00 in the morning and hustled through the La Guardia terminal to catch a taxi for an 11:15 AM meeting at the U.S. Attorneys' Office in Brooklyn. John Lauro was the picture of calm, a seasoned veteran who remained steady at all times. By stark contrast, I was nervous, like a lame mouse gimping across a back alley inhabited by hungry cats looking to fill their bellies. After all the years of fast living and riding on the edge, I no longer felt invulnerable. To the contrary, I felt defeated, whipped, and humbled to the core. They say turnabout is fair play, and I was about to be on the receiving end of some serious turnabout. Much to my surprise, my other attorney, badass Greg Hagopian, wasn't looking so badass. As we traveled through Queens and entered Brooklyn, Greg unexpectedly declared some reservations about the situation.

"I'm not too thrilled about going into New York City and being in the middle of a case involving organized crime," he said.

Now why the hell would he say something like that? I'm looking for a little support and he's worried about the mob. Way to put a client at ease!

We pulled up to the office building and took an express elevator to the 18th floor. Stepping into the lobby, my eyes landed on a large round seal affixed to the opposite wall, emblazoned with the words "United States Attorney for the Eastern District of New York." My chest started to pound and my throat went dry. For a few seconds I was frozen, unable to move, eyes staring straight ahead like a deer in headlights.

John Lauro announced our arrival to the receptionist and we all took a seat. A bulletproof glass window separated the lobby from the main office and I felt like a monkey on display at the Bronx Zoo. Secretaries and other staff members would occasionally walk past the reception area and grab a quick glimpse into the cage.

Eventually Assistant U.S. Attorney Tom Seigel walked briskly to the lobby and introduced himself. When he shook my hand, he looked at me intensely, as if to deliver a silent message that he was running the show and that I was now on his turf. He appeared to be in his mid- to late forties, a short man with small hands and tiny fingers, his hair rumpled like a schoolboy's. With no fanfare, he escorted us into the inner sanctum, leading us down a long hallway to a conference room cluttered with dozens of legal storage boxes stacked high along the walls, all labeled "Gotti Trial." On a large dry-erase board fastened to the wall near the foot of a long rectangular table, someone had listed various crimes and prison sentences that I presumed might apply to me:

Gambling	5 years
Wire Fraud	20 years
Money Laundering	20 years
Racketeering	20 years

Before I could choke down my next swallow, Seigel instructed us to have a seat and then promptly excused himself.

Money laundering? Racketeering? It was clear to John Lauro and Greg Hagopian that the feds were messing with me, getting into my head, and setting the stage for a real come-to-Jesus revival with me as the repentant sinner and Brother Seigel as the preacher standing at the River Jordan, fully prepared to wash away my filthy indiscretions. Perhaps my attorneys were calm enough to see the forest through the trees, but I was under a physiological siege, blinded by the onslaught of the most remedial of interrogation techniques. Remedial or not, I was prepared to confess to the Lindbergh kidnapping just to get out of the room. That's when Seigel returned with FBI Special Agents Phil Scala and Paul Harris, and we got down to business.

Seigel explained that we were in a "proffer" session, whereby I would subject myself to an interview and then he would evaluate my level of cooperation and eventually make a decision on prosecution. At the time, I wasn't exactly sure what he meant by "make a decision on prosecution." Was he suggesting that I might possibly avoid prosecution and a criminal conviction? After all, wasn't he the guy who told Greg several days earlier that if I went to them, I might only lose my job? It didn't really matter. I flew to New York with the full intention of spilling my guts, and after the initial mind games, I couldn't do it fast enough. Seigel asked most of the questions during the early going.

"Do you bet?" Seigel asked.

"Yes," I said, realizing that I had just popped my cherry.

"Who do you bet with?" he asked.

"Well, I'll tell you the whole story," I began. "Originally, I started betting with Jack Concannon."

Before I could continue, Seigel abruptly stopped taking notes and looked up at me.

"Who is Jack Concannon?" he asked, trying to mask his surprise at my answer.

Who is Jack Concannon? I thought, stunned by Seigel's question. These guys still don't even know who Jack Concannon is? What *do* they know, or better yet, what else *don't* they know? For a moment, I thought I had made a huge mistake. Maybe I should have listened to my lawyers and not said a word. Hell, even my wife told me to keep my mouth shut! For that brief moment, I regretted flying to New York, meeting with Seigel and his henchmen, and putting my size-10 foot into my big mouth. Maybe, just maybe, they had nothing but a few phone calls between me and Tommy. Hell, we'd been friends since the ninth grade, and what's wrong with calling a close friend on the phone? If Tommy really had lied before the grand jury and covered my back, they had nothing on me.

My juices were starting to flow and I was coming alive. Maybe it's not too late to change my story and lie my way out of this mess. Maybe I…

And then I caught myself. The lies and deceit were a thing of the past; those days were over. It was time to shed the cocoon of dishonesty and fly into the storm with a clear conscience. *Don't go back, Tim. This may be your last chance,* I thought to myself. What did Willy Shakespeare say? "Into the breach!"

I took a deep breath, cleared my mind, slowly leaned forward, and proceeded to tell the prosecutor everything. I started with Jack and explained how we began with golf, cards, and casinos and then made the jump to betting on college and professional sports, including pro basketball. I explained my connection to Tommy, his connection to Ba Ba, the threats against my family, the 2,000 apples, the payoffs in hotel rooms, the secret codes, the whole thing. After 45 minutes, it was all on the table. I just leaned back in my chair and waited for the questions, but Moe, Larry, and Curly just sat there, mouths agape in total shock.

These guys had interviewed hundreds, if not thousands, of criminal suspects during their careers, but perhaps never one like this. At this stage of the investigation, they were doing nothing more than fishing. Oh, they had suspicions and some phone calls, but that was pretty much it. They probably expected me to do the dance and talk in circles, never quite admitting to any wrongdoing. That's how it usually went with confidence men, scam artists, and low-level knuckleheads—lots of talk, nothing to say. Well, not this time, boys!

Finally breaking free from his trancelike stare, Seigel, with the dwindling appearance of a man in charge, opened his mouth and meekly asked for a timeout.

It was perfectly clear that they had no idea of the scope of my involvement in betting on pro basketball, let alone any evidence upon which to build a case. Seigel and his pals had to regroup for a few minutes and come up with a new plan. So the prosecutor asked me and my lawyers to step into the hallway for a short break, but before I stood up from the chair, Seigel, in his best effort to appear unrehearsed, turned to Special Agent Phil Scala and asked if he had anything to say.

Scala, in his late fifties with gray hair and a meticulously groomed beard, reminded me of the actor Sean Connery. He appeared to be in very good physical shape, but the lines on his face revealed a man that had been around the block more times than he might have preferred—too many criminals to chase, too many cases to crack. Nearing mandatory retirement, he was called in to handle a potential bombshell of a case involving big-time sports gambling and corruption inside the ranks of the NBA. Not since the Pete Rose gambling scandal or the exposure of steroid use in Major League Baseball had an investigation into professional sports been potentially more explosive. Phil Scala was the right man for the job, a patient yet relentless pit bull who could direct the course of an investigation through the sheer force of his personality. I suppose it didn't really matter how much evidence they had when I walked into the room. Wherever the investigation started, Scala and company had worked their way to Tommy, and that meant I was next. If there was any lingering notion that I could have beaten these guys and walked away unscathed, it was about to disappear for good. The moment I heard Phil Scala's voice, I knew there was no way I would have survived the hunt. He was coming at me, and he wouldn't be denied.

They were playing "good cop, bad cop," and Scala was more than ready to do his part. Strangely, it wasn't even necessary, as I was anything but a reluctant interviewee. Still, whether it fit the situation or not, there was a point to be made and a message to be delivered.

Pointing his thick index finger directly at my face, Scala said, "You're sitting in the same fucking seat that John Gotti sat in, so don't think you can con me. I've been around a long time and if you're going to bullshit me, get up and leave right now! Don't waste my time!"

Scala is an intimidating man, and he made no bones about his tenacity to get the answers he wanted. During my career in the NBA, there were lots of players and coaches who got in my face and attempted to intimidate me, but with them, I always had the last word. Not anymore, and certainly not with Phil Scala and Tom Seigel. The rules of the game were forever changed, and they had me on my heels.

During the five-minute break, John Lauro tried to give me a boost.

"You're doing fine, Tim, just be honest and we'll get through this," he assured me.

In my opening narrative, I identified four names that became of great interest to the prosecutor and investigators: James "Ba Ba" Battista, Tommy Martino, Jack Concannon, and Pete Ruggieri. Add my name to the list and we had a starting five, a virtual all-star team of graft, vice, and corruption. Seigel did most of the talking, and he pounded me with questions about every aspect of the operation. He seemed particularly interested in Ba Ba and Tommy and any possible connection to the Gambino crime family. It was as though I was on the witness stand, being grilled by a veteran prosecutor with the jurors' eyes scrutinizing my words and my every twitch and turn. Phil Scala was sitting in for the jury that day, and I could feel his gaze studying me. First impressions are everything at a time like that, but I held a trump card that would ultimately give me great credibility—I was telling the truth.

The meeting lasted almost five hours, and when it was through, I finally asked a question of my own.

"Am I going to be charged with a felony?" I said.

Seigel put down his pen, straightened up, and looked me directly in my eyes.

"I don't know how I can't charge you with *something*. It's just too big," he said.

As we all stood to leave, I turned to Scala.

"What would have happened if I had kept my mouth shut? Would you have gotten me?" I asked.

He nodded, and said, "It would have taken another two or three months, but we would have gotten you, definitely. We would have gotten you."

We all shook hands and I headed for the exit with my lawyers. On the elevator, I felt totally drained. I had barely eaten or slept in days, and my thoughts were jumbled. During the flight back to Tampa, I sat transfixed, consumed with worry and fear. Greg noticed my unusual silence and tried to be pragmatic.

"Tim, we've got to play this out and see where it goes," he said. "You're doing the right thing. We'll wait to hear from them and go from there."

I arrived home after midnight to find my wife waiting for me with a look of grave concern on her face. We stared at each other in silence for what seemed like an eternity, neither one of us anxious to start a conversation that would be very disturbing—a conversation that would not, could not, have a good ending. Kim finally realized the magnitude of my crimes and broke down in tears.

"How could you do this to us? How could you do this to the girls? We're ruined; you've ruined everything," she cried.

Kim ran out of the room furious and overwrought with emotion. For the first time in our relationship, I was speechless. No comebacks, no off-the-cuff remarks, no tired excuses. I tried to comfort her but she would have none of it.

"Leave me alone, you selfish bastard!" she shouted.

Later that night, I went to the bedrooms of my four daughters. Standing in the hallway, I peered in to see my little angels. They looked so peaceful and innocent in their sleep, unburdened by troubles and completely unaware of how their lives were about to change. I felt shame, absolute and total shame, for failing them, for letting my selfishness guide my actions, and for setting in motion events that would destroy our precious family. Never in my life had I felt so small and so pathetic. Still, I resolved to turn the tragedy into a lesson learned, a lesson in humility, a lesson in grace, and a lesson in perseverance. It would be a very hard lesson for all of us, but during those early morning hours, it was all I could cling to.

For the next several days, the tension in my house was palpable. Kim's anger and feelings of betrayal simmered while I was racked with worry. I was in limbo, waiting for the government to make the next move, waiting for the other shoe to drop. My career was over, the paychecks would soon dry up, the media would descend upon my neighborhood, and I might actually go to jail. It was overwhelming and I got lost in the enormity of it all. The only good news was that I no longer carried the secret. My lawyers knew, the U.S. Attorneys' Office knew, and so did the FBI and my wife. There was only one more person who needed to be told before the entire world knew—my father. The thought of telling him that I gambled on basketball, including games that I refereed, was unimaginable. My dad's entire life was built on a foundation of honesty and integrity. There were no shortcuts, little fibs, errors in judgment, or honest mistakes. He was a straight shooter who played it by the book and could never be compromised.

I spent virtually all of my life attempting to measure up and be like my dad. A tall order for any son, but in my house, one that was worthwhile and deserving of a man's very best effort. Of course, I failed miserably. Everyone knows that failure is a relative thing, often apportioned in varying degrees. It's one thing to earn less money than your father, or to hold a job that is not quite as important. Even general underachieving can be offset by redeeming personality characteristics and a good heart. However, disgracing the family name and inflicting undeserved shame and humiliation go well beyond the bounds of routine failure. Disgrace required an element of purposeful aberrant behavior, or at the very least, gross recklessness bathed with indifference or a cavalier attitude. Disgrace transcends mere failure; it stinks like a rotting corpse and leaves a bitter taste in the mouths of its victims.

And so on Father's Day in 2007, I called my father and feebly choked out a holiday greeting, inviting a response of concern, the type of concern that any decent parent exhibits for a child in distress. That concern was undeserved as I was about to reveal the vestiges of a troubled life, one that would most certainly bring disgrace to the Donaghy name—my father's name.

"What's wrong?" my father asked. "You don't sound like yourself."

Dead silence.

"Dad, I'm in some trouble, a lot of trouble," I replied.

"What happened?" he said with the calm voice of a parent who had been down this road before.

But he hadn't been down this road before, not even close. I told him the whole story and he never once interrupted. He was absorbing it all, maintaining his trademark composure, just as he had done so many times before on the basketball court.

"Dad, please don't tell Mom yet," I pleaded. "I just can't put her through the pain. I don't want her to worry."

"She has a right to know," he responded. "Don't worry, Tim, we'll get through this together. I'll do whatever I can. Just keep me posted."

We spoke for a minute or two and then he asked the question that was troubling him most.

"Did you fix the games?" he said.

"No, Dad," I replied. "I never fixed a game."

"Okay, we'll get through this," he said with a tone of relief in his voice. "As long as the games weren't fixed, we'll get through this."

The distinction between gambling on pro basketball and fixing games seemed to be monumental to my father. In his mind, fixing a game was like lying, cheating, or stealing. Perhaps the distinction was his way of coming to terms with my conduct; not justifying it, but understanding how it could happen. In any case, he had said the words I longed to hear, and I felt like a young boy again, comforted by my father and believing I could face the world with him at my side.

* * *

While I was dealing with problems at home, the FBI was contacting the NBA to inform league officials that they had a problem as well. FBI Agents Phil Scala, Paul Harris, and Kevin Hallinan met with NBA Commissioner David Stern and briefed him on my startling disclosures of June 15.

"We have resources throughout the country. We ran it down and it checks out," Scala said.

Stern was given a thorough rundown of my gambling activities, along with information about bookies with mob connections. It was a nightmare for David Stern, and he knew a major scandal shaking the NBA to its very foundation was sure to follow. Armed with the damning disclosure of my involvement in betting on pro basketball, the commissioner would naturally terminate my employment immediately, generating inquiries from the NBRA, many of my colleagues, and various media outlets. A press conference would be called, questions would be asked, and the media circus would begin. Before the last syllables of bad news rolled off Phil Scala's tongue, David Stern was in full damage-control mode. The wheels were falling off the team bus, and the only way out was some quick thinking by the commissioner and a little luck. At the conclusion of their meeting, Scala instructed Stern to sit on the information for a while, as the investigation was continuing and more leads had to be pursued. Stern graciously obliged.

Before Stern was broadsided by the shocking news from Scala, his attention had been focused elsewhere. For starters, the NBA Finals had just concluded, and the commissioner was taking a victory lap, basking in the glow of another successful season. More importantly, the league was about to announce contract extensions with broadcast television partners ESPN/ABC and TNT for the exclusive rights to televise NBA games. The last thing David Stern needed was an unseemly referee corruption scandal as he tried to seal the deal, but thanks to an official directive from the FBI to sit on the information and keep it quiet a little longer, Commissioner Stern was generously, if unwittingly, given a window of opportunity.

On June 27, 2007, just a few days after Stern was briefed by the FBI, the NBA announced the signing of eight-year contract extensions with ESPN/ABC and TNT, ensuring a lucrative broadcasting partnership through the 2015–16 season. Interestingly, the new deal was inked a full year before the original contract expired. Prior to the signing, my employment had not been terminated, there was no press conference to address the gambling scandal, there were no questions for reporters to ask, and there was no media circus. Instead, secrets had been kept and deals were struck. However, as the ink dried on the newly signed contracts, all hell was about to break loose.

* * *

By the beginning of July, I was feeling enormous pressure. There was still no word from the FBI, and absolutely nothing from the NBA. I was scheduled to train prospective NBA officials at a clinic in Utah the following week, but obviously I could not participate. The days went by and there was still no word from the authorities or the league. On July 9, 2007, after 13 years working in the NBA as a highly rated referee, I faxed a one-page letter of resignation to league officials.

July 9, 2007
To: Joel Litvin
Stu Jackson
From: Tim Donaghy
  Please be advised that effective immediately, I am resigning my position as an NBA referee.

Sincerely,
Tim Donaghy

That was it. It was over. Thirteen years of living my dream flushed down the drain with one short sentence. Of course, the dream didn't vanish solely because of the words I had typed on a piece of paper. Rather, it was what those words represented, an out-of-control, reckless lifestyle punctuated by an addictive personality and a full-scale surrender of basic values. Greed and arrogance had conquered the day, ending a promising career and destroying a reputation. After sending the fax, I just sat back and waited.

Over the next few days, word of my resignation leaked out to my fellow referees, and emails and phone messages poured in. I ignored them all. Eventually, Commissioner Stern issued a gag order to all referees—no talking with me, the media, or anyone else. After that, the calls and emails stopped and I was on my own, no longer a member of the exclusive fraternity of NBA referees, no longer a part of one of the most exciting organizations in the world.

In the days leading up to my resignation, I received many calls from Scott Foster. We were both on summer break from the NBA and planned on playing some golf together. Scott had been calling to remind me of a member-guest golf tournament at a country club in Maryland that we were going to enter. After my initial meeting with the FBI in New York, I just couldn't face Scott and I avoided his calls. He finally tracked me down a few days before my resignation from the league.

"Tim, where the hell have you been?" he asked excitedly. "Why haven't you returned my calls?"

It was very unusual for either one of us to not return a phone call. Even during the off-season we spoke on the phone almost every day.

"I've had a few issues around the house. I'm sorry," I replied.

"Are you ready for the tournament? When are you coming up?" he inquired.

"Oh, yeah, the tournament. I'm not gonna be able to make it. My back is acting up and I can barely swing a club," I responded.

"What? We've had this planned forever. Since when does a sore back stop you from playing golf?" Scott asked sarcastically.

"Look, this is different. It's really bad and I've got to take it easy for a while. I'm sure you can find someone else to fill in," I said with an uneasiness in my voice.

We went back and forth for a few minutes, but he finally gave up.

"Okay, pal. I guess I'll catch you next time. Take care of that back," he said.

I wanted to say something. Scott had been my best friend for 15 years and we shared everything. If we had family problems, we talked. If we had job problems, we talked. Hell, if we had any kind of problem, we talked. Now, at the most problem-filled moment of my life, I couldn't pull the trigger. More than anything, I was ashamed of what I had done. As NBA referees, Scott and I had a connection, a bond that only a handful of others shared. Beyond that, we were true friends, the kind who stick together through thick and thin, the kind who weather the storm and never look back. I betrayed all that, and I simply couldn't face up to it.

"Scott?" I started softly.

"Yeah," Scott replied.

"Nothing. Take care of yourself," I said, saddened by the knowledge that we might never speak again.

We never did.

After the scandal broke, there were no more calls from Scott Foster. I eventually asked my father to contact Scott and tell him I would call when things quieted down, but Scott was unreceptive to future communication. He likened hearing the news of my involvement with gambling to arriving home unexpectedly and finding his wife in bed with another man.

He was right, of course. For anyone close to me, the news was sickening, a sharp blow to the head, a hard punch in the gut. Scott was the latest victim of my misdeeds, and a great friendship was lost forever. What could possibly happen next?

How I Picked the Games

"Fixed! NBA Ref in Mob Betting Scandal."

That was the headline in the July 20, 2007, edition of the *New York Post*. How the *Post* broke the story didn't matter, and the identity of its anonymous source was irrelevant. The story was out, and everyone in sports journalism and broadcasting wanted a piece of the action.

When I read that headline, I was crushed. Yes, I bet on NBA games. Yes, I used inside information to make my picks. Yes, the mob was involved. But I *never* fixed a game! I was about to learn a cruel lesson, one that revolves around the sale of newspapers and the push for increased television ratings: never let the facts get in the way of a good story, or at least a good headline. Of course, the distinction between betting on games and fixing games means nothing to the average reader or viewer, but it does to me, and it certainly does to my father. But I quickly had to accept the fact that when you play with fire, you sometimes get burned—and sometimes you get incinerated. As I languished over the public perception that I fixed games, I came to realize I had no one to blame for this misconception but myself. For years, I was on a collision course with disaster, a path toward self-destruction, yet I kept pouring gasoline on the tinder of my life, waiting for someone to toss a match. In the fast-paced era of the 24-hour news cycle, my world suddenly became very small—and so did my front yard.

Late June in central Florida can feel like the inside of a pizza oven, and the summer of 2007 was no exception. But that didn't stop dozens of reporters, cameramen, technicians, and still photographers from descending on my sleepy little neighborhood, looking for a scoop. They were relentless! Satellite trucks lined up around the corner waiting to broadcast the latest exclusive updates from ground zero—the Tim Donaghy residence.

Two days after the story broke, I received an ominous call at my home. As Kim prepared supper and my daughters played in the family room, a male caller with a steely coolness pronounced my sentence: "That's it, you're done, you're dead."

The caller had an East Coast accent, and his tone was all business. It rattled me to the core, and my fingers trembled as I hung up the phone. My thoughts immediately shifted to Ba Ba and Tommy. Could they possibly be behind the call? Worse yet, were Ba Ba's bosses shooting a warning shot across the bow? Either way, it was too late for warnings from tough guys; I was already cooperating with the authorities. I filed a report with the local police and the FBI, and from that night on they maintained a presence in my neighborhood. Special Agent Phil Scala reassured me that he had his eye on me and that no one would dare make a move against me. Scala also told me that the Gambino crime family was in an uproar over the situation involving Ba Ba and me. Apparently, good little soldiers like Ba Ba had not been passing important information up the ladder to the lieutenants and capos. Word on the street was that Ba Ba had been a bit selfish with his golden goose and hadn't shared the profits with the big boys. Too bad for Ba Ba, and too bad for me.

Phil Scala knew these types better than anyone. For years, he had been tracking, investigating, and busting underworld punks and thugs with a vengeance. When Gambino family crime boss Big Paul Castellano was gunned down outside Sparks Steak House in midtown Manhattan, Phil Scala was called in to investigate. Scala didn't know it at the time, but as he worked the crime scene around Castellano's blood-soaked body, the future Don himself was speeding away from the area into the crowded city. John Gotti and his No. 1 henchman, Sammy "the Bull" Gravano, had just witnessed the execution, ensuring Gotti's ascendancy to the throne of New York's underworld. Over the next seven years, Scala was on Gotti's trail, from the Teflon Don's Howard Beach home in Queens to the Dapper Don's favorite haunt in lower Manhattan, the Ravenite Social Club. Scala was there when Gotti got his cold-blooded start, and he was there when his luck finally ran out. Scala was a straight shooter, the ultimate G-man, a no-nonsense, this-is-our-town-not-yours kind of guy. He loathed mobsters who intimidated and threatened the weak, hiding behind their shadowy reputations or the barrel of a gun. If the world was the Wild West, Phil Scala was Matt Dillon, the kind of sheriff who couldn't be corrupted and always got his man. Hell, he got me, but now I felt like we were on the same side, working together for some greater purpose. I often thought he viewed me as a pawn of the mob, someone that could be easily exploited and then discarded into the East River like yesterday's trash. I was the right kind of pinch for a gangster: a little cocky, a little greedy, and very reckless, the careless guy who gets in over his head and needs two extra hands and a rope to get pulled out. I was out in the open now, exposed to the world, linked to the mob, and desperately trying to protect my family. With Phil Scala on the case, I felt safe, and I was more than willing to do things his way. I suppose I had no choice.

Kim didn't feel as safe as I did, so we decided that she and the girls would stay with a friend until things quieted down. They would occasionally sneak into our house at night so we could see one another, but the separation was eerily troubling for me. I privately feared that what was intended to be temporary would become permanent.

Four days after the story broke, NBA Commissioner David Stern held a press conference to address the media. It had been a full month since Phil Scala first briefed Stern on my illegal activities, 28 days since the commissioner inked lucrative contract extensions with the NBA's television partners, and 15 days since I resigned as a referee. Stern held the podium for an hour and 10 minutes, repeatedly stressing that a "rogue" NBA referee had engaged in illegal gambling activity. When one reporter asked the commissioner to comment on my overall job performance as a referee, Stern said, "Indeed, as a matter of his on-court performance, he's in the top tier of accuracy…"

And then there was this exchange:

> Reporter: So they are looking into other referees as well?
>
> Stern: Not exactly. But we don't know exactly. We know a little bit and we know that at this point, that we understand that it's an isolated instance, but I don't want to comment about their investigation or what they are doing because I've been asked not to.

Later, in response to a reporter's question about the NBA's policy concerning referees who gamble, Commissioner Stern offered the following:

> Oh, yes, you are not permitted to bet if you're a referee. You're not permitted to bet legally and you're not permitted to bet illegally. The legal betting will cost you your job. The illegal betting, depending upon the context, may cost you your freedom.

I couldn't help but wonder about all of my former colleagues who played golf and cards for money, bet on ponies at the racetrack, and gambled at casinos with impunity. Did Commissioner Stern's comments send a chill up and down their spines? Were they circling the wagons, waiting for the onslaught, and getting their stories straight? It wouldn't be the first time the NBA had to deal with referees who violated league rules.

In the early to mid-1990s, a number of NBA referees were indicted in federal court on tax evasion–related charges stemming from an airline ticket reimbursement scam. As part of its ongoing operation, the NBA paid referees first-class airfare for traveling from game to game. The indicted referees routinely downgraded the first-class tickets to coach and pocketed the sizeable difference in fares. In all cases, the referees failed to report the fraudulently obtained money on their income tax returns. The offenses were crimes of dishonesty, all perpetrated in an effort to pocket extra income, tax free. Penalties for the convicted defendants ranged from fines and restitution to probation, home confinement, and prison. The list of those convicted included: Joe Borgia, Don Vaden, Mike Mathis, Ronnie Nunn, Jess Kersey, Joe Forte, Derrick Stafford, Eddie F. Rush, Bennett Salvatore, Joe Crawford, Darell Garretson, Blane Reichelt, and Ken Mauer.

The NBA's response to the roundup of basketball's top officials was conciliatory. While emphasizing the league's uncompromising standard for honesty and integrity—a standard all NBA referees are expected to meet—the fall from grace for these standard-bearers was largely ignored by the league. All of these convicted referees retained their jobs and many would go on to receive promotions, effectively moving up the corporate ladder into one of the sporting world's most prestigious organizations. Joe Borgia became a Vice President in the league office, Donnie Vaden a Group Supervisor of Officials, and Jess Kersey a Group Supervisor. Vaden, Mathis, Mauer, Nunn, Salvatore, Forte, Rush, and Crawford all refereed in the NBA Finals *after* their convictions.

The facts underlying Jess Kersey's felony conviction illustrate the gravity of his offense and that of all the others, offenses that presented a sizeable dilemma for NBA Commissioner David Stern. At the time of his guilty plea in federal court, Kersey submitted a written statement of fact to the court for consideration at sentencing. He specifically admitted obtaining fake airline ticket receipts from a travel agency in South Carolina and implicated 15 other referees for doing the same thing. Kersey reported that he and the others were very much aware of what they were doing and that they openly discussed methods to cheat the system and line their pockets. He also informed the court that he handled many of the ticket transactions in cash so they would not be traceable by the IRS. Finally, Kersey admitted that he initially lied to IRS agents when questioned about his involvement in the scam.

Despite Jess Kersey's criminal activity off the court, he was a good referee and a favorite of the front office; hence, David Stern's dilemma. The commissioner had to make a choice—uphold the league's high standards for honesty and integrity and enforce its own rules of conduct, or look the other way for the good of the game. Stern chose the game.

Kersey's career as an NBA referee continued and he was eventually promoted to a supervisory position. The same was true for many other convicted referees. When deemed to be in the league's best interest, the commissioner selectively enforces league rules and policies, even when a lack of integrity and honesty among referees is revealed in the light of day. (This pattern continued following my downfall, as the league chose not to punish any of the referees that its own internal review showed had gambled in violation of the NBA's rules.)

All of this meant nothing in my case, nor should it. Betting on games in which I officiated was both a crime and a mortal sin in the NBA. Still, in his continuing effort to paint me as a "rogue" referee and shield the NBA from further scrutiny, the commissioner was turning a blind eye to the broader problems of gambling and favoritism by NBA referees. The gambling habits of other referees were never an issue for me, but they soon became a major concern for someone else: FBI Special Agent Phil Scala.

* * *

John Lauro finally heard from Tom Seigel—they wanted another meeting on July 27. The prosecutor stressed the need for total confidentiality. No one, not even my wife, could know about the meeting or the nature of our discussions. Despite the admonition, I immediately told three very important people in my life—my wife, my mother, and my very good pal, Vito Bavaro.

I first met Vito when we moved to Florida three years earlier. Like me, Vito was from the Northeast; New Jersey to be specific. He loved to eat rich foods, drink top-shelf liquor, drive expensive cars, play golf, deal cards, shoot dice, talk smart, and laugh like hell. We hit it off instantly! Vito was 35 years old and heavyset, a laid-back guy who didn't pay much attention to fashion or personal appearance, at least not his own. He and his family lived in a million-dollar home on the golf course four doors down from mine. Vito told me he was a baker, and that's where he made his dough.

So I called Vito and asked for his help in escaping undetected from my house. Vito, undeniably titillated by the prospect of participating in a game of catch me if you can with the national press corps, immediately signed on.

"Here's the plan, Tim," he said. "I'll pick you up in my golf cart in the backyard after dark and we'll drive through the golf course until we get to Mike Wolf's house. You can stay there for the night; I'll take care of everything. Then I'll pick you up at 6:00 AM and we'll go to the airport. Piece of cake, no sweat."

It sounded good to me, so we synchronized our watches for 10:00 PM and said good-bye.

"Vito," I said.

"Yeah, T.D.," he replied.

"You can't tell anyone about this, not even your wife," I insisted.

"Got it, don't worry about me," he promised.

That was it. I packed my bag and spent some time on the telephone with Kim and the girls. I was nervous about the meeting the following day, but that evening, I was focused on evading the press and keeping my picture out of the papers.

Just a few minutes before 10:00 I heard the muffled sound of an electric-powered golf cart zigzagging across my back lawn. It was already dark, but I could still make out the silhouette of a hefty Italian guy cruising up to the porch in full stealth mode. What a sight! Here's Vito, wearing dark pants and a black shirt with a blue floppy hat hanging down over his eyes. Subtle Vito, real subtle.

"Get in, my man, the midnight express is ready to roll!" Vito whispered excitedly.

I quietly locked my back door and then got in next to Vito.

"Let's move, Kato!" I instructed my getaway driver.

"Roger that, T.D. These fucks will never know you left the house," Vito boasted.

With that we were off toward my friend Mike Wolf's house. As Vito pushed the gas pedal to the floor, he turned the wheel sharply to the right and immediately ran over a large oscillating sprinkler connected to a 25-foot garden hose. The hose became entangled around the right rear wheel and we spent several minutes fumbling in the dark trying to break free.

"Way to go, Ace!" I said sarcastically. "Can we please be a little more careful?"

"What do you expect?" Vito snapped back. "I can't see a fucking thing."

Off we went, through backyards, around trees, perilously close to the Carabias' swimming pool, through the Keublers' award-winning flower garden, over the Comitos' pink flamingo lawn ornaments, and into the night. It wasn't exactly like Steve McQueen attacking the streets of San Francisco in *Bullitt*. No, it was much more like *Driving Miss Daisy*, which I suppose made me Miss Daisy.

Despite encountering a few obstacles on the ground, we were making progress in our attempt to slip away from the media knuckleheads sipping burnt coffee and eating stale doughnuts on the other side of my house. Then, driving through backyard after backyard, a strange thing occurred. One after another, motion-sensitive floodlights burst on, creating a synchronized light show that illuminated the two dummies trying to sneak away in the dark. It was like watching the light and water show extravaganza in the reflecting pool outside the Bellagio Hotel in Las Vegas. All we needed was Beethoven's Fifth Symphony and the scene would have been complete.

In a panicked effort to get off the stage, Vito swerved violently toward the golf course adjoining my neighbor's backyard and dove into the darkness of a pitch-black night. As we plodded along, skirting ponds, trees, sand traps, and ravines, I found myself thinking about the classic children's bedtime song, "Three Blind Mice"—minus one, of course.

Mike Wolf's house was on the other side of the golf course, a 20-minute walk in broad daylight. Forty-five minutes after Vito and I set out for adventure, we were lost, trying in vain to navigate the darkness and find our final destination. And then, at last, there it was, the familiar sight of Mike's house about 100 yards away. As we drove closer, it appeared that a low-lying swampy marsh separated us from the safety and comfort of Mike's sun porch. We drove up to the edge of the tall grass and my chauffeur wasted no time.

"Okay, pal, there you go," Vito stated. "Just walk through there and you're home free."

"What do you mean, walk through there?" I said, pointing to the murky black sinkhole in the ground. "I'm not walking through there!"

"Don't be a chicken," Vito scolded. "So your feet get a little wet. So what?"

As Vito disappeared into the night, I pulled up the legs of my trousers and made a dash through the swamp, kicking up muck and stagnant water, until I reached Mike's porch. Man, a Bacardi and Coke has never tasted so good!

* * *

After a rough night's sleep and a smooth flight to New York, I strolled into the U.S. Attorneys' Office in Brooklyn right on schedule. John Lauro and I met with Tom Seigel and Special Agents Scala and Harris, and this time they wanted details. Phil Scala tossed a copy of my referee schedule for the 2006–07 NBA season onto the conference table and asked me to identify the games I picked for Tommy and Ba Ba. The investigators specifically wanted to focus on games that I officiated, a clear signal to me that they were not yet persuaded by my claims that I didn't fix games. The season was still fresh in my mind, so I calmly pointed to the schedule and tapped my fingertip on the listing of each contest where I made the call to Tommy. Between December 13, 2006, and March 18, 2007, there were 12 games that I described for them in detail.

December 13, 2006
Boston at Philadelphia

This was where it all started, the first game I picked for Ba Ba and my first payout of 2,000 apples. I worked the contest with referees Matt Boland and Derrick Stafford. During our pregame meeting earlier that day, the three of us discussed how bad the 76ers were without their former star guard, Allen Iverson. Derrick Stafford also stated that Philadelphia coach Mo Cheeks didn't know what he was doing and that forward Chris

Webber was washed up. I knew that Philly had been losing lately and Boston was playing hard, so I told Tommy to bet Boston.

On the floor that night, the 76ers shot poorly from the field and generally played flat. Chris Webber shot a miserable 4-for-17 and sharpshooter Kyle Korver went 3-for-14. It was clear to me that the entire team was lost that night, and Boston won easily 101–81.

Special Agent Paul Harris focused in on a traveling violation I called against Philadelphia. He had previously watched game tape and read reports filed with the NBA front office and implied that it had been a borderline call that many referees would not have made. I told him that there was no gray area with a travel; it either was or it wasn't. If the ball was not out of a player's hand before the pivot foot was lifted, it was a travel. I went on to tell him that although the definition of a traveling violation is crystal clear, the issue of enforcement is a totally different matter. Some officials enforced the rule, but most didn't. The NBA keeps statistics as a means to track the tendencies of referees, and those stats revealed that while some referees called as many as 200 traveling violations in a given season, others called as few as 20. My numbers were consistently on the high side of the equation.

My point was further corroborated by the supervisory reports filed for the Boston-Philadelphia game. The site supervisor in the arena that night reported that I made an "incorrect call," while the group supervisor who later reviewed game tape in slow motion changed the report to reflect a "correct call."

As the discussion continued, the investigating agents began to shift gears and expanded the conversation beyond my role. They started asking questions about other referees and the biases, quirks, and tendencies that could affect the outcome of a game. That's when I explained to them that my system for making a pick wasn't that complicated. I simply checked to see which referees were assigned to work a game, and then I utilized my knowledge of those referees' tendencies to make a pick. I explained that a referee who had a special relationship with a certain player or coach could affect the score by as much as five points. In the betting world, even a slight edge can seriously change the odds, and knowing the other referees gave me that edge.

December 26, 2006

Memphis at Washington

When I learned that referees Joe Forte and Eli Roe were working this game with me, I immediately picked Memphis to win. Forte and Memphis coach Mike Fratello were good friends and had been for years. Forte had a "free dinner" card for Fratello's sports restaurant in Atlanta and he loved to share it with his friends. Forte lived in Atlanta, and whenever we worked a Hawks game together, I was Joe's guest for a delicious meal, compliments of Coach Fratello.

Joe's special relationship with the coach was all I needed to know, so I called Tommy and told him to bet Memphis.

A couple of hours before the tip-off, a longtime employee of the Wizards stopped by the referees' locker room to check on us. During the visit, he informed us that he had just spoken with Coach Fratello, who stated that his team was really battling injuries and he hoped he would have enough players to finish the game. This revelation was a game changer for me, and I felt that even Joe Forte wouldn't be able to help his old pal.

Armed with the new information, I decided to change my pick to Washington. I grabbed my cell phone to make a frantic last-minute call to Tommy, but I couldn't get any reception down in the bowels of the MCI Arena.

"Can you hear me now?" I repeated over and over.

I quickly borrowed Eli Roe's cell phone and found a quiet corner to make the call.

"Tommy," I whispered. "Switch the pick. Bet Washington."

The Wizards came out on fire, racking up a 45–18 first-quarter lead. It was one of those nights where Washington could do no wrong, and all of its players got to pad their stats. Memphis was hapless, and Coach Fratello went through the motions of coaching in a losing effort. Even the Grizzlies' best player, Pau Gasol, only played 23 minutes, obviously struggling with a nagging injury.

Washington won big that night, and I owed it all to a low-level employee of the home team who just happened to stop by for a quick chat and to see if we needed more ice.

Scala and Harris couldn't believe it was that simple, and they questioned me about the flow of inside information available to referees prior to a game. I told them that we regularly obtained information from a variety of sources, some of which were very unusual, such as team mascots and ball boys. Our locker room was wide-open and well traveled by many, like Times Square on a Saturday night. It was rare not to receive some type of inside information, and it didn't take any effort on my part. Typically, it just walked right through the door.

January 1, 2007
Minnesota at Charlotte

This was a New Year's Day game and I was in Charlotte for a matchup between the Bobcats and the Minnesota Timberwolves. Before the game, I spoke with my group supervisor, Jim Wishmier. Jim mentioned that Minnesota's star forward Kevin Garnett had been getting away with a lot of traveling violations and that no one was paying attention to his footwork. Jim expected us to keep an eye on Garnett and to start enforcing the rule.

I worked the game with referees Joe Forte and Marc Davis, two veteran officials who weren't afraid to take on a superstar player. Prior to the game we specifically discussed Jim Wishmier's comments and decided to watch Garnett closely and rein him in on traveling violations.

In addition to the anticipated crackdown on Garnett, I liked the way Charlotte coach Bernie Bickerstaff had his squad playing high-energy basketball most nights. I called Tommy and told him to bet Charlotte.

The Bobcats played well early but fell apart during the second half, getting outscored 34–18 in the fourth quarter. Garnett played exceptionally well for Minnesota, while Charlotte's players were arguing amongst themselves all night. Much of the angst was directed at the Bobcats' Adam Morrison, who took several off-balanced, ill-advised shots down the stretch in what had been a fairly tight contest.

Minnesota kept its composure and pulled out the road win 102–96. It was a loss for me, Tommy, and Ba Ba, and there were no apples coming my way.

The investigators once again expressed amazement at the seemingly subtle factors I used to make the pick, albeit a losing pick. I reminded them that we often received directives from supervisory staff to key in on certain players, enforce certain rules, and generally change the dynamics of a game. The experience and strength of an officiating crew was also a critical factor, especially when it came to interpreting those directives. It was all rather uncomplicated, but the Minnesota-Charlotte game reinforced the fact that there was no such thing as a guaranteed winning pick. Still, the inside information was reliable enough that I was right on the money seven or eight times out of 10.

January 5, 2007

Miami at Phoenix

I had flown from Bradenton, Florida, across the country to work a game in Phoenix with referees Bernie Fryer and Gary Zielinski. During our pregame meeting, we discussed how banged up Miami was; both Shaquille O'Neal and Dwyane Wade were out of the lineup. Even coach Pat Riley was out, on a leave of absence after hip-replacement surgery. Filling in for Riley was assistant Ron Rothstein, a journeyman coach not highly regarded around the league. We agreed that it would be a blowout for Phoenix and an easy night for us. I told Tommy to bet Phoenix.

Miami had a terrible night, scoring just nine points in the fourth quarter and losing the game 108–80. The Heat looked like a high school team that hadn't practiced over the Christmas break, very sloppy and wildly overmatched.

During the contest, Gary Zielinski threw Heat guard Jason Williams out of the game after Williams argued a call that didn't go his way. Scala and Harris were particularly interested in Zielinski's actions on the court that night and repeatedly asked me if he was on the take.

"Was Zielinski a part of this?" Scala asked. "Don't bullshit me, I want to know the truth!"

"No, never," I said. "Gary would never do something like that."

The investigators were starting to see the big picture, recognizing that referees could, and often did, influence the outcome of an NBA game. Sometimes it was subtle; other times it was embarrassingly obvious. Enlightened to this phenomenon, Scala and Harris initially had a difficult time accepting that I was the only one who bet on pro basketball. They would eventually reach the conclusion that I acted alone, but along the way, they would develop serious questions about the honesty of many NBA referees and the integrity of the game.

As an aside, Harris informed me that the spread on the game had gone all the way up to 18 points before tip-off.

Wow! That was the biggest line I'd ever heard of. Someone was betting major money on Phoenix and the oddsmakers were in a panic. Of course, 18 points wasn't nearly enough that night, as the Suns easily covered the spread with a 28-point blowout victory.

January 6, 2007
Utah at Denver

Immediately after the game in Phoenix, I flew to Denver with the same referee crew for a contest between the Nuggets and the Utah Jazz. During our pregame meeting, Bernie Fryer, Gary Zielinski, and I discussed the situation involving referee Steve Javie and Nuggets guard Allen Iverson. I knew Denver was at a disadvantage, so I called Tommy and told him to bet Utah.

In the first quarter, Iverson was whistled several times for palming the ball and never seemed to get in a rhythm, shooting a lousy 5-for-19. The Jazz started fast and led 27–16 at the end of the first quarter. Carlos Boozer shot the ball particularly well that night, hitting 10-of-12 from the field. At halftime, group supervisor Jim Wishmier came into our locker room laughing about the message that had been delivered to Iverson. The boss knew exactly what we were doing and actually thought it was funny.

As with the previous game, Scala and Harris again took notice of several strange calls made by Zielinski and demanded to know if he was betting on games. I told them that if there had been a priest on the staff, it surely would be Gary Zielinski. He may have joined in with the rest of us and enforced the rules against Iverson, but he didn't bet and he would never fix a game.

January 15, 2007

Toronto at Philadelphia

Back home in Philly, I worked a 76ers-Raptors game with referees Ron Garretson and Eli Roe. The normally mild-mannered Roe had been having problems with Sixers coach Mo Cheeks all year. Cheeks was tough on Roe, riding him every chance he got, and Roe was fed up. On top of that, the 76ers were still reeling from the trade of Iverson to Denver, and the Raptors were on a hot streak. I called Tommy and told him to bet Toronto.

During the game, Raptors forward Chris Bosh and guard T.J. Ford were unstoppable. At the same time, Philly was rotating its lineup, trying to find a combination that would generate some offense. They never did and were run out of the building 104–86.

January 19, 2007

New Orleans at San Antonio

After a leisurely stroll along the Riverwalk in downtown San Antonio, I headed off to the AT&T Center for a contest between the Spurs and the visiting New Orleans Hornets. Earlier in the day, I had lunch with Jim Wishmier. We agreed that it would be a relatively easy game to work, especially considering that New Orleans' best player, guard Chris Paul, was injured and out of the lineup. Plus, San Antonio was arguably the best team in the league. I worked the game with referees Joe DeRosa and Eli Roe, and DeRosa specifically commented that the Hornets had been playing poorly as of late. I placed the call and told

Tommy to bet San Antonio.

The game was physical from the start and both teams argued just about every call we made. Admittedly there were a few questionable calls against San Antonio early in the contest, resulting in the usual heated exchanges, technical fouls, and ejections. Of particular note, I tossed San Antonio coach Gregg Popovich for his profanity-laced tirade, and the complexion of the game changed—advantage New Orleans. The Hornets kept the game fairly close, but San Antonio won 99–86. Despite picking the right team, I lost the bet as the Spurs failed to cover the spread.

Tommy called to tell me Ba Ba was pissed that I tossed Popovich out of the game. After all, I picked the Spurs to win, so why would I toss their coach? I heatedly explained that I wasn't fixing games, just making my best educated guess.

That was the game that helped to convince the FBI that I wasn't fixing games. Not only did we lose the bet, but I actually ejected the coach of the team I picked—in the first quarter!

January 24, 2007
Philadelphia at Cleveland

The January referee schedule had me working my way back across the country with a stop in Cleveland for a game between the Cavaliers and the Philadelphia 76ers. I worked the game with referees Duke Callahan and Eli Roe, and Roe was still smarting over his ongoing battle with Mo Cheeks. This was LeBron James' backyard and the sinking 76ers were clearly overmatched. I called Tommy and picked Cleveland, a real no-brainer.

Surprisingly, Philadelphia came out with a purpose, and despite a 39-point performance by King James, the Sixers stole one on the road 118–115 in double overtime. In a bizarre exchange, Philadelphia center Sam Dalembert approached me during the second overtime and told me he was playing well that night because he'd eaten a second plate of goat meat for lunch—his favorite meal. But I was the real goat in this one; that made two losses in a row, and Ba Ba had grown restless.

February 3, 2007

Los Angeles at Washington

The Wizards were hosting the star-studded Los Angeles Lakers in the nation's capital. I worked the game with referees Dan Crawford and Courtney Kirkland, a couple of veteran officials who knew the ropes and had strong opinions about certain players and coaches. For me, the Lakers-Wizards matchup had less to do with the players and more to do with the dislike between Crawford and Lakers coach Phil Jackson. In our pregame meeting that day, Crawford was deriding Jackson, calling him an arrogant attention grabber whom he would not talk to during a game. I was well aware that many NBA referees felt the same way about Jackson; there was a perception among referees that Jackson hated them and would attempt to embarrass them during the game or in the press. True or not, that was the common perception held by the refs, and I personally witnessed efforts to screw Jackson many times during my career.

It was a home game for the up-and-coming Wizards, and Dan Crawford was the beat cop patrolling the court that night—look out Lakers and look out Phil Jackson. I told Tommy to bet Washington.

To my surprise, it was all Lakers that night. Kobe Bryant lit it up on 14-of-26 shooting. Meanwhile, Gilbert Arenas of the Wizards couldn't buy a bucket, hitting only 3-of-15 beyond the three-point arc.

Once again, I made the wrong pick and the Lakers prevailed 118–102. I don't know why I *ever* bet against Kobe Bryant. It was the third loss in a row and Ba Ba was livid. I tried to reassure Tommy, but the phone call turned nasty and I hung up. I needed a win badly to break the losing streak and get Ba Ba off my back.

By this time, Scala and Harris were becoming more convinced that I hadn't fixed games. Yes, I used inside information to make picks, but I didn't take affirmative steps to influence the outcome. Scala repeatedly asked if my stake in the outcome of a game could have subconsciously affected my objectivity. I would have to admit that yes, it could have. It would be a matter of further discussion and contention, but they were starting to see my involvement for what it was.

February 10, 2007

Sacramento at Seattle

Flying to the Great Northwest, I was crossing the country again, scheduled to officiate a contest between the Sonics and Kings. I reunited with Gary Zielinski, and we were joined by Joe DeRosa.

Seattle's season was starting to slip away and the buzz around the referee staff was that the players were quitting on coach Bob Hill. I also knew from experience that Gary Zielinski liked Sacramento coach Eric Musselman. I picked Sacramento that night and gave Tommy the green light.

Sacramento was red-hot in the first half, jumping out to a 63–46 halftime lead. The Kings stayed hot, shooting 50 percent from the field throughout the game, and Seattle just couldn't get anything to drop, with Rashard Lewis hitting only 2-of-11 and Earl Watson going 1-of-6.

Sacramento put Seattle away early and finished strong with a 114–93 win. The losing streak was over—I was back in business.

February 26, 2007

Miami at New York

Madison Square Garden was the place to be for a marquee matchup between the Miami Heat and New York Knicks. I worked the game with Derrick Stafford and Gary Zielinski, knowing that the Knicks were a sure bet to get favorable treatment that night. Derrick Stafford had a close relationship with Knicks coach Isiah Thomas, and he despised Heat coach Pat Riley. I picked the Knicks without batting an eye and settled in for a roller-coaster ride on the court.

During pregame warm-ups, Shaquille O'Neal approached Stafford and asked him to let some air out of the ball.

"Is this the game ball?" O'Neal asked. "It's too hard. C'mon, D, let a little air out of it."

Stafford then summoned one of the ball boys, asked for an air needle, and let some air out of the ball, getting a big wink and a smile from O'Neal. I immediately started second-guessing my pick and seriously contemplated running back to the locker room and calling Tommy. But it was too late. The buzzer sounded and it was time to start the game.

Stafford was more than obvious in his effort to favor the Knicks, and I breathed a sigh of relief. Thanks in large part to his quick whistle against the Heat, the team fouls, technicals, and free throws were completely out of whack. New York went to the line 39 times compared to only eight trips for Miami. Free throws made the difference that night and the Knicks won 99–93.

Special Agents Scala and Harris were dumbfounded by the impact a strong referee or coach relationship can have on a game and began to realize that referee manipulation was not only commonplace, but rather easy. In the Knicks-Heat game, Miami was clearly the superior team. However, 31 extra trips to the free-throw line for New York proved to be a tremendous equalizer in a slim six-point win.

March 18, 2007

Orlando at Miami

This was the last NBA game I bet with Tommy and Ba Ba. The intrastate rivalry between the Magic and Heat always resulted in a hotly contested game, and my officiating crew was ready. I worked the action with referees Joe Crawford and Leroy Richardson, and once again, I was confident that personalities would play a role in the outcome. During the previous season, Joe Crawford had a profanity-filled run-in with Miami's radio announcer, prompting Heat owner Mickey Arison's attempt to get Crawford fired. Crawford didn't take Arison's attempt lightly and was always looking for an opportunity to dish out some payback. I called Tommy and told him to bet Orlando. The Magic jumped out to a 28–16 first-quarter lead and never looked back, winning the game 97–83.

I didn't know it then, but my run with Ba Ba and Tommy was over.

Now, we were all running for our lives, and I felt my best chance for survival was to cooperate with the government and tell the truth. That's exactly what I did.

I had already confessed to my crimes, but now the investigators wanted to look more closely at other referees and determine if there was a wide-scale gambling problem in the league. Beyond that, the FBI wanted to know if a culture of game manipulation and fraud existed in the NBA. Special Agent Phil Scala was determined to get the answer.

CHAPTER

"Swish"

After two explosive meetings, complete with my full confession, Assistant U.S. Attorney Tom Seigel was anxious to seal the deal. I was given one choice: plead guilty. A hearing was quickly arranged for the morning of August 15, 2007, at the federal courthouse in Brooklyn, where I would stand alone and answer to felony charges of wire fraud and conspiracy to transmit wagering information.

There had been talk of leniency all based, of course, on my full cooperation and testimony against Ba Ba and Tommy. There was nothing concrete, just vague references to me "helping" myself. To be perfectly clear, I knew the score: the feds were going to bleed me dry, soak up and scrutinize every word I spilled, and then unilaterally decide my fate.

Ba Ba and Tommy were trying to work out deals of their own, but opted for a different approach—playing hardball. Ba Ba, in particular, was never one to roll over easily, and he continued to play the tough guy. He had an image to protect, not to mention a few unhappy bosses who were watching him closely. As for Tommy, the prosecutor always believed he lied to the grand jury, and my confession proved it. Tommy, like Ba Ba, was in a world of shit, but they both had one thing in their favor, or so they thought—me.

Ba Ba and Tommy knew that I was the ultimate prize for the prosecutor and undoubtedly planned to hold out for sweetheart deals before agreeing to testify against me. Of course, they had no way of knowing that their testimony wouldn't be needed. In fact, they had no idea that I was working with the authorities and planned on testifying against *them*. I was the only significant witness against Ba Ba and Tommy, and while the testimony from a codefendant is always viewed with a suspicious eye, I did have something every prosecutor wants: lots of facts, lots of details, and the ability to deliver in a convincing way. Going to trial would be a real crapshoot for Tommy and Ba Ba, and if convicted, they would be facing serious time in prison. It was another game of chicken, a dangerous bluff that had the potential of exploding in their faces. Whether he liked it or not, Tom Seigel needed me, at least for the moment.

The FBI had a different agenda, and Phil Scala and Paul Harris quickly got down to business. They demanded to know the full scope of the gambling and game manipulation problem in the NBA—they wanted names. Scala presented a list of all active referees and instructed me to identify anyone who bet on golf, cards, horses, or sporting events, and anyone who gambled in casinos. Out of 60 referees, I pointed to approximately 50 names. Scala and Harris were shocked. Like any veteran investigator, Scala wasn't going to accept my word at face value; he had to follow up every lead and make a judgment for himself. That's how the probe of wide-scale abuses in the NBA began. After grilling me for hours in the first two interviews, the FBI smelled blood, and under the direction of Phil Scala, the investigation expanded. Agents fanned out across the country, following up on my information and interviewing dozens of prospective witnesses, including referees, coaches, and players. They watched hours of game tape, scrutinized every call, and reviewed dozens of game reports filed with the NBA front office by referees and referee supervisors.

I became the FBI's star witness, the inside guy with inside information. They wanted to get the whole truth about professional basketball, and I told them what I knew. Scala gave me the code name "Swish" and went to great lengths to shield me from the press and preserve the confidentiality and integrity of the investigation. I was instructed to avoid speaking with anyone about any aspect of the investigation unless he or she knew the secret code name. It was all a bit cloak and dagger to me, but they were dead serious. There was much work to be done and relatively little time to act. Seigel wanted to lock in my guilty plea and then go to work on Ba Ba and Tommy; he was in a hurry and on a mission. Scala had to move fast and make a case that would stick. I was along for the ride.

The days leading up to my August court date were nerve-racking. I dreaded the idea of walking into a courtroom and further humiliating my family, especially my father. He and my mother remained unwavering in their support after the shocking news broke. At the same time, I could sense a cloud of disappointment hanging in the air. I could sense it in every phone call and on every visit. I was ashamed for having done this to them, for tarnishing a family name that once stood for integrity and honesty. Most of all, I let my parents down and caused them to suffer needlessly. As I reflected back on my years of reckless and selfish behavior, I couldn't help but finally realize the depth of my immaturity. At 40, it was time to grow up.

At home, Kim and I were in full scramble mode. I was constantly on the phone with FBI agents, assisting with the investigation. The press continued to dog my every step. Friends and neighbors started to disappear. For the first time since high school I was out of a job, and the bills were piling up. On top of all that, I was preoccupied with a fear of going to prison. It added up to a grim realization that my life was falling apart, and I was dragging my family down with me. My relationship with Kim suffered greatly, and I could tell that the point of no return was fast approaching. All that was needed to push us over the edge was a little spark, like a single match dropped in a forest that erupts into an all-consuming sea of flames. I was hanging by a thread, and people all around me were making decisions about my future. In many respects, I just wanted to get it over with. I just wanted it to end.

Out of the blue, Tom Seigel called for another meeting one week before my plea hearing. John Lauro and I made the trip to New York thinking we were going to tie up a few loose ends and hopefully formalize my plea deal. But from the moment Seigel walked into the room, he was all over me, making accusations that I hadn't told them everything, that I had left important facts out of my story. I had no idea what he was talking about and the conversation quickly got out of hand. Seigel was screaming at me when Lauro finally intervened and demanded to know what he was talking about.

"Let's start with the SATs!" Seigel screamed.

The SATs? I couldn't believe what I was hearing. These guys were going way back, constantly digging and looking for anything to trip me up. Yes, 25 years earlier, I had a guy take the SAT college admissions test for me. My grades weren't quite good enough to get me into my hometown Villanova University, so I recruited the services of a rather bright upperclassman to take the test on my behalf. Unfortunately, he scored so high that the results were questioned and I was denied full-time admission. Eventually, I was allowed to attend night classes and prove myself. I did, and was subsequently enrolled in the regular full-time program.

As Seigel continued to berate me, I grew increasingly irritated. What in the hell did my actions as a stupid 17-year-old kid have to do with the current case? Well, it sure seemed to matter to Seigel, who pushed and pushed. I know he was just doing his job and was worried about my credibility, but at one point I'd had enough and snapped back.

"Hey, I also stuffed a kid in the closet back in the sixth grade and told the teacher he jumped out the window! Do you wanna talk about that, too?" I said.

Phil Scala came to my rescue and suggested we take a break. We walked down the hall and talked for 10 or 15 minutes.

"You know, Tim," he started, "you've given us a lot of explosive information and most of it checks out. Other stuff is harder to nail down. A lot of these guys aren't talking. I think they feel pressure from the NBA. Your credibility is very important, so when I say we need to know about anything negative in your past, I'm not kidding around. The news media is going to turn over every stone in your life, so we've got to know anything that might be front-page news."

Scala was a true professional. I could sense that he believed me, but he also had to make a case that would hold up in court. He was painfully aware that Seigel would have the final say on going forward against other subjects of investigation, so he had to get as much information as possible.

"Tim," he continued, "would you be willing to take a polygraph test?"

"In a New York minute," I immediately replied.

"That's all I had to hear, kid," Scala said.

Just like that the crisis passed, and I was back in the conference room poring over details, answering follow-up questions, helping Scala build the case. It was my last meeting with the FBI before going to court. Next up was a date with a federal judge and a very public admission of guilt.

In the days prior to leaving Florida for my plea hearing in New York, a quiet sadness descended over our house. Even the kids seemed to know that something bad was looming. I walked around like a zombie, going through the motions, consumed by worry. It was the beginning of a self-induced pity party, the kind where it seems as though the entire world is out to get its victim. Of course, I wasn't the victim. I was the one who brought this mess into my life and the lives of my loved ones. I constantly fought the doom and gloom and tried to put on an upbeat face, especially for my daughters. I may have fooled them, but I couldn't fool Kim—not this time, anyway. The roof was caving in and the inevitable was at hand. We decided that she would stay in Florida with the girls; they needed her support more than ever. Besides, I didn't want Kim to face the public humiliation of standing by my side and being viewed as the pathetic wife of a crooked referee. We had previously seen television coverage of doting wives standing stone-faced next to their fallen celebrity husbands, and wondered how they could do it. No, I just couldn't stomach the thought of Kim assuming the dreaded solitary pose while wisecracking pundits took potshots at a woman they knew nothing about. Kim and I said good-bye and I headed for the airport. As I drove away from my house, I had no idea what would happen to me or what would be waiting for me upon my return. I was still clinging to the hope that eventually there would be no jail time, but the prosecutor's unwillingness to make a firm commitment was troublesome. For now, I would admit my guilt and throw myself on the mercy of the court. I was about to make the once unthinkable transformation from regular citizen to convicted felon. Heaven help me!

* * *

Two FBI agents, Beth Ambinder and Chris LaManna, were waiting for me at the gate at La Guardia Airport. They whisked me away in an unmarked black sedan and tucked me in for the night at the Brooklyn Bridge Marriott Hotel. After a restless night's sleep, I was driven to the federal courthouse and entered the building through an underground entrance. The media was out in full force, hungry for a glimpse of the disgraced NBA referee and anxious for the gavel to drop and the fun to begin. I entered the jail reception area of the federal building complex and was promptly fingerprinted, handcuffed, and placed in a holding cell. After weeks of special treatment by the FBI, I hadn't fully anticipated the stark processing procedure of the federal court system.

Sitting in a 4' x 6' cement-block cell for over an hour, I was alone with my thoughts as sounds of doors clanking and guards shouting commands echoed through the hallway. It was the most embarrassing and humbling moment of my life. When it was time to face the judge, a group of five federal marshals escorted me through a maze of hallways and corridors to the courtroom. An outside observer would have thought I was the boss of a major crime family or the leader of an international drug cartel. The long walk was silent, and I couldn't help but think of the shame I brought to my family, my profession, and myself. I kept thinking that it was all just a bad dream, that I would wake up, grab a shower, and go referee a game. Madison Square Garden was a mile or so away, just across the East River, in the heart of Midtown. Spike Lee would be there, carrying on like a one-man cheerleading squad, whining, jawing, and screaming at the refs while cheering on his beloved Knicks. Yes, indeed, they would all be there, and I would be right in the middle of the action, center stage, and the center of attention.

But it wasn't a nightmare I was going to wake up from; it was reality, and more importantly, it was far from over.

Right before the hearing, Phil Scala pulled me aside and told me it would all work out.

"You made the right decision, Tim," he said. "It's painful now, but in the end you'll be a better man for having told the truth. You can walk with your head held high."

I wasn't ready to do that, but I found some comfort in Scala's words. He even offered to call my parents and let them know how it went in court. At last, I was ready to face the judge and get it over with.

Upon entering the courtroom, I took a quick glance around and observed the gallery overflowing with spectators. All of the FBI agents working on my case were sitting in the back row, offering simple nods of reassurance. The major newspaper and television sports journalists were jostling for position, feverishly trying to get a small logistical advantage over one another. Off to the side were two women, their legs straddling artists' easels covered with sketch paper. Although they were only 10 feet away, they peered at me through small binoculars, the kind used by patrons of the opera.

The bailiff quieted the crowd and announced the arrival of Federal District Court Judge Carol Amon. Looking directly at me, Judge Amon began to speak.

"Are you here to plead guilty, Mr. Donaghy?" she asked.

"Yes," I responded.

"You know the government has the burden of proof in every criminal case? And that you're entitled to a trial and you don't have to plead guilty?" she said.

"Yes, I know that," I replied.

Then, in an effort to make sure I was making my plea voluntarily and that I was of sound mind and judgment, Judge Amon continued.

"Are you currently taking any medications?" she asked.

"Antidepressants," I admitted with embarrassment. "I've been taking Xanax."

My reply drew a collective chuckle in the courtroom and plenty of media coverage over the following 24 hours.

Satisfied that I knew what I was doing, the judge asked one more question.

"Do you plead guilty?"

"Yes," I said. Just like that, it was over.

Sentencing was scheduled for November 9 and I was quickly hustled out of the courtroom and down a back service elevator to a waiting car.

Special Agent Harris drove me to La Guardia, flashed his badge, and brought me to the front of a long security screening line. I avoided the press altogether and was on a flight back home within a couple hours of the plea hearing.

Flying coach on a Delta Airlines 707, I was sandwiched between an elderly woman and a large man who weighed about 320 pounds. As I carefully sipped a Coke, the gentle giant tried to start a conversation.

"Where you headed?" he asked.

"Tampa," I replied.

"Me too, then I'm off to Vegas for a few days," he continued. "You been to Vegas?"

"Couple of times," I responded.

"Like to gamble?" he pressed.

"Used to. Not anymore."

"Got the best of you, huh?"

"You might say," I stated, turning away to look out the window.

I closed my eyes and pretended to be asleep. That was the end of our conversation. Once again I was alone with my thoughts, and my mind drifted to that winter day in 1992 when I first saw Kim on a commuter flight to Chicago. I remembered how captivating she looked in her flight attendant uniform and the bright smile she flashed as I boarded the plane. Neither one of us knew that fate would bring us together that day, or that we would ultimately pledge our lives to one another and bring four little girls into the world. Of course, neither one of us knew that I would eventually ruin everything and become a convicted felon, setting in motion a series of events that would alter the course of our lives. On the final approach to Tampa, I felt a sense of renewed excitement about my wife. I wanted to hold her and thank her for standing by my side. I wanted to start fresh, just the six of us. More than at any time since Tommy dropped the bombshell about the FBI, I was seeing things clearly and getting my priorities straight. I couldn't wait to get home.

After my guilty plea in federal court, the wire services and sports blogs were churning out the latest round of speculation and gossip. At least one journalist got it right. Chris Mannix of SI.com wrote a thought-provoking article entitled, "Trouble Ahead—Stern to Face More Backlash if Donaghy Fingers Others." The word was out that I was cooperating with federal officials in a gambling probe targeting NBA referees. Mannix wrote:

> What if Donaghy is right? What if nearly 20 officials have spent time at the craps table in Las Vegas or spent one of their off days in the casino in Milwaukee? What if a handful of them participate in a Sunday football pool?... If Stern chooses not to take action, it will only serve to increase the level of distrust the public feels toward the league. For many people, allowing officials to break *any* rules in the wake of the Donaghy scandal would be tantamount to condoning their actions. This is something the league simply cannot allow to happen. Stern may have wanted this crisis to be over, but it looks like he is about to be painted into a corner.

For me, reading the Mannix article was like listening to Phil Scala. During our many conversations, Scala often spoke of his interest in preserving the integrity of the game and restoring the public's confidence in NBA basketball. He didn't know where the investigation would lead, but it was a hand that had to be played, and like any good investigator, he was all in, consumed by the probe and dedicated to getting answers, whatever they may be. Scala told me point blank that he didn't believe I was the only referee who was a source of inside information. He insisted that if it was as easy as I described, others were doing it, too.

It wasn't the first time I had heard such a statement. Watching ESPN one evening, two former mobsters were interviewed about the scandal. Mike Franzese was a former captain in the Colombo crime family, and Henry Hill was a reformed wiseguy, once portrayed by the actor Ray Liotta in the movie *Goodfellas*. Both were commenting on the mob's connection to the case and the ramifications of my cooperation with the FBI. Franzese and Hill told ESPN that I would be looking over my shoulder for the rest of my life. As if things weren't bad enough, these guys are telling the world that I was a dead man walking! The comment was so upsetting to me that I Googled Franzese and located his email address. We subsequently had upwards of 10 telephone conversations, wherein Franzese told me he was a born-again Christian and that he was hired by Major League Baseball to lecture umpires on the dangers associated with gambling. In one particularly sobering discussion, Franzese stated that he had two NBA referees on his payroll in the mid-1990s. He refused to identify the referees, claiming it was in the past and that he would never hurt a former business associate.

This was the question on everyone's mind in the summer of 2007: just how big was the scandal? The media wanted to know, the prosecutor wanted to know, and Phil Scala wanted to know. Perhaps the only person who didn't want to know was NBA Commissioner David Stern.

* * *

As the investigation continued, I was playing Mr. Mom to my four daughters. Kim was forced to take a job at a local hospital, and I was hiding in our house desperately trying to avoid the media. The vigil outside my front door was in full swing—a virtual block party for the wandering band of gypsies. Kids from the neighborhood sold lemonade, a neighbor baked cookies, and the Good Humor truck canvassed the neighborhood in search of sun-baked reporters eager to spend their per diems on some frozen relief. It was like the circus that never left town.

My four daughters grew increasingly frustrated with the intrusion. They couldn't play outside, friends couldn't (or wouldn't) come over, and summer vacation became the summer of their discontent. It was time for revenge, and the girls conjured up a plan of attack. As two reporters and a photographer from the *New York Post* sat in a car at the end of our driveway, my 10-year-old daughter Shannon set the bait. She pressed the automatic garage-door opener and raised the door a couple of feet before pressing the button again and quickly lowering the door. As soon as the noisy door started to rise, two things happened. First, the occupants of the car jumped to attention and fumbled around, pen and pad in hand and telephoto lens in full focus. At virtually the same time, my three other daughters—Meghan, Bridget, and Molly—were giggling uncontrollably in the foyer near the front door. After the garage door closed, the reporters settled back and continued with their monotonous routine of listening to talk radio, playing a game of hearts, or catching 40 winks. Shannon repeated the gag two more times, enticing the same clumsy response. Up and down, up and down, went the door; up and down, up and down, went the three amigos. Finally, Shannon opened the door all the way and left it opened. The reporters roused slowly and cautiously made their way to the front of the driveway. Shannon seized the moment and loudly opened the interior garage door leading into the house. The unsuspecting newspaper crew took the bait and rushed up the driveway, ready to get an exclusive report for the next day's edition.

"A little closer, wait until they're a little closer," whispered Molly as she peeked through a front window at the doomed trespassers. "Now!" she shouted.

Her sister Bridget flipped the switch for the front-yard sprinkler system, dousing the intruders and sending them running for their lives—and a change of clothing. The pranksters had a good laugh, and so did their victims. Later that day, in a gesture of temporary reconciliation, all of the girls marched out the front door and waded into the crowd, handing out cold bottles of water to the press corps. The incident broke the tension, but nothing changed. The press wanted a story; they wanted a piece of me.

Kim and I sat down with our girls on many occasions during that summer, explaining the situation and reassuring them that everything would be all right. These were very confusing times for all of them, especially the youngest. Many of their friends suddenly disappeared, and as school resumed in mid-August, they heard whispers from some and outright taunts from others. "Your dad is a cheater!" was one of the more hurtful statements; "Your dad is going to jail!" was the knife through the heart.

Kim and I did our best to insulate the girls from the nasty press coverage, but kids can be very curious, especially when they know something big is taking place right in their front yard. I told each of my daughters that I had done something wrong and that I was going to be punished. I attempted to explain the details, including giving "secret" information about my job to bad people, betting on games, and breaking the law and the rules of my job. It was difficult to explain the intricacies, so I focused on concepts that are understandable to children ages seven through 12. I suppose that parents occasionally fail to realize that children are smarter and savvier than we give them credit for being; I know I surely did. I anguished over telling the girls, and labored over finding the right words to say what needed to be said. When it was done, I wasn't sure if I had satisfied their curiosity, let alone answered their questions. The statements that seemed to have the most impact were ones of reassurance and love—that's all any of us really want to hear during difficult times. When I was home that summer, the girls reveled in spending time with me. We were inseparable, the five of us clinging to one another, cherishing every moment spent together, and collectively taking on the world.

In one particularly poignant exchange, 10-year-old Shannon demonstrated a maturity beyond her years that almost left me speechless. Shannon is the second-oldest, a strawberry blonde with her mother's eyes and a heart of pure gold. Only a fourth grader at the time, she's the expressive, outgoing, always cheerful little girl that is liked, or loved, by everyone. Like me, she was into sports at an early age, playing softball and basketball on a team I coached.

Shortly after I entered a guilty plea in federal court, Shannon and I were alone watching television in the family room. Sitting on the couch, my arm around her and her head resting on my chest, I noticed that she seemed distracted and glum.

"What's on your mind Shannon?" I asked. "Is something bothering you?"

"No," she replied unconvincingly.

"Are you sure?" I gently persisted. "You know you can tell me anything, right?"

"I know," she said softly. "Dad, you didn't bet on games you reffed, did you?"

Stunned by her question, I tried to mask my amazement at the sophistication of the inquiry. I could hardly believe that my little girl could appreciate the distinction between betting on a basketball game that I didn't officiate versus a game that I did. I immediately thought of my Father's Day conversation with my dad. He wanted to know if I fixed games, and was openly relieved to learn that I did not. Distinctions! Shannon obviously perceived a difference between my reffing a game and not reffing a game. I wanted to ask what the distinction was, in her mind, but left it alone. She asked a question, an intelligent question, a tough question, and she deserved an honest answer.

"Yes, Shannon, I did. I shouldn't have done it, any of it, but I did," I said.

There was a pause, and I watched her eyes as she digested my response. Finally, she squeezed me tight and nestled a little closer.

"That's okay, Dad. I love you," she said.

"I love you too, sweetheart," I replied.

It was an unbelievable moment for me. I wished that none of this had happened, that I hadn't brought this tragedy to our lives, that my little girls weren't burdened with such concerns. At the same time, I witnessed the love and strength of my daughters under trying circumstances. I witnessed Shannon blossom into a thoughtful and caring young girl. I witnessed the bond I shared with my girls grow stronger—and I knew that we could weather any storm and remain a family.

CHAPTER 12

Judgment Day

As late August rolled around, I was breathing easier and enjoying the brief respite between my plea hearing and the looming sentencing scheduled for November. Kim was finding her groove at her new job, the kids were in school, and I was still assisting the FBI. The press was camped outside my door, as usual, but the coverage had tapered off and I lowered my guard. After all, the cat was out of the bag—what else could possibly happen? Unfortunately, I was about to find out.

I received an unexpected phone call from John Lauro on August 26, and he informed me that the *New York Post* was running a story the next day identifying an Arizona woman as my girlfriend and suggesting that she was being investigated by the FBI as part of its ongoing NBA gambling probe.

"Well?" John asked, after a short pause.

"I know her, we've been friends for a couple of years," I replied.

Her name was Cheryl, and we met at a sports bar and restaurant she owned in Phoenix. The place was a popular watering hole for referees and players, and we started a conversation that blossomed into a friendship. I usually stopped by for dinner when in town to work a Suns game, and on several occasions I gave her two game tickets, which she shared with a friend. I never told Kim about my friendship with Cheryl, and that alone was wrong. More importantly, it is always inappropriate for a married man to have a secret relationship with another woman, even if it's of an innocent nature. Of course, the moment John told me of the *Post*'s intentions, I knew that my already strained and increasingly fragile marriage was about to be put to the ultimate test.

The headline read, "Dirty Ref's 'Sideline Gal' Eyed by Feds."

The source for the story was anonymous, but I had a good idea who it was—Tommy Martino. Tommy and I had dinner together at Cheryl's restaurant back in January. Tommy was in Phoenix to deliver my 10,000 apples and have a night on the town before heading back to Philly. I introduced him to Cheryl and the three of us had some drinks as Tommy told one hilarious story after another. It was quite an evening, one that obviously made an impression on Tommy.

If Tommy was the source, it wasn't hard to discern what his reason for talking to the *Post* was. Reports of my cooperating with the FBI had been swirling for weeks, and the guilty plea confirmed my status as a government witness. With my guilty plea on the books, Ba Ba and Tommy no longer had any leverage to work favorable deals for themselves. They knew I was prepared to testify against them and expose the entire operation. For Tommy, my testimony would be particularly problematic, as it would contradict what he told the grand jury. It's one thing to commit a gambling crime—it's another to take the oath and perjure yourself to the grand jury, the Assistant U.S. Attorney, and God above.

Boxed into a corner, Tommy's last option was to strike back and attack my credibility. In typical fashion, he let the *New York Post* do his bidding. It didn't matter; Tommy did what he thought he had to do, for self-preservation, for spite, for whatever. As for me, I was left with the aftershocks of a Richter scale–busting earthquake, the kind of jolt that can tear a house apart.

When Kim read the story, she was livid. It was one more humiliating revelation, one that no woman wants to hear let alone read in the tabloids. Before I could say a word, she told me it was over. She had endured the entire ordeal with a certain strength and determination, but this was too much—this was personal. The drama in our lives had gone from the ridiculous to the sublime and my wife of 12 years had had enough.

Once again, the pain and heartbreak rested on my shoulders, but this time I couldn't make it go away. Ten days later, Kim filed for divorce; our marriage was over.

* * *

Back in New York, Tom Seigel suddenly left the U.S. Attorneys' Office for a turn in private practice. I had mixed feelings about Seigel's departure. Although we never got along very well, he struck me as a dedicated public servant prepared to do whatever it took to get the truth. More importantly, he wasn't afraid to step on a few toes to get the job done. Seigel was replaced by Assistant U.S. Attorney Jeffrey Goldberg, a professional but hard-nosed career prosecutor who didn't appear to be emotionally invested in the case. Seigel had been on the case from the onset, and now Goldberg was being called upon for mop-up duty. Some mop up! Big decisions still had to be made. Ba Ba and Tommy were holding out, Scala's investigation was steaming along, and the entire sporting world wanted to know what was going on in the NBA. The only matter ready for closure was mine. With sentencing just a few weeks away, the heavy lifting was done. I did my part, Scala was doing his—it was up to Goldberg to take care of the rest. The first orders of business were Tommy and Ba Ba.

Tommy was in a sticky situation. As a result of my guilty plea, he was no longer in a position to offer up his testimony against me in exchange for a lighter sentence. He quickly turned to Plan B and agreed to testify against Ba Ba. By FBI standards, Tommy was a small fish in the operation, a low-level hack stuck in the middle between the big prize (me) and the boss (Ba Ba). Tommy's decision came with certain risks. Ba Ba was holding tight, not naming names and protecting his bosses. Loyalty like that has to be rewarded, and Tommy undoubtedly knew he was playing a dangerous game. Tommy had concerns, but he wasn't about to take one for the team. No sir, if someone had to be sacrificed, it wasn't going to be Tommy. Besides, Ba Ba stiffed Tommy on his cut of the apples one time too many times. So Tommy cut the deal, and on April 16, 2008, he became the second piece to fall, pleading guilty in federal court to wire fraud. Charges of perjury and conspiracy to transmit wagering information were dropped.

As defense lawyers are known to do, Tommy's attorney, Vicki Herr, put a good spin on the situation: "Martino allowed himself to be used by people he considered to be very good friends who he knew all his life."

Sure, Tommy, okay.

With Tommy assuming the title of convicted felon, Ba Ba was next. A deal for his guilty plea was tentatively reached, but at the last minute, Ba Ba backed out. It was a strange development, one that usually irritates a prosecutor and forces him to quickly shift gears and get ready for trial. The strangest aspect of Ba Ba's change of heart was the lack of any realistic prospect of winning at trial. Both Tommy and I were prepped and ready to go. We knew the whole story and were prepared to expose the operation, including Ba Ba's major role, in great detail. I had a lengthy session with FBI agents and prosecutors in Brooklyn, reviewing the investigation, going over the details, and answering questions that would likely be posed on direct and cross-examination.

Despite the fact that Ba Ba was running out of time and seemingly out of luck, he didn't flinch. It made no sense. He wasn't just holding a bad hand; he didn't even have a card to play! Ba Ba wouldn't dream of being a rat. If I had been in his shoes, I would've been worried about my health and the well-being of my family. I knew that Ba Ba knew the drill as well as anyone and would never cooperate with the feds. Besides, for a gambling beef he was only looking at three to five years at the very worst. Who knows? The time away from the pills, the booze, and the casinos might do him some good—a real rehab.

So what was his angle? If he had no leverage, why was he messing around? Why not end this thing and enter a plea? Everyone knows that you get a better sentence on a plea. Hell, you're admitting your guilt, taking responsibility, and saving the system the time and expense of a jury trial. Going to trial and getting convicted by a jury is an entirely different matter.

Just when I thought Ba Ba's behavior couldn't get any more bizarre, his lawyer, Jack McMahon, turned up the heat and took the game to a new level. In a surprising statement to the press, McMahon upped the ante and sounded like he was *daring* the prosecutors to take them to trial, where he would get the chance to question me on the witness stand.

"I look forward to him testifying for a very, very long time," he boldly proclaimed.

That kind of bravado by the captain of a sinking ship is typically unheard of in legal circles, but McMahon wasn't exactly a conformist. My father used to say that it didn't take a Philadelphia lawyer to read the writing on the wall, but I remained baffled. Jack McMahon, on the other hand, *is* a Philadelphia lawyer, and he knew exactly what he was doing. So did Special Agent Phil Scala.

Scala knew of McMahon's reputation as a guy who represented defendants linked to organized crime. He also knew that McMahon was nobody's fool and always played to win. In the legal system, winning comes in various forms, and it doesn't necessarily take an acquittal to achieve victory. No, sometimes victory comes on a smaller scale, like a reduced sentence or avoiding a large restitution order. No doubt any victory sounded pretty good to Ba Ba, in light of the circumstances. Even so, any form of victory had to be cultivated, and when Jack McMahon went public, he was sowing the seeds.

"He's sending a message to the NBA," Lauro said. "The last thing Stern wants is a trial with you on the witness stand."

If Ba Ba went to trial, the gloves were coming off. I would likely spend several days on the witness stand, painstakingly detailing the games, the wagers, and of most importance to the NBA, how I was able to make successful picks 70 or 80 percent of the time. Imagine the litany of questions I would face on direct examination:

Q: Mr. Donaghy, how did you make the picks?

A: I focused on the Master List of Referees to locate game assignments for certain referees.

Q: Why were you looking for certain referees?

A: Because after many years in the league, I knew their biases, tendencies, and special relationships that could affect the outcome of a game.

Q: Give us an example, please.

A: Do you have a preference?

Q: Let's start with Dick Bavetta.

A: Okay, but this is going to take a while.

Q: Take as much time as you need.

After Dick Bavetta, there would have been questions about Joe Crawford, Steve Javie, Jess Kersey, Derrick Stafford, and on and on. The NBA's dirty little secret would be fully exposed, not in some second-rate tabloid report, but in a federal court of law.

The prospect of a courtroom exposé on the culture of fraud in the NBA would be David Stern's worst nightmare. Because of my actions, the league had already suffered a black eye. With my testimony, the hemorrhaging would be almost uncontrollable. It was time to stop the bleeding.

Shortly after McMahon's public statement, a deal was struck, and the man who had no card to play walked away with the pot. Ba Ba entered a plea to a single gambling charge with sentencing scheduled for the summer. The full extent of his victory wouldn't be known for several months, but any way you sliced it, Ba Ba did well for himself. But the biggest winner in the reputation sweepstakes never set foot in the courtroom: NBA Commissioner David Stern finished the fast break with an easy layup.

I will never know exactly how or why things with Ba Ba turned out the way they did. All I know is that my cooperation with the FBI left him without any leverage or cards to play, yet he somehow got a favorable deal after his attorney floated the idea of taking the case to trial where he knew I would be a key witness. Maybe Ba Ba thought he had a better chance at trial than he really did. Or maybe there's a less charitable explanation. All I know is that my potential testimony in open court would have proved hugely embarrassing in certain quarters.

For a variety of reasons, my November sentencing date was scratched and eventually rescheduled for May 22, 2008. The FBI investigation was still ongoing, and Assistant U.S. Attorney Goldberg didn't want me sentenced until my cooperation had been completed. The same rationale was applied to my role in Ba Ba's and Tommy's cases: no sentencing until I fulfilled all of my obligations. Since Ba Ba and Tommy didn't enter guilty pleas until April of 2008, I was in limbo for months.

Meanwhile, my divorce proceedings were also in the court system, so I was dealing with another lawyer and a different set of issues. During the week, I took care of the kids while Kim worked at the hospital. We were suddenly living separate lives as though we had never been married, as though the previous 12 years had never occurred. I did my best to stay strong for the girls, but there was so much uncertainty about the future and so many issues to be resolved.

* * *

Phil Scala had his hands full. Thousands of pages filled with interviews and investigative reports were contained in case folders bulging at the seams. The legwork was finished, and Scala was convinced that more prosecutions were not only appropriate but necessary to root out and expose the underlying culture of fraud that had permeated, and eventually saturated, the game. Still, he knew there would be obstacles to systemic change, and he believed that the NBA would make every conceivable effort to resist that change.

"Listen, I'm telling you right now," he said. "The NBA's in a lot of trouble. Don't take hush money from them, because they're gonna offer you hush money. They have no way out from this, other than to keep you quiet."

The day after Scala filed his report, he called to tell me he was retiring. At age 58, mandatory retirement had arrived. My initial reaction was despair and panic. Scala started out as my adversary, but through every step of the prosecution against me, I had come to realize what an honest and decent man he is. As much as anyone, Scala showed me how to handle adversity with honesty and dignity, not to mention boatloads of humility. He was the captain of the ship, and I feared all of his hard work would drift away and eventually disappear on the horizon. It was his concern too, but someone else would have to carry the torch—he was officially off the clock.

Shortly after Ba Ba and Tommy entered their pleas in federal court, the NBA went on the offensive. John Lauro received a call from a high-priced, high-powered lawyer named Larry Pedowitz. Pedowitz, the former chief of the criminal division in the U.S. Attorneys' Office for the Southern District of New York, had been hired by the NBA to conduct an independent investigation and to file a report of his findings with Commissioner Stern. In the call to Lauro, Pedowitz demanded to interview me; the NBA was not privy to the FBI's investigative report, and Stern and Pedowitz wanted to know what I knew before it was made public in court.

Despite Pedowitz's demand, Lauro took a firm stand and declined his request. The FBI investigation, although completed in principle, was still ongoing. Additionally, Ba Ba, Tommy, and I had yet to be sentenced, and that meant no cooperation with any organization outside of law enforcement.

Pedowitz didn't take kindly to the rejection of his demand. He fired off a letter to Lauro informing us that if I wasn't immediately made available for an interview, he would notify the court, on behalf of the NBA, that I had refused to assist in his investigation and therefore was refusing to assist the "victim" of my crimes. It sounded like a threat, one that I didn't take kindly to. The FBI had stressed confidentiality in the investigation from day one—I was to speak with *no one*. The NBA had a separate agenda, and I chose to honor my commitments to the FBI.

As May approached, Federal District Court Judge Carol Amon raised concerns about the disparity in sentencing recommendations for me, Ba Ba, and Tommy. Once again, sentencing was postponed, this time to June 29, 2008.

In early June, Lauro met with then-retired Phil Scala at a restaurant in Manhattan. Scala told him that the investigation yielded at least five to six other individuals of interest—including NBA referees—who could have been further investigated but that time, scarcity of resources, and statute issues had precluded it. Around the same time, Larry Pedowitz sent Lauro an email again demanding to know what I told the FBI and threatening to appear at my sentencing.

As a former federal prosecutor, Larry Pedowitz had sway, the kind of juice that provides unique access to the people who make decisions about things like whether or not to pursue a prosecution. The FBI, however, is independent of the U.S. Attorneys' Office, and even in the world of criminal justice, turf battles are commonplace. The FBI, thanks in large part to Phil Scala's personality, wouldn't play the game. Nevertheless, the U.S. Attorney had the final say. Further prosecutions would be a "no-go."

To this day, I don't fully know why the individuals Scala felt were worthy of investigating escaped further scrutiny. Maybe the U.S. Attorneys' Office felt that my conviction sent an appropriate message, or that while more investigation might uncover wrongdoing, they would not be prosecutable offenses. Maybe the fact that my story had broken removed the element of surprise that could have aided an extended probe. Maybe the departures of Scala and Seigel caused the investigation to lose its momentum. Maybe political strings were being pulled to make sure I was cemented in the public's mind as the "lone assassin." Or maybe it was a combination of all of them.

With my sentencing fast approaching, the NBA filed court papers demanding that I be ordered to pay more than $1 million in restitution as part of my sentence. John Lauro was more convinced than ever that the NBA wanted to punish me for not assisting with its unofficial investigation, while simultaneously keeping pressure on the U.S. Attorney to refrain from charging others in the growing scandal. It was all about portraying me as the rogue referee who violated the public trust and tarnished the reputation of a proud American sporting institution. More importantly, Lauro felt that Pedowitz, as the NBA's point guard, was attempting to influence the court's perception of me, thereby extracting a more severe penalty, one that would keep me in prison—and off the front page—for years. This was Lauro's biggest fear: that my months of cooperation with the FBI would be forgotten. Despite my wrongdoings, I had voluntarily agreed to cooperate with the FBI from the very beginning, and did so for a grueling 10-month period. I admitted my guilt and was prepared to receive a just punishment. I simply wanted the court to know all the relevant facts.

Lauro had had enough of the NBA's meddling and filed public documents with the court challenging the demand for restitution and outlining, in some detail, facts underlying the extent of my cooperation with the FBI. Lauro was determined to trump the shenanigans of the NBA and proceed to sentencing with full disclosure to the court.

Lauro's filing triggered a nationwide response from sports journalists who were shocked by the explosive disclosures about bias, manipulation, and fraud in the NBA. It was out there, in the court of public opinion, a tangible glimpse into the inner workings of a league that survived largely because of its reputation for integrity. *Sports Illustrated* basketball writer Phil Taylor summed up the feelings of many in the sporting world:

> Stern can shout from the top of the Manhattan skyscraper that houses the league's headquarters that none of Donaghy's allegations are true, but the real problem for the NBA is that hardly anyone would be surprised if they were.

In an interesting commentary on the disclosures made in Lauro's submission to the court, none other than Los Angeles Lakers coach Phil Jackson voiced his opinion in a *New York Post* article:

> You know, a lot of things have happened in the course of the Tim Donaghy disposition. I think we have to weigh it as it comes out, and we all think that probably referees should be under a separate entity than the NBA entirely. I mean, that's what we'd like to see probably in the NBA. It would just be separate and apart from it. But I don't think that's going to happen. That's just a want and desire in the area of having everything apart from the NBA that can be apart from the NBA.

Of course, Jackson's Lakers team was the beneficiary of the NBA's broken system against Sacramento in Game 6 of the 2002 Western Conference Finals. When the *Post* reporter brought up the controversial 2002 series, Jackson's response was cautiously revealing: "A lot of things have been suspicious."

In response to Lauro's bombshell release of information, Assistant U.S. Attorney Goldberg demanded that I return to New York on June 24. It would be my last meeting with the prosecutors and federal agents working the case. Goldberg was visibly upset, reeling over the disclosures contained in Lauro's public filing. He had worked hard to keep the damaging information under wraps, but after one fact-packed letter from Lauro, the genie was out of the bottle. Goldberg was careful not to reveal the real reason for his angst; he just stammered through a general admonition against further disclosures. Then he awkwardly changed focus and began cross-examining me about whether or not I had taken a lie detector test without his knowledge. The answer was a resounding "Yes!"

Ever since Phil Scala had raised the notion of administering a lie detector test, I was anxious to get strapped to the box and answer a few questions. I always knew there would be questions about my credibility, something a polygraph test could help address. Unlike so many defendants who talk a good game about taking a test and then politely decline, I actually viewed a test as an opportunity to prove my truthfulness to the authorities, and on May 14, 2007, I did just that.

The test was conducted by the firm of McDuffie, Jones & Associates in Sarasota, Florida. After a lengthy pretest interview, the examiner selected four specific questions for the actual test:

1. Did Dick Bavetta tell you the NBA put him on certain games throughout the years to make sure a certain team won?
ANSWER: Yes

2. Did Don Vaden make contact and discuss confidential information with Jeff Van Gundy about the 2005 playoff series?
ANSWER: Yes

3. Did Mike Marso tell you that "incorrect calls" were changed on the computer system for certain referees to keep their stats up?
ANSWER: Yes

4. Did referees bet on who would call the first foul in an NBA game?
ANSWER: Yes

Examiner Joe McDuffie scored the test and indicated I passed with flying colors:

> Test Findings: Based on chart interpretation, there was no reaction indicative of deception on subject's polygraph examination when he answered the above listed questions.

I couldn't help but wonder why Goldberg was so concerned about my taking a polygraph test. Surely he would love some scientific corroboration of my claims…or would he? Without the test, an allegation could be dismissed rather easily as one person's word against another's. With the test, it was an entirely different story. Granted, polygraph examinations are not permitted in court, but the court of public opinion isn't bound by the same rules. More importantly, prosecutors routinely utilize polygraphs to test the veracity of witnesses' claims and allegations. Goldberg should have been elated with the result. He wasn't.

The meeting ended with a flurry of pleas to refrain from further public statements—for the "good of the case." There was a definite shift in demeanor toward me, and I began to feel as though the period of my usefulness to the prosecutor had passed. Despite all of the time we spent together, despite the FBI's unqualified support of my claims, despite the polygraph results, the prosecutor was cutting the cord and washing his hands of me. Sentencing was next, and once again, I was on my own.

On July 24, Judge Amon sentenced Tommy to a year and a day. With good behavior, he would be out in nine months. Ba Ba was next, and he received 15 months in prison. He was required to repay just a fraction of the money he earned on the back of my picks. Pete Ruggieri and my old friend Jack Concannon were never charged. July 29, 2008, was judgment day for me.

For the previous six months, I had been sleeping on a couch in a friend's condo. With no income, no reserves, and no family in Florida to fall back on, I was at the bottom, constantly thinking about all the wrong moves I had made over the years. It wasn't so much self-pity as a cold evaluation of a life gone wrong. With no one to blame but myself, I had lost many things that can never be retrieved. In the Catholic faith, Saint Anthony is the patron saint of lost souls, and as my day of reckoning drew near, I prayed to him for mine.

I was also receiving court-ordered treatment for my gambling addiction, regularly seeing an individual therapist and attending weekly group meetings. Night after night I would listen to stories of havoc and devastation brought to people's lives through gambling addiction. Sometimes the stories seemed so pathetic and far removed from my own; when I was honest with myself, the stories were no different at all. Despite recurring thoughts and temptations, I stayed clean and sober. I haven't placed a bet since the spring of 2007, not because I didn't want to, but because I wouldn't allow myself to make one.

My parents urged me to fly to New Jersey the day before my sentencing and spend the night at their home in Sea Isle City. They also suggested driving to New York together on the morning of sentencing. I had initially planned to face the music alone, but they insisted on attending—I was their son, and we would go as a family. I couldn't say no. I didn't want to.

I arrived in Atlantic City and was greeted by the reassuring embrace of my mother and father. After a quick 30-minute drive to Sea Isle City, I breathed easy. It was good to escape all the madness for a few hours and feel the warmth and security of a seaside retreat that had been in our family for years. My parents tried to keep the mood light and upbeat. Familiar ocean smells drifted through the open windows and the scent of a home-cooked meal wafted out of the kitchen. I felt like a kid again, safe from the outside world, lost in the comfort of my parents' love.

I excused myself and went to my father's office to check my email and make a last call home to the girls. Dad's office was a shrine to his long career as a college basketball referee, the walls covered with framed photos of him in action on the court or posing with colleagues and lifelong friends. These images represent the treasured memories of a storied career for a man who cherished the game of basketball and profoundly appreciated the many wonderful opportunities it afforded him.

I was proud to share a prominent place on the wall with my father. Shortly after beginning my career in the NBA, our Pennsylvania hometown newspaper ran a huge front-page story featuring the Donaghy family tradition of officiating college and pro basketball. It covered my father's impressive career and talked about me assuming the mantle and continuing his legacy. The newspaper ran a great picture of me and Dad, side by side, him brimming with pride. My father has always been a stoic person, a man of few words, and one not quick to heap glowing praise. In the story, he spoke with uncharacteristic public affection, complimenting me and touting my abilities.

"He deserves to be there," he boasted with the enthusiasm of an obviously proud father.

I loved that newspaper story and treasured it as much as he did, probably more. The day it went up on the wall was a great day for me. It signified a rite of passage, an acceptance into the fraternity, and the respect of a man whose respect I had craved all my life.

As I leaned back in my father's well-worn swivel chair, I smiled with great contentment, fondly reviewing the photos with which I was so intimately familiar. The smile slowly faded and my heartbeat quickened as I suddenly noticed a sizeable void on the wall, a void punctuated by a solitary picture frame hook, surrounded by the remaining collage of happy memories. *It was gone.* I looked around the room, opened a few drawers, and peered into the crack between the desk and the wall. *It was gone.* My heart sank—he was silently ashamed of me and could no longer bear to include the story, our story, in his sacred collection. I just sat there, stoned with devastation, the final lash of a severe whipping. I knew that all of the pain endured by my family rested at my feet, but I was stunned by the simple removal of a treasured photo from the wall of my father's private office. After several minutes of sitting in solitary silence, I gathered myself and joined my parents for dinner. The conversation was light yet strained, and for the life of me I cannot remember what we ate. All I could think about was that missing picture. I occasionally stole a glimpse of my father as he ate his food, desperately wanting to ask the question, but I couldn't do it. I never said a word.

The drive to New York was quiet. The time for fear and anxiety had long since passed. I fully submitted myself to the process and was resigned to the inevitable result. There would be no strategy, no ploys, no endgame, just simple contrition and an acceptance of my personal failures. In many respects, the prospect of losing my freedom paled in comparison to my other losses. My boyhood dream of being in the NBA was over. I disgraced myself and dishonored my family name. I betrayed my father's legacy and broke my mother's heart. I lost my marriage and the love of my life. I caused four beautiful little girls to join the sad ranks of children everywhere who come from a broken home. I lost my way.

Finally, with my head held steady, I entered the chamber, prepared to give to Caesar that which belonged to Caesar. Judge Amon was sharp with her rebuke, but not unfair. I agreed with all of her words, and understood that they weren't meant just for my ears. It was important to hold me to a higher standard and to make an example of my transgressions. She sentenced me to 15 months in prison and ordered me to pay $217,000 in restitution. I was particularly alert while she pronounced sentence, almost like an observer in the gallery, hanging on her every word. Regrettably, the prosecutor made no mention whatsoever of my lengthy cooperation with the FBI in its probe of the NBA. It was as though the months of investigation had never taken place.

The court process was finally over, but my adventure was just beginning. Prison was next, and although I didn't fully know what to expect, I sensed that for the first time in a very long time, I was actually moving forward. The court system calls it punishment and justice. My faith calls it penance and salvation. Call it what you will; for me, it was time to pay the piper.

On my previous trips to New York for meetings or court appearances, the prosecutor's office and the FBI rolled out the red carpet. I was picked up at the airport, chauffeured to my destination, and secretly transported into buildings. No effort was spared to protect my privacy and keep the hungry media wolves at arm's length…but not this time. With the sudden thud of a cadaver hitting the pavement after a 20-story fall, I was left to fend for myself. I suppose it had something to do with Lauro's letter, the polygraph test, and the prosecutor's new attitude.

I walked out of the courtroom accompanied by my parents, family friend Father Rob Hagan, and retired FBI agents Phil Scala and Warren Flagg. Immediately diving into a sea of reporters, television cameramen, and jeering courthouse rubberneckers, I told my parents to hang back until I was well out of sight and the media had their fill. My father, however, insisted on walking the gauntlet at my side, and as we weaved our way through the horde, he put his arm around my shoulder and gave me a squeeze. Whatever shame or humiliation he felt was overshadowed by his natural instinct to be a father and to comfort a troubled son. From that point, I walked a little taller and was ready to face the world.

On my other side was Phil Scala. He had been there from the very beginning and insisted on standing with me to the bitter end. It was extraordinary. A crusty, seasoned veteran who had once intimidated me with tales of standing toe-to-toe with John Gotti was now my cherished friend. Scala, of all people, knew what I had gone through, and he believed in me. Expressions of friendship come in all shapes and sizes; Phil Scala's simple gesture was the biggest and brightest of them all.

A few days later, the *New York Daily News* ran a story lauding Scala's involvement in some of the biggest crime investigations in New York history, including mine. Scala was asked to comment on whether he believed I had been honest with investigators.

"Donaghy told us the truth," Scala said. "He was as emotional and remorseful as I've ever seen a cooperator. In the course of my relationship with him, I had the insight that he was intent on repaying his debt to society, restoring his family's faith in him and trying to make something better out of his life."

I returned to Bradenton and the couch in my friend's condo. Around the same time my divorce was finalized. A letter from the United States Marshal would arrive in a few weeks, an official notification of my designation to the Federal Prison Camp in Pensacola, Florida. I began the process of preparing myself for prison, and the expected fears and anxieties set in. For the most part, I was determined to enter prison with the goal of spending my time in a positive way, continuing with my treatment for gambling addiction, maintaining my health and fitness, and utilizing the time away from home to reflect on the man I was and the man I wanted to be.

In an unexpected but greatly appreciated gesture of kindness, Kim invited me to spend my last night of freedom at her new home with my daughters. As I lay down to sleep that night, my girls, one by one, hopped up onto the bed and snuggled close, as if holding on for dear life. For just a moment, a brief wonderful moment, it was like old times—we were together, five sleeping souls comforted by the warmth of each other's love.

CHAPTER

Life Behind Bars

"All right Donaghy, bend over and grab those ankles. Let's see some chicken eye!"

Those words, spoken by a gruff corrections officer as I stood buck naked on a cold concrete floor, signified my crude introduction to the federal prison system. Chicken eye, of course, is a euphemistic reference to the opening of a certain body cavity located on one's backside. In prison, any orifice is subject to inspection, and mine was no exception.

"C'mon, spread 'em!" the officer barked. "I ain't got all day!"

After years of running up and down the court in the NBA, I was in fairly good shape, but I wasn't a human pretzel. As the blood rushed to my head, I could hear the sound of a flashlight clicking on and off and I noticed an intermittent flash on the wall. When he was good and satisfied that I was contraband-free, the guard tossed a one-size-fits-all orange jumpsuit in my direction and instructed me to get dressed. Gladly!

Before my release into the general population, I was fingerprinted, photographed, and given an identification card that boldly stated that I was the property of the Federal Bureau of Prisons. In the course of a quick 45 minutes of intake screening, I was stripped, probed, rolled, flashed, and renamed. My new identity was simply Inmate Donaghy, No. 75377-053.

The Federal Prison Camp in Pensacola is located in the extreme western section of the Florida panhandle, near the Florida-Alabama state line. Pensacola is a navy town and home to a massive naval air station on the Gulf of Mexico, better known as a training facility for navy pilots and the famed precision flying team, the Blue Angels. Naval Air Station Pensacola is supported by several smaller satellite bases located in the surrounding area, one of which is Saufley Field. Used heavily as a training facility during the Vietnam War, today Saufley Field is a slowly evaporating installation that currently leases space to the Bureau of Prisons for a federal prison camp.

At first blush, the camp looks similar to any aging, second-tier university campus in America. The tranquil setting, however, belies the pain, heartache, mental illness, and simmering anger that inhabit the inner bowels of the institution. FPC Pensacola is, after all, a prison, and prisons are filled with criminals.

Back in the day, the camp was regarded as a country club, the population relatively small and the clientele predominantly white-collar. Lawyers and bankers and Wall Street traders were sent to Florida from all around the country, sentenced to little more than extended vacations on the Gulf Coast. With the stepped-up war on drugs in the mid-1980s, the federal prison population exploded, and bed space became scarce. To curb overcrowding, prison camps were opened up to a massive influx of drug dealers and other nontraditional invitees. The camps changed forever; they were edgier, overcrowded, unpredictable, and more dangerous. That's exactly the world I stepped into on September 23, 2008.

Walking around the compound in a blaze-orange jumpsuit, I stood out like a sore thumb. As I passed by other inmates, their eyes looked me over with distant curiosity, and I heard lightly spoken mutterings.

"Fresh fish," someone whispered.

The word was out around the camp that the disgraced NBA ref was coming to Pensacola, and ESPN broadcast my arrival throughout the day. There were whispers and fingers pointed in my direction.

"That's him, that's the ref," another inmate said.

Some of the last advice I received before leaving Bradenton to travel north was to fly under the radar, attract no attention, and disappear into the prison population. I quickly learned that there was no chance of that. The population was young, mostly African American and Hispanic inmates from South Florida. This group loved to sit in front of the television sets located throughout the camp for hours at a time, watching sports television all day and all night. They knew NBA basketball, and they knew my case. Many had been talking about my arrival for weeks, eager to force a confrontation and to provoke a response.

I was given a room assignment on the third floor of the main housing unit, the farthest point from the control center guard station. The building was laid out dormitory style, with a long corridor running in each direction from a center lobby. Adjoining rooms—the actual living quarters—were small, approximately 15' x 20', stuffed with six metal-framed industrial-strength bunk beds occupied by 12 grown men of every size, shape, and color. Add in 12 short-stack metal lockers and the fit was tight and too close for comfort.

After a quick trip to the prison laundry to get "dressed out" in green institution-issued work pants and matching shirt—complete with name tag and registration number—I made my first foray into the housing unit. Walking up three flights of stairs crowded with loitering inmates gawking at my every step, I realized that all eyes were on me. I was carrying a bundle in my arms, including a bedroll and various towels and institutional toiletry items, but no one was in a hurry to clear the hallway or to let me pass unmolested. Several rather large men with tattoo-covered arms and bulging biceps stood their ground as I passed, forcing me to hug the wall and slide by in an effort to avoid physical contact. Up and down the hallway, antagonizing comments were thrown my way.

"Rat bastard!"

"It's the refereeeeeeeee!"

"Hey, Zebra!"

As I inched closer to my room, one particularly tough-looking con with a toothpick protruding from the corner of his mouth walked by and lowered his shoulder into mine, causing me to jerk back and momentarily lose my balance.

"You owe me money!" he exclaimed.

I just dropped my eyes and kept walking.

"I want my money, bitch!" he yelled.

Spotting my room number on a small placard above the heavy solid-oak door, I turned around and backed my way in without further incident. For the moment, I found safe haven in my new digs, surrounded by 11 stone-faced inmates, my "cellies," who were not particularly pleased with my arrival.

I looked around the room and spotted an open bunk, an upper, in the middle of the room, and began to organize my things. Initially, there was silence; I had no idea if it was appropriate for me to introduce myself and start asking questions. Eventually someone broke the ice.

"You the ref?" he asked.

"Yeah, that's me. Tim Donaghy," I said, extending my arm for a handshake.

The other inmate appeared caught off guard and clearly didn't want to shake hands. Instead, he reluctantly extended his arm with a closed fist. I likewise made a fist and we butted knuckles like baseball players celebrating a home run in the dugout. There were a few follow-up questions about where I was from and the length of my sentence, but not much more. One cellie explained a few "rules of the room," and offered to loan me a pair of shower shoes until I could purchase my own. The rest of the guys went about their business, playing cards, listening to music, and reading magazines.

I went looking for a bathroom and immediately noticed that the hallway was filthy and cluttered with trash. The bathroom was considerably worse. Toilet paper, soap wrappers, empty shampoo bottles, ripped canned-food labels, and other items of debris were strewn about the floor. The toilet seats were spotted with droplets of urine and the bowls were caked with dried feces. The sinks were stained with a variety of disgusting substances including dried and fresh toothpaste, nasal excrement, blood, and lots of hair follicles, clippings, and shavings. I couldn't imagine where all the hair was coming from until I noticed a young shirtless inmate meticulously shaving his entire body with a handheld electric hair trimmer. I would later learn that this was a common practice of the Hispanic population, a sort of metrosexual approach to personal grooming. Of course, all of the arm, leg, abdomen, and chest clippings were left where they fell.

After a long and emotionally draining day, I was exhausted and decided to turn in as early as possible. I made one last trip to the bathroom to use the facilities and brush my teeth. As I stood over the sink, an elderly inmate to my left was coughing up phlegm and spitting globs of mucus into the sink. At the same time, he was feverishly scrubbing something in the palm of his hand with a toothbrush. I looked a little closer and realized it was a plate of dentures. I looked up at the old guy and he flashed a big toothless grin, never breaking stride down below in the sink. I'd had enough for one day; I was going to bed.

As I lay in my upper bunk that first night, my face only 12 inches from the ceiling, I realized I was in for the experience of a lifetime. I wanted to kick myself for being stupid enough to be in this position, but it was too late for that. All of my energies would now be directed toward living life one day at a time. I was certain that each day would present new challenges, and my goal was to settle in and simply persevere. It would all begin with a good night's sleep.

Shortly after the lights went out, my new living quarters came alive with the sounds of a nocturnal orchestra, a steady rhythm of grunting, snoring, throat clearing, spring squeaking, and, of course, farting. A guy known as Fat John, who suffered from sleep apnea, was strapped to a breathing apparatus. He reminded me of Hannibal Lecter in *The Silence of the Lambs*; all I could see were the whites of his eyes peering through the mask and his naked belly bobbing up and down like a buoy in the ocean. There was a huge man named Raul a couple of bunks over, snoring so loudly that most of the guys in the room had to wear earplugs to get any sleep. A hillbilly from rural Georgia named Grady didn't make a peep in his sleep, but his pungent body odor made my eyes burn. It was a toxic mixture of grease, grime, sweat, oil, and tobacco chew. The chaos in the room was further punctuated by the evening body counts, performed like clockwork by late-shift guards at 10:00 PM, midnight, 2:00 AM, and 4:30 AM. With no desire to have well-rested inmates, the guards clumsily entered our room, threw on the lights, and chatted at daytime volume as they counted each man. Most guards turned the lights off on their way out; a few sadistic ones didn't.

Then there was a 50-year-old guy referred to as Stinky, a well-deserved moniker for a nonstop farter who could literally conjure up a blast of gas at will. Out of politeness to his roommates, he never farted in the room while he was awake. However, when the lights went out and he drifted away to sleep, all bets were off. Stinky's farts hung in the air like mushroom clouds and forced me to spend the entire time sleeping with my head under the covers. I knew I was in for a rough ride until Stinky was either released or subjected to a colon cleansing.

I tried to blend in with the crowd and avoid trouble over the next few days, but the edgy comments continued and left me uneasy. One particular evening I found several whistles hanging from my bedpost and my pillow was soaked with what appeared to be urine. Around the same time, someone told me about a brutal attack that had taken place outside my room a few weeks earlier. A mild-mannered bespectacled man in his late fifties had been labeled a "rat" by a group of young Puerto Rican inmates. Early one morning as he lay in his bunk, he was savagely beaten about the head by hooded assailants wielding heavy locks stuffed into the toe section of tube socks. Suffering from severe lacerations, contusions, and loss of blood, the victim dragged himself into the dark hallway where he passed out, only to be found by guards some time later. He was rushed to a hospital where he was diagnosed with a life-threatening concussion and collapsed lung. Despite an intensive investigation by the FBI, the attackers were never apprehended and remained incarcerated at the institution. For that reason alone, the victim was not permitted to return to FPC Pensacola and was shipped to another facility. The "lock in the sock" attack was all the buzz for weeks. It was particularly sobering news to me, especially in light of the many taunts of "rat" that were hurled my way.

The chilly reception followed me wherever I went. In the chow hall, other inmates would purposely avoid sitting at my table or got up and left if I sat at theirs. When I was initially assigned to do light grounds maintenance, no one would work with me. A few inmates who didn't know who I was introduced themselves and tried to be friendly. Later, after someone had filled them in, they would walk right past me without saying a word. Just when I thought it couldn't get any worse, I made a major blunder that created even more problems.

As I walked around the institution, it became painfully evident that gambling was everywhere. High-stakes card games, mostly Texas hold'em, were played every evening and all weekend long in a game room located above the library. Sometimes 10 or 15 inmates would encircle the card table, watching the action and waiting for a chance to play. Since possessing money is not permitted in prison, inmates found other ways to pay gambling losses, losses that were often heavy. The most common form of currency was a variety of food products for sale in the prison commissary. Cans of tuna, 12-packs of soda, chips, and ice cream were often used to settle debts. For the high rollers, a few snacks could never begin to cover the losses. Losses that ran into the hundreds or thousands of dollars were typically handled on the outside, with the family of one inmate cutting a check to the family of another. It's a reliable system, because slow pay or no pay is a big mistake in prison.

With time on my hands, I was drawn to the action and hovered over the tables like a bee waiting to pollinate a flower. I fought temptation night after night until I realized something bad was going to occur if I didn't seek help.

FPC Pensacola has a drug and alcohol treatment program for inmates with a documented history of abuse, so I approached one of the treatment specialists and asked if the institution provided treatment for gambling addiction. Incredibly, the answer was no. Prior to arriving in prison, I had been involved in court-ordered treatment for over a year, and I was making progress. In fact, Judge Amon ordered that I continue with treatment during my sentencing. But there I was, surrounded by temptation with no access to treatment and seemingly nowhere to turn.

In an innocent yet ill-conceived move, I wrote to warden Scott Fisher and asked for treatment. In support of my request, I pointed to the widespread illegal gambling that was occurring in the institution and the temptation I was experiencing as a result. I also referred to my previous treatment history and the judge's order for continuing treatment. Finally, I mentioned that if treatment was not available, I would like to be transferred to a halfway house in Tampa so that I could reenter the treatment program in which I was previously enrolled.

It all seemed reasonable enough to me, but I was dead wrong. My first blunder was to discuss my request with another inmate. While temporarily assigned to work in the prison laundry, I simply needed someone to talk to and I confided in my fellow inmate. Big mistake!

Shortly thereafter, two things happened. First, my "coworker" blabbed to anyone who would listen, and the story spread like wildfire. Second, despite years of indifference to illegal gambling in the institution, the warden instituted a crackdown on gambling, sending guards to conduct unexpected raids on card games and to search the lockers of suspected ringleaders. It was pure pandemonium and all eyes were once again staring at me.

Inmates who formerly made comments under their breath were now loudly proclaiming their anger. I was openly jeered in the hallways of the housing unit and began to hear rumblings about physical retaliation. Late one afternoon, I was pulled aside by the lieutenant in charge of internal security at the institution and told to watch my back. She informed me that inmates had anonymously sent threatening letters to her office, indicating that something bad was going to happen to me if I wasn't removed from the prison.

Scott Fisher had no intention of sending me to another facility. A chunky bulldog of a man with a bald head, Fisher had spent two and a half years at FPC Pensacola in his first job as a warden and was probably ready to move on to a higher-security institution and a bigger paycheck. I was the most high-profile inmate he encountered during his time in Pensacola, and it probably would do his career little good to tell his superiors that he couldn't keep me safe. No, I wasn't going anywhere, not on his watch.

On a warm afternoon in the fall of 2008, I was working my regular job assignment in the prison laundry. Midmorning, my supervisor directed me to pick up dirty laundry in two of the housing units, so I set off to complete the mundane task, not knowing what I was about to encounter. Walking along, I noticed two inmates painting the curb adjoining the sidewalk with paint rollers attached to long wooden handles.

As I passed within a few feet of them, one lowered his head and grumbled at me.

"Rat, rat, rat!" he said.

The comment took me by surprise and I stopped.

"Are you talking to me?" I asked.

"You heard me, you rat fuck!" he repeated while lifting his head and stepping toward me.

He immediately came at me, wildly swinging the wooden-handled pole in a violent manner and repeatedly striking me on the legs and torso. I felt a sharp pain in my right knee and stumbled back, but he kept charging. In a thick New York accent, he screamed threats at me, all the while striking me with the pole.

"I'm from New York, and I have friends in the mob!" he shouted.

With a wild look in his eyes, he placed his index finger on his temple and elevated his thumb, simulating a gun. He stared directly into my eyes.

"I'm gonna get a gun and blow your fucking head off. Then I'm gonna cut your balls off and shove 'em up your ass," he threatened.

His tirade continued with a threat to break my kneecaps until suddenly a corrections officer came flying out of the adjacent administrative building. Covered with yellow paint and thoroughly beaten, I limped away to the safety of the control office before being promptly taken to the medical office for treatment.

My assailant, who was known in the camp as Big Paulie, was quickly escorted to the hole and eventually shipped to a higher-security institution, never to be seen by me again. I have no idea if he intended to carry through on his threats, and I also can't say for sure whether he was taking orders from someone on the outside or was just angry I had pointed out the prison's gambling culture to the warden. But the incident was a sobering reminder of the dangers that lurk in prison, even a minimum-security prison camp.

Within a few days, I was transferred from the prison laundry to the grounds maintenance crew—the very same crew that my attacker had come from. His former partner, the other painter working on the day of the attack, shot me a look of rage when I walked into the maintenance shop. He was pissed and seemed anxious to take a shot at me. A few days later, our paths crossed and he threatened to kick my ass. This was a defining moment for me because I was left with a simple choice: back down and forever be the target of threats and physical abuse, or stand up for myself and gain some measure of respect. I was in no hurry to get my ass kicked, but I'd been in a few fights in my life, and I decided to stand my ground.

"Let's do it," I calmly stated.

"Tough guy, huh?" he responded.

"Nope, but I'm not taking any more of your shit!" I replied.

About that time, another inmate stepped between us and suggested we take the fight to a secluded location where the guards wouldn't get in the way. He recommended we wear gloves so there wouldn't be any marks on our knuckles and hands, and that if we were questioned by the corrections staff to say each of us had fallen in the shower. The entire situation felt like it was right out of the movies.

"Okay, let's go!" I said eagerly.

"Fuck you, I'm not going to waste my time," replied my prospective opponent.

Just like that, it was over. He walked away and we never spoke again. It wasn't the last time someone made a wisecrack aimed at me, but I never had another physical confrontation.

A few weeks later, a dead squirrel was found on the driveway leading to the chow hall. Someone had placed it in the supine position, arms and legs spread, head tilted back. Over its chest was draped a piece of paper with the following words penned in black ink:

RIP

THE REF

* * *

I wasn't the only one having problems in prison. My brother Jim is a friend of Tommy Martino's brother Johnny, and the two of them stay in regular contact. According to Johnny, Tommy and Ba Ba were serving their prison sentences at the Metropolitan Detention Center in Brooklyn, New York. Although they were housed in different units and didn't have access to one another, a rumor spread that Tommy's life was in danger, so prison officials transferred him to a prison in Massachusetts "for his safety." The news was very disturbing to me to say the least, and I kept thinking about Mike Franzese's prediction that I would spend the rest of my life looking over my shoulder. But there was no time to worry about the future; I had enough problems dealing with the present.

Early in my term, a fellow roommate offered the use of his cell phone so I could call home whenever I wanted to speak to my children. Cell phones are strictly prohibited in prison but readily available, and my room was a regular Verizon outlet store. Almost everyone had a phone, used by night, hidden in mattresses and above ceiling panels by day. Other inmates throughout the various housing units would find their way to my room for the purpose of making a quick call or ordering a pizza. Yes, some inmates actually called Domino's and had pizza delivered to nearby family or friends. The inmate would then sneak off to a remote area on the prison grounds, where his connection would slide the pizza under the 10-foot-high chain-link security fence. Of course, pizza was just the beginning. At various times I saw inmates chowing down on steak, shrimp, fried chicken, Big Macs, Whoppers, and an occasional serving of moo goo gai pan. It was straight out of an episode of *Hogan's Heroes*.

Cell phones and food weren't the only contraband items floating around FPC Pensacola. If you had money, you could get just about anything you desired, including cigarettes, chewing tobacco, liquor, watches, pornography, designer sunglasses, and expensive tennis shoes. The prison commissary had two brands of tennis shoes available for sale to inmates: one in white, one in black. These were the only shoes that could be legitimately purchased at the prison. But on any given day, it was common to see inmates walking around the prison grounds in red, blue, yellow, orange, or gold high-end, brand-name basketball shoes. Nike, Puma, Adidas, New Balance, and all the rest found their way into the prison and could be purchased at an affordable price—just like going to Wal-Mart.

In an environment where meal portions are strictly monitored, inmates are always looking for a means to beef up their diet and satisfy their palates. In the quest for more food, the prison kitchen was ground zero. Everything from a few eggs to boxes of chicken mysteriously disappeared into the night from the FPC Pensacola chow hall. Kitchen workers were the "couriers" who established sophisticated methods of larceny and diversion to remove food items from the kitchen and transfer them to the housing units. There were many occasions when the kitchen staff would run out of food before all the inmates were fed. This was particularly common on an evening when fried chicken or ribs were on the menu. Sure enough, later that night the thieves would troll the hallways with trays of chicken or platters of ribs, selling the stolen goods like crack dealers in a back alley.

Tangible goods weren't the only things for sale in the camp. If you needed an adjustment of your spine, a deep muscle massage, or perhaps a brand-new tattoo, you were definitely in the right place. The prison population wasn't comprised exclusively of drug dealers and pimps. No, there was the usual array of personal service practitioners, including chiropractors, doctors, lawyers, accountants, tattoo artists, personal trainers, and even a masseur! The corridors of the housing unit often resembled an urban version of a street bazaar in old Marrakesh.

The top masseur on campus was a short, skinny, bald Puerto Rican doing a 10-year bid for running drugs across the Mexican border. For the reasonable price of two cans of mackerel, he would gladly provide the rubdown of your life. For four, he would happily be your wife—for the night, anyway. At first, I didn't believe this story, but a late-night visit to the third-floor bathroom was all the proof I would ever need. Just before 1:00 early one morning, I got up from bed to use the facilities. While standing at the urinal, I heard a commotion coming from a nearby shower stall and turned my head to look. To my great surprise, the masseur strolled out of the single-person shower stall in the naked company of another short, skinny, recently shaved Puerto Rican with a full head of hair. The companion looked particularly relaxed, no doubt the result of a full-body, muscle-relieving, "four-can" rubdown. When the happy couple noticed my presence, they just giggled and scampered out the door. I returned to my room and promptly recalculated my release date, more anxious than ever to get out of the zoo that was my home.

There were many days and nights during the early months that pushed me to the edge. Prior to my incarceration, I had been taking Xanax to keep my emotional stability in check. I wasn't proud of the fact that I needed chemical help, but it did provide a measure of relief that was crucial to maintaining my sanity. During a medical screening at the prison health services department, I informed a doctor of my situation and the need to continue the medication.

"No, we don't do that here," he flatly stated.

"Well then, what do you recommend?" I asked.

"I suggest you sit outside and stare at the sun," he replied. "Yes, I prescribe plenty of sunshine."

Well, if the good doctor prescribed sunshine, it was sunshine I would get. My job on the grounds crew consisted of raking leaves and picking up pinecones on the military base that stretched for several hundred acres. At times it was monotonous, but at least I got to work outdoors and enjoy the beautiful fall weather in northern Florida.

While raking leaves early one December morning, my right knee throbbed with a debilitating pain, a recurring problem since I was whacked with a wooden pole by the angry curb painter. I had been in excruciating pain that morning and was sitting on the ground when my supervisor happened to drive by and see me nursing my knee. He took one look and could plainly see the onset of swelling. With that, he rushed me to the prison infirmary for treatment.

I sat in the lobby for about 15 minutes, my knee throbbing, when the doctor who prescribed me sunshine casually strolled down the hall.

"What's the matter with you?" he asked incredulously.

"My knee has been giving me trouble," I replied. "It's been swelling up."

"Let's have a look," he said.

I raised my pants leg and revealed a badly swollen right knee.

"I don't see any swelling," he declared.

"There, it's right there," I insisted.

With that, he suddenly grabbed my right knee with his hand and squeezed tightly, sending excruciating pain through my entire leg.

"What the hell are you doing?" I screamed. "Get away from me!"

My outburst startled the good doctor, and he backed away and retreated to his office. The commotion sent office staff running to the area, followed by the on-duty lieutenant who demanded an explanation.

"He assaulted me!" I exclaimed.

I was promptly escorted to a holding cell where I sat in isolation for the next six hours without treatment. Later, I was issued a disciplinary citation for causing a disturbance in the doctor's office and punished with a 30-day restriction from shopping at the commissary. The citation was eventually reversed and removed from my record, and I was belatedly prescribed medication for my aching knee. I took the medication intermittently, only when I was experiencing pain, but it never seemed to afford any relief. Months later, X-rays and an MRI would reveal a severe injury to my knee that required surgical repair.

Over the ensuing months, I began to experience strange mood swings—one day feeling great and the next wanting to break down in tears. After several months on this roller-coaster ride of emotions, I was unexpectedly called to the health services department. To my surprise, the warden and office administrator were also in the room. The doctor proceeded to tell me that an error had been made with my prescription for the pain and swelling in my knee: I was mistakenly given an *antidepressant* medication, not an *anti-inflammatory* medication.

I couldn't believe it! No wonder my knee was still hurting and my emotions were all screwed up. To top it off, the doctor wanted me to sign a document claiming that I knew I was receiving an antidepressant. I refused.

After the incident with my knee, I was no longer permitted to work in the field and was reassigned to cleaning toilets and urinals. Sometimes, when I scrubbed toilet seats and cleaned toilet bowls, my mind would wander to memories of lavish casinos and state-of-the-art sports arenas. It occurred to me that my entire life had been about journeys—a journey to the NBA, a journey into a secret life, and a journey to the bottom of the barrel. I was tired of journeys and simply wanted to go home and live a normal life.

As Christmas approached, I was missing my girls and desperately trying to stay connected to their lives. I wrote letters often and called home three times a week. Still, there was no substitute for seeing their beautiful smiling faces and watching them laugh and have fun. To my great surprise, Kim told me she was going to make a road trip and bring the girls for a visit. I initially had mixed feelings; as much as I wanted to see them, I dreaded the thought of them seeing me in a prison uniform. During a phone call with my parents, my mother reassured me that the girls wouldn't care about my green pants and shirt; they just wanted to see their dad and know that I was all right.

Walking to the visiting room that Saturday morning, my heart raced with excitement. It had only been a few months since I left home, but it seemed like years. I entered the room and searched for my family in the large crowd, hoping that my girls wouldn't be embarrassed by the sight of me in my green uniform. They weren't. Before I took three steps into the room, they came running at me shouting, "Dad! Dad! Over here!" All four hugged me and held on until we lost our balance and almost fell over. We had a good laugh and then a good cry before finding a few chairs and settling in for the most amazing four hours of my life. There were updates about Shannon's softball team and Meghan's soccer games. Bridget was all smiles and Molly was her usual hyper self, bursting at the seams with enough energy for three people. Kim was kind and gracious, offering a warm hug and telling me how much I was missed. We talked and walked and ate snacks and carried on like we were on a day trip to Disney World. The time went by so fast that we were all shocked when the guard in charge announced that visiting hours were over for the day. All of us had a look of surprise, and then exasperation, as people began to shuffle toward the exit.

The good-byes were heart-wrenchingly painful, and one by one, my girls broke down in tears. After more hugs and more tears, I managed to get a few chuckles out of them. Molly was the last to let go. She cried so hard that everyone in the place took notice, but I didn't care. It was our moment, and I wanted to reassure her. I wanted to let her know how much I loved her. Just before she let go, Molly pulled close to my ear.

"What do you want for Christmas, Daddy?" she asked.

"To be home with you and your sisters," I whispered. "That's what I want."

We both knew that I wouldn't be home for Christmas that year, but the time we shared that afternoon was going to carry all of us a little further and get us closer to a very happy reunion.

At Christmas, I always showered my daughters with gifts. Kim used to say that I spoiled them rotten, but I didn't care; they were my little princesses, and all princesses should be spoiled. That year, unable to shop for toys or dolls or dresses, I found a quiet place in the prison yard away from the madness and wrote a holiday message to my girls. Later, they told me it was the best gift they ever received.

Dear Meghan, Shannon, Bridget, and Molly:

It's almost Christmas and all of you are in my thoughts. So sorry that I won't be home this year to see you open your presents on Christmas morning. You'll never know how much I will miss seeing your smiling faces. Still, it's Christmastime and I hope you are as excited as ever.

I don't know if I ever told you this, but Christmas has always been my favorite holiday. When I was a little boy, I couldn't wait to open my presents on Christmas morning. Mom-Mom Joan and Grandfather always insisted that no gift could be opened until everyone in the family was present. I was up by 5:00 in the morning, but my sleepy brothers didn't get up until 10:00 or 11:00. The wait was excruciating, but always worth it.

Even when I grew up, Christmas was always special to me. My favorite Christmas was the one when I asked your mother to marry me. Mom and I were in Detroit at the time because I had to referee a game.

Before I asked her, I called Grandpa John on the phone and asked him for his daughter's hand in marriage. There was a long pause of silence and then he told me that he was impressed that I had called to obtain his blessing. He gave me his blessing and I couldn't wait to pop the question.

That year, Mom told me she wanted a new coat for Christmas, so I picked out the fanciest one I could find and wrapped it up in a beautiful box. When she opened the box on Christmas night, she loved the coat and immediately tried it on. She brushed her fingers over the fabric, slid her hands deep into the pockets, and looked up at me with a curious expression on her face. She slowly pulled a small wrapped box out of the pocket and opened it up. Can you guess what was in the box? That's right, it was a sparkling diamond engagement ring. I asked her to marry me and she said, "ABSOLUTELY." It turns out that we both received a wonderful gift that Christmas and eventually we received four more. Of course, I'm referring to four baby girls named Meghan, Shannon, Bridget, and Molly. Since it all started on that special day, I suppose you could say that each one of you is a Christmas gift to me and Mom each year.

You know, girls, Christmas gifts come in many different forms. I'm talking about things such as a big present under the tree, a kind gesture, a warm and reassuring hug from your mother or father, the birth of the baby Jesus, or even a pleasant memory you will never forget.

Since I cannot be with you this Christmas, my gift to you is this letter and my memories of Christmas past. And don't forget, next year we will all be together again. I don't care if I have to dash through the snow in a one-horse open sleigh, I'll be home for Christmas...You can count on me...

MERRY CHRISTMAS!

Love, Dad

* * *

The new year came and went with little fanfare at FPC Pensacola. As the weeks and months rolled by, things started to cool down and my problems subsided. The little comments and threats were a thing of the past, and I was finally blending into the woodwork. I established a routine of rising early, working hard, staying in good shape, and going to bed by 7:00 or 8:00 PM.

I made a few acquaintances, guys who became my friends for the duration of my stay. There was a consultant named Walt, a building contractor named Raul, a heavy equipment operator named Welch, and a former prosecutor named Joe.

They all had stories similar to mine. You know, promising careers, great families, and some personal shortcomings that derailed their lives and their dreams. I came to view these guys as decent men who made very poor choices, men who would one day make the most of their second opportunity in life—men like me.

As time passed, I came to the conclusion that there were three basic categories of inmates. By far and away the most prevalent were the inmates who claimed to be innocent, aggrieved victims of a system that worked tirelessly to screw people who were in the wrong place at the wrong time. The lies, excuses, explanations, and rationalizations piled up ad nauseam. The second category, a tiny percentage of inmates, admitted their guilt and took full responsibility for their actions. These were the guys who really got it, the ones who stood a fighting chance of successfully rejoining society someday. The third category, a hefty group, consisted of inmates who, regardless of their culpability, had been given too much time behind bars. These men endured a punishment that in many cases defied logic and functioned only as an inhumane reaction to some undefined societal goal of retribution.

There was one inmate in particular whose case was both tragic and typical. His name is John, a 40-year-old from Georgia who formerly worked for a telecommunications company. When he first joined the company, he had no idea that the owner and several other executives were defrauding customers out of millions of dollars. After just six months on the job, he was indicted, along with the rest, and put on trial. The main culprit, the CEO, copped a plea and took a deal for five years in prison.

John, who denied any involvement during his brief time at the company, went to trial and was convicted. He was promptly sentenced to 17 years in prison. *Seventeen years!*

I came to know John as a peaceful and considerate person who wouldn't harm a soul. He had gone to college, paid his taxes, married his high school sweetheart, called his mother twice a week, and never once got into any trouble with the law. He was one of the few who had the courage to sit with me at dinner or take a walk with me around the jogging track. He may have been convicted of a crime, but he was no criminal. On several occasions I asked him whether he was bitter about the events that had transpired. He told me that in addition to his imprisonment, his wife had left him and his family had disappeared, but that he still had to get up every day and live his life. John said he looked to the simple things in life to find meaning and purpose. With 10 years down and seven to go, he was in no particular hurry. There would come a day when he would be released, but until then, there would be thousands of other days, days that had to be lived to the fullest.

My conversations with John really hit home. I thought about all that he had lost, but realized in some ways he had become a richer man. From my experiences with John and many others, I rededicated myself to a fuller appreciation of the many blessings I have. For most people, my personal failures and my fall from grace will always define me, but I choose to look at it a bit differently. The many failures most certainly impacted and redirected the course of my life, but they would never define me. Rather, the manner in which I accepted those failures and learned from them would be the real measure of my worth. As the date of my release inched closer, it was almost time for my second chance, and I was more prepared for a fresh start than ever before.

In the NBA, when a player misses a shot but gets the offensive rebound, the team gets a new 24 seconds to take another shot. With my second chance in life, I've been given a new 24—a new 24 hours every time I wake up to live an honest and meaningful life, devoted to the people I love most, always mindful of the past and wary of the demons that occasionally call my name. Just about anyone can get a new 24, a fresh start, a second chance. All they have to do is blow the whistle, take a step back, and start over. For me, it's time to put the ball in play and get back in the game.

AFTERWORD

Fixing the NBA

On July 1, 2008, the NBA hired a retired U.S. Army General to fill the newly created position of Senior Vice President of Referee Operations. Ronald L. Johnson, formerly the Deputy Commanding General of the U.S. Army Corps of Engineers, would be responsible for "all aspects of the NBA's officiating program, including recruiting, training and development, scheduling, data management and analysis, and work rules enforcement."

Johnson was to report to Joel Litvin, the NBA's President for League and Basketball Operations. You may recall that Litvin is the individual who described my allegations of a culture of fraud among NBA referees as "the desperate act of a convicted felon who was hoping to avoid prison time," though that skepticism does not seem to apply to the convicted felons still employed as NBA referees.

I found especially revealing a July 6, 2008, Associated Press report quoting an email from Lamell McMorris, the spokesman and lead negotiator for the NBRA. McMorris told the AP that Johnson would have to "rework the officiating program" and referred to the "many challenges left by his predecessors. These challenges include poor vision, a lack of focus and direction, mixed messaging, a flawed evaluation system, a misguided reliance on statistical analysis to measure performance, blatant favoritism, and a dispirited and demoralized staff."

In other words, even the referees' union understood the problem was bigger than one "rogue" referee.

On July 21, 2008, the NBA announced with great fanfare that General Johnson would have three individuals reporting to him in a restructuring of the Referee Operations Department. Bernie Fryer was named Vice President and Director of Officials; the other two individuals the NBA selected are no strangers to anyone who has read this far: Joe Borgia and Ronnie Nunn. Yes, the same Joe Borgia who wouldn't call a sixth foul on Chris Webber in a game I described earlier in the book. And yes, the same Ronnie Nunn who was involved in the airline ticket scam and hired relatives of his favorite refs regardless of their abilities. As The Who once sang, "Meet the new boss, same as the old boss." If I were an NBA fan, I wouldn't know whether to laugh or cry. I can understand the NBA hiring General Johnson to straighten things out. But does he have any idea who his eyes and ears are?

* * *

One of the questions raised in the aftermath of my actions was whether it was possible to referee an NBA game with 100 percent accuracy. To put it simply, it's not. In a perfect world, if the referees were perfectly trained and did not have vendettas and/or alliances with the players and teams involved in the game that night, a game could be called, in my opinion, 93 or 94 percent accurately. And that's good enough. That's a respectful, professional product with integrity. However, you can show me the tape of any NBA game and I can find at least 10 obvious calls— traveling, missed fouls, players stepping on the end line—that are just plain wrong. If there are 50 calls in a game and 10 are wrong, that's 80 percent accuracy. That's about the average of an NBA game. But once you layer in the friendships and hatreds between the referees and the players, coaches, and owners, the percentage drops even further, down to maybe 65 or 70 percent accuracy. Because the referees are able to make calls or ignore violations with impunity, they can hide a whole lot of love or hate for players or a team with their calls. If you think that 60 percent accuracy is acceptable, then I've got a new job for you.

Commissioner of the NBA.

In point of fact, the refereeing staff is the NBA's single biggest headache. For every 10 problems the NBA has, nine of them center on refereeing. It's crazy, but that's just how it is. And yet the league has done practically nothing to improve the caliber of referees or refereeing. It's hard to imagine any other highly visible corporation in the marketplace having such a "problem child" division and not doing something about it. Actually, David Stern has been aware of the poor quality of refereeing in the league for a long time. His solution? Get rid of the third referee on the court. In his mind, a third ref was actually making things *worse*. I guess he thought the referees were doing such a bad job that by getting rid of the third ref every night, you could eliminate a lot of the dead weight on the staff. Ronnie Nunn told me personally that it took enormous lobbying on his part to keep Stern from making that move. In my opinion, it would make more sense to add a fourth referee for each game, one that could review the action on video and could alert the on-court referees about any mistakes.

* * *

Sometimes people ask me what I would do, if I were David Stern, to eliminate the culture of fraud that many believe permeates the NBA.

The answer has a lot to do with the fact that the NBA is called a "players' league." Most of the time, that expression is understood to mean that the players are in charge of things—they can get a coach fired or maybe even get a teammate traded if they have enough juice. But the other meaning of the phrase "players' league" is that the NBA's marketing focuses on its star players.

It stands to reason that if the NBA is marketing individual players, it doesn't want to see those players racking up fouls, collecting technicals, sitting on the bench for long stretches, or getting tossed out of games. So the first thing I believe the NBA has to do is make up its mind about whether it's putting on real games featuring real competition, where the referees have the power to enforce the rules in the rule book, or whether it's putting on a show. If you're paying $1,500 for a courtside seat, are you there to see a game or a show? Even if you're sitting at home watching a game on TV, ask yourself what attracts you to the NBA. Is it the chance to watch a legitimate athletic competition, or is it the opportunity to see some of the world's most amazing athletes perform physical miracles that you and I can only dream of? The first step is simple honesty. Is it a game or a show?

If it's a show, fine. Let's admit it. The same general basketball rules apply in high school, college, and the NBA. Those same rules just aren't enforced in the NBA. You don't see college players taking an extra hop, skip, and a jump to the basket. They can't palm the ball, travel, or flop. In college, the rules are enforced. If the NBA is a show, simply change the NBA rule book to reflect that certain players get special treatment, marquee players get 10 fouls instead of six, and global icons are permitted to move their pivot foot. At least we'd be telling the truth. The problem with enforcing the rules as written, of course, is that scoring would drop 20 points a game, stars would get in early foul trouble, and those fans that spring for the luxury boxes may end up watching games played by the 12th men on NBA benches instead of the Kobe Bryants of the world. If it's going to be real basketball, then let them play by the rules. If it's going to be a show, then let's change the rule book to reflect that reality so that everyone—referees, players, fans, announcers, coaches, and owners—are all on the same page.

* * *

At one point during my court proceeding, a newspaper published my home address. As a result, I received hundreds of letters of support, and my attorney received several emails. I found this one particularly interesting because it was from a pastor who was obviously taken aback by some of David Stern's comments.

> My name is Bill Jakeway. I am currently a children's pastor in Peoria, Arizona. I am sickened by Stern's comments today that the NBA game is never manipulated.
>
> During the time that I refereed, the AIA [Arizona Interscholastic Association] would hold yearly camps and trainings. On several occasions

the camps were held during the summer at Arizona State University (ASU). During these camps, in addition to getting hands-on experience on the floor, AIA would bring in NBA referees to talk to us about various aspects of the game. Habitually there would always be a time of Q&A for the AIA refs to ask the NBA refs whatever they wanted. Invariably, the question would come up as to why some players would get away with stuff more than others. I particularly remember two answers that have stuck in my mind ever since.

The first answer was "because the NBA is about the money and the show." The second was "because people don't pay that much money to see Michael Jordan and Shaq sit on the bench." The discussion was clearly that the policy was not to foul out the stars. My impressionable son, about 9 or 10 at the time, was quite disillusioned.

Bill

Even casual basketball fans are aware that the way the game is being handled is not quite kosher. Some things have to change.

One consideration would be limiting the amount of time that an NBA referee can work to 20 years, and even subjecting them to periodic lie detector tests. Some referees have just been around too long; they have too many alliances and/or grievances with regard to too many players, coaches, and owners for them to change their ways. Everybody in the NBA knows which refs call games to the beat of their own drummer. It's an open secret, to say the least.

Moreover, I would also suggest a complete overhaul of the way referees are managed by the league. To start, I would pay them all the same salary. There's no reason for one referee to be making three times what another is being paid. This kind of salary gap just creates the incentive to do whatever is necessary to earn a higher salary. The NBA should also hire more referees to avoid having the same referees going to the same cities to referee the same teams as often as they do today. The hiring, training, and promoting process is broken. A better system to hire and promote the most qualified referees must be installed. Currently too many referees are hired and promoted because of who they know and not how qualified they are.

I would also suggest relocating all of the referees to a central hub during the NBA season; Chicago, Atlanta, Dallas, or some other city near a major airport that would make it easy for them to fly out to the various NBA cities. With a central headquarters for the referees, the NBA could develop its referee training process in a much more meaningful way than is currently the case. How much education and training can referees really get sitting in a hotel room watching plays that the NBA sends over the Internet? The smarter course would be to have all the referees in constant training sessions throughout the year so that everybody is consistent in how they officiate the game. If a player who resides in Miami, Florida, is playing for the Portland Trail Blazers, he is expected to live in Oregon during the NBA season; is it too much to ask referees to make the same sacrifice? Likewise, players lift weights, work on their skills, and receive instruction year-round from their coaches; why shouldn't NBA referees follow the same regimen? And if you're worried that basing referees too close to Chicago or Atlanta or Dallas would leave them vulnerable to influence from fans in those communities, then base the NBA referees out of Wichita, Kansas, or Lincoln, Nebraska. Would I have moved to Kansas to become an NBA ref or to keep my job if they established a headquarters there? You better believe I would.

I would also recommend recruiting the best referees from the college game, paying them enough so that it's *worth* coming over to the NBA, and letting them call an honest game based on the infractions. The politics of the referee assignment process, the subjective nature of rating referees, and the carrot-and-stick approach to advancing referees in the playoffs have negatively impacted the NBA's ability to recruit top college referees. In many cases, Division I referees earn more than their NBA counterparts, more easily advance to the postseason tournament, and are less subjected to manipulation by higher-ups. More importantly, there is a public perception that college basketball is more honest and legitimate than the pro game. Many referees in the college ranks regard the game as a contest of skill and ability, not just as a show to be packaged and sold. As a result, some of the best college referees prefer to stay at the college level, and the result is predictable. Old-guard NBA referees continue to suckle on the league's teat, playing ball and spinning the company line with the hope of garnering coveted playoff assignments and earning more money.

Another positive step would be to do away with the practice of having coaches and general managers rating the referees. This practice partly explains why referees do favors for coaches or do what they can to help them avoid embarrassment during games. The refs want the best rating possible, so many would try to stay in the good graces of the coaches and general managers. After all, they're the ones with a direct line to the NBA office.

It makes me cringe when I hear an NBA fan or announcer say, "You're just not going to get that call from a referee in that situation." Why is that? Why would you not get a call if a foul was committed against you, just because a particular referee was standing there? Is it a foul, or isn't it a foul? Why do we have to take into account which referee is in position to make the call? That's why we have a rule book; everybody is supposed to enforce the same rules, evenly and fairly, throughout the game. The game shouldn't be controlled by the referees; it should be controlled by the illegal actions. If fouls are committed, the ref should blow the whistle, plain and simple. There shouldn't be identical situations resulting in different outcomes.

* * *

Everybody knows the problems in the NBA are much bigger than just one "rogue" referee. The FBI knows it. The prosecutors know it. And now you know it, too.

You've got to give David Stern his due. He's the one who marketed this league and made it an international game. He brought it back from the ashes when he took over in the early 1980s. He embraced the concept of superstar players being known on a first-name basis all over the world. He made everybody a lot of money—the owners, the players, the networks, and the sponsors. And while they fail to punish past offenders and do little to change the NBA's culture of fraud, two recent reforms—publishing the Master List of Referees each day and relaxing the rules regarding referees legally gambling—are positive steps. But as accomplished as Stern is on the business side of things, he never really had a feel for the game of basketball, and it has caught up with him. They're not putting a good product on the floor, but the NBA is marketing the game so effectively in every corner of the world that nobody seems to care.

I don't see anybody rising up to challenge David Stern, either. The owners got so comfortable with all of the money they were making, they looked past the major problems they're now being forced to confront. There's a need for someone who will enforce the rules, someone who will concentrate on protecting the integrity of the game and not just the marketing and the expansion. It's not just how well you're selling the product—it's about thinking through what kind of product you're putting on the floor in the first place.

I'll tell you who my first choice would be for a new commissioner: Mark Cuban. His business track record speaks for itself. He's implored the NBA office to make improvements since he took over the Dallas Mavericks, but obviously his requests have fallen on deaf ears. He simply wants the game called the right way. And if you think it's crazy to have an owner step up to become a league's commissioner, I would refer you to Bud Selig, the commissioner of Major League Baseball. Mark Cuban would do a terrific job leading the NBA. I'm sure he has little interest in giving up his stake in the Mavs just for the chance to try and clean up the NBA, but I believe he'd have the guts to throw out the people who are wedded to the old ways, and he loves the game enough to make sure the product on the court is all it could be.

Do I anticipate the NBA taking advice from a disgraced ex-referee who gambled on games? I'm not holding my breath. But just because I may not be the perfect messenger doesn't discredit the ideas I'm putting forth. These are my thoughts about how to turn the NBA around, and I know they're shared by many. The question remains, will anybody listen?

Acknowledgments

Thanks to my four daughters—Meghan, Shannon, Bridget, and Molly—for keeping me strong and pushing me to fight through my long days. They kept me motivated and going when I thought it wasn't possible. I can't tell you how lucky I am to have such wonderful children. Thanks to my mom and dad, for being there when I really needed them. They've counseled me, stood by me, and lifted my spirits. I am fortunate to have them as my parents. I also want to thank my brother Jim for lending me his ear during my difficult days.

Thanks also to John Lauro and the Lauro Law Firm—I owe everyone there my deepest gratitude for everything they did for me; Warren Flagg, who was always there when the phone rang—I will always remember the "FLAGGMAN" and his words of wisdom; my friends Kip, Joe P., Mike, Jimmy, and Vito, special people who stayed with me from the beginning; Phil Scala, for his understanding and help through my poor choices; and Father Rob Hagan, who shared an unforgettable dinner and the sacraments with me on March 22, 2008—thanks for your constant support. To everyone who sent a letter or card, thanks for the love and support. You made me keep fighting, even when I felt totally crushed. Finally, thanks to Executive Prison Consultants, as well as Shawna Vercher, Benjamin Daniel, and all the fine people at VTi-Group.

Index